P9-CBJ-831

A Team *for the* Ages

Baseball's All-Time All-Star Team

A Team for the Ages

Robert W. Cohen

Illustrations by J. Michael Jordan

THE LYONS PRESS
Guilford, Connecticut
An imprint of The Globe Pequot Press

The Lyons Press is an imprint of The Globe Pequot Press.

10 9 8 7 6 5 4 3 2 1

Printed in the United States of America

Designed by M. A. Dube

Baseball card designs based on "Baseball Cards, 1887–1914" from the American Memory Collection of the Library of Congress. [http://memory.loc.gov/ammem/bbhtml/bbhome.html] [bbc1468, bbc1477, bbc1492, and bbc1518] (January 9, 2004).

Courtesy of "Taking the Long View: Panoramic Photographs, 1851–1991" from the American Memory Collection of the Library of Congress. [http://memory.loc.gov/ammem/pnhtml/pnhome.html] [3c22692, 6a29720, 6a29726, 6a29735, and 6a29764] (January 9, 2004).

ISBN 1-59228-402-7

Library of Congress Cataloging-in-Publication Data is available on file.

To my dad, who instilled in me at a very young age a love of the game and an appreciation of its history and all the great players whom I never had a chance to see.

And to my mom, who nurtured me and gave so much of herself to allow me to pursue my interests.

CONTENTS

PART ONE

PART TWO

PART THREE

PART FOUR

PART FIVE

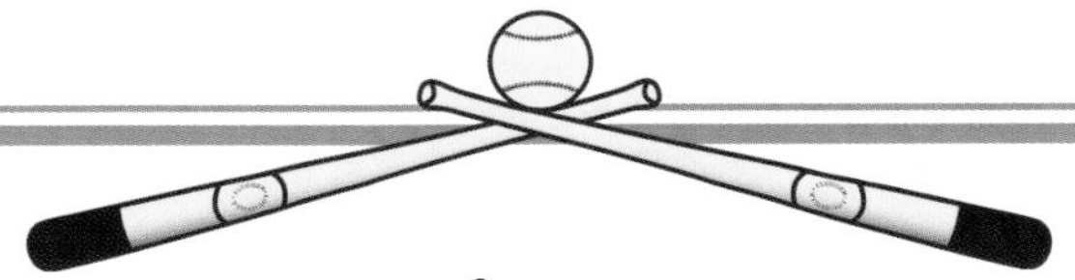

Contents

PART ONE

Selecting the All-Time All-Star Team

Reasons for Writing This Book

I DEVELOPED A LOVE OF THE GAME OF BASEBALL AT A RELATIVELY YOUNG AGE—PROBABLY about seven or eight. My earliest recollection as a fan goes back to the 1964 World Series between the Cardinals and Yankees. The two things I remember most about that Series are Mickey Mantle's home run off of Barney Schultz in the bottom of the ninth inning to win Game 3 for the Yankees, and the end of Game 7, when the Cardinals finally prevailed. Even though I had not been much of a baseball fan up to that point, having grown up in a household that was definitely pro-Yankees, I was nevertheless extremely upset at the result.

I'm not sure why, but for some reason I didn't become interested in football for at least another two or three years after that. My earliest years as a sports enthusiast definitely revolved around baseball. This can be applied not only to my interest as a fan, but also as a participant. In fact, my fondest memories from my childhood are the times spent with my father just having a catch or hitting fungos to one another. We would get up early in the morning on the weekend, go down to the schoolyard, and spend hours hitting the ball to each other and chasing after fly balls. As a young boy growing up in the Bronx, I suppose it was my secret desire to eventually play center field for the New York Yankees.

I also found that these were the times I felt closest to my dad. For those few hours, we were more than just father and son...we were buddies and best friends. My dad would tell me stories about some of the great players from his time. Born in 1919, he was very familiar with the exploits of some of the all-time greats, and I delighted in hearing stories about the likes of Babe Ruth, Lou Gehrig, Jimmie Foxx, Lefty Grove, and the rest. He would also tell me about some of the great teams from that era—the dominant Yankees teams of 1927–1928, the great A's teams of 1929–1931, and the superb Yankees squads that won four world championships in a row from 1936–1939.

FASCINATION FACTOR

FOR SOME REASON, I DEVELOPED A PARTICULAR FASCINATION WITH JIMMIE FOXX. THIS was probably because everyone seemed to know about Babe Ruth and Lou Gehrig and those great Yankees teams. There were always stories being written about them, film clips being shown of them on

TV, and even movies being made about them. But you never seemed to hear much about Foxx. Maybe it was because he didn't play in New York. Or maybe it was because he and those great A's teams were overshadowed by Ruth and his Yankees. But everything my dad told me about him indicated that Foxx was on the same level as Gehrig as a player—maybe just a notch behind Ruth—and, with the possible exception of the Babe himself, the most feared hitter in the game at that time. So I suppose it was this fascination with Foxx, as well as with some of the other players my father told me about, that encouraged me to acquire as much knowledge as I could about the great players of the past.

I began to read books about them, familiarizing myself with their statistics (in some cases, even memorizing those stats). With this knowledge base, I reached a point that, as I got older, I viewed things quite differently than many of my contemporaries. Most of them seemed to feel that players such as Willie Mays, Hank Aaron, Roberto Clemente, and later Reggie Jackson, Rickey Henderson, and Mark McGwire had to be better than the Ruths, Gehrigs, Cobbs, and DiMaggios who preceded them. After all, they were for the most part bigger, faster, and stronger. And hadn't the players improved over the years in the other major sports of football and basketball? I agreed without question that the players had gotten better in football and basketball, where size, speed, and athletic prowess play such an important part in the ability of the player. However, while these attributes certainly contribute to the success of a baseball player, there are other qualities that are very important as well, qualities such as quickness, agility, concentration, hand-eye coordination, dedication, and the ability to hit a baseball—probably the most difficult thing to do in all of sports.

Born in 1956 and, as mentioned earlier, having become a baseball fan around 1964, I'd been able to see the likes of Mays, Aaron, and Clemente, albeit in the second half of their illustrious careers. Having done so, I certainly have a great appreciation for what these players accomplished and for their vast abilities. And having seen them, I can tell you that I haven't seen anyone since—and keep in mind that we are talking about almost forty years—who I would say has surpassed them as all-around players. There may be some who run faster or who hit longer home runs, but as far as sheer ability as baseball players, they rank with the best I have seen. Is it therefore fair to presume that, just because these players came along thirty, forty, or even fifty years after some of their predecessors, they were superior to them as players?

It is a very difficult thing to compare players from different eras since the game has changed so much over the years. Things seem to go in cycles: the game is dominated by pitching for a number of years, then the rules change and suddenly the hitters seem to take over. We will discuss some of these changes later, but needless to say, they make selecting an All-Time All-Star Team from all eras a difficult task. However, that is what this book will attempt to do.

DISSATISFACTION WITH OTHER EFFORTS MADE TO SELECT AN ALL-TIME TEAM

ASIDE FROM MY FASCINATION WITH AND LOVE FOR THE GAME, I HAD TWO MAIN REASONS for writing this book. First, a few years ago, when Major League Baseball ran a campaign to have the fans select the All-Century Team, I was disappointed in several of the selections. Now, I realize that these

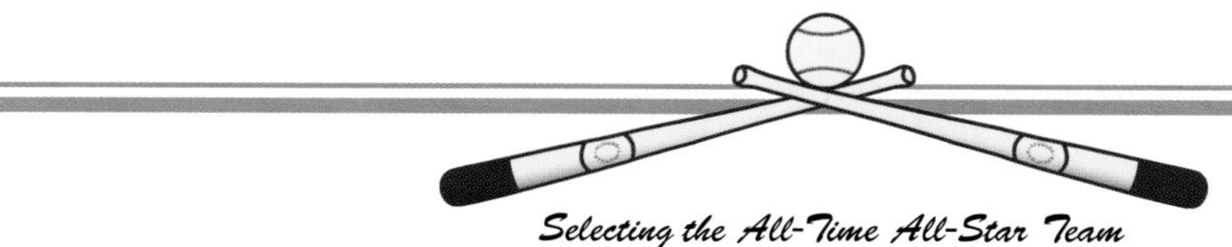

types of thing are usually based on popularity and that the majority of fans have a tendency to vote for those players with whom they're most familiar. I also realize that since the majority of the votes were submitted over the Internet, most were cast by people from a younger generation—people who never saw players such as Joe DiMaggio or Ted Williams. I am also aware that the vast majority of people who choose to participate in such a ballot are not true students of the game, and most do not know very much about players such as Tris Speaker, Bill Dickey, or Josh Gibson. But when I saw players like Jimmie Foxx, Frank Robinson, and Juan Marichal excluded from the team and replaced with the likes of Mark McGwire, Pete Rose, and Nolan Ryan, it just galled me. Now, don't get me wrong, I am not taking anything away from McGwire, Rose, or Ryan; they were all very gifted players. But, to me, the All-Century Team should be just that—a collection of the truly greatest of the great—and I don't think that any of them qualify as such.

For example, Mark McGwire, while a great slugger, was an extremely one-dimensional player for the first half of his career. It wasn't until the second half that he was finally able to get his career batting average over the .250 mark. And it wasn't until his last four or five years that he became a truly dominant offensive player.

Rose was an exceptional player who got everything he possibly could out of his somewhat limited natural ability. But longevity was the thing that truly made him stand out. During his playing career, he was never looked upon as a dominant player, at least not to the degree that his rivals Mays, Aaron, and Robinson were.

As for Ryan, while he had tremendous "stuff" and could dominate a game on any given day, he was more of a thrower than a pitcher for the first half of his career. It wasn't until the later years, when he gained better control of his pitches, that he became a true pitcher. Maybe that explains why, for his career, his win percentage was only slightly over .500.

In addition, I have read other books attempting to put together an all-time *dream team,* and I found that they were, in some ways, lacking. Too many relied on mere opinion, while others placed too much emphasis on statistics. Some took it a step further and came up with complicated formulas to adjust players' statistics based on factors such as the team on which they played, the statistics of other players from their era, and the ballpark in which they played their home games. I found this "park effect" to be particularly ludicrous, and here's why:

The proponent of this theory suggested that a hitter who played his home games in a ballpark that was "pitcher-friendly" should have his batting statistics adjusted upwards to compensate for the negative effect that the ballpark had on his actual numbers. Conversely, a hitter who played his home games in a ballpark that was "hitter-friendly" should have his statistics adjusted downwards. In theory, this seems rational. However, there are circumstances that cause this approach to lose all credibility. As an example, the advocate of this theory referred to the "old" Yankee Stadium as a pitcher-friendly park, which it was, and to Fenway Park as a hitter-friendly park, which it always has been. For someone like Joe DiMaggio, who was a right-handed, dead pull-hitter playing all his home games for thirteen seasons in spacious Yankee Stadium with its "Death Valley" in left-center field, this theory would hold true. However, this particular writer adjusted the batting statistics of Ted Williams downwards to compensate for the positive "park effect" Fenway had on Williams, and adjusted the statistics of Yogi Berra upwards to compensate for the negative effect playing in Yankee Stadium had on Berra. However, Williams was a left-handed, dead pull-hitter who hardly ever took advantage of Fenway's "Green Monster" in left field. Instead, he was constantly swinging for the right field stands, which were 380 feet away. Berra, also a left-handed, dead pull-hitter, got to swing for the much cozier, short right field porch in Yankee Stadium, which was only 344 feet from home plate. Needless to say, Williams was hurt playing all his home games in Fenway and Berra was helped considerably playing in Yankee Stadium.

When all was said and done, factoring in this "park effect" and making other adjustments to offensive statistics based on other criteria, Williams was ranked *behind* Mickey Mantle as an offensive player. While Mantle was a great player, there is no way he should be ranked above Williams, offensively. Also, using these formulas, the top fifty offensive players of all time wound up including the likes of Daryl Strawberry, Norm Cash, Frank Howard, and someone named Ross Barnes, who in 1,032 major league at-bats from 1871–1878 had 2 home runs and 111 RBI.

So, while statistics are very important in determining who the greatest players of all time are, *too* much emphasis can be placed on them. They will therefore be used here as a measuring stick, but not be relied upon exclusively.

Methodology

THE GAME OF BASEBALL HAS UNDERGONE MANY CHANGES OVER THE YEARS AND WAS NOT always played as it is now. Most of these changes have resulted from alterations in the rules governing the game, but virtually all of them have caused the sport to constantly evolve, and the style of play to evolve along with it.

Prior to 1884, pitching was underhanded, similar to fast-pitch softball. Prior to 1893, the pitcher stood only forty-five to fifty feet from the batter. When the pitcher's mound was pushed back to 60.5 feet in 1893, the National League batting average, only .245 in 1892, rose to an all-time high of .309 in 1894. In fact, the Philadelphia team's outfield of Billy Hamilton, Ed Delahanty, and Sam Thompson all hit over .400 that year. Fielding percentages in the early days, when fields were rutted and often unmowed and when balls were torn and scuffed, were below .900 (as opposed to the typical league average of about .970 these days). Walks were awarded only after nine balls, slowly decreasing to four balls over a ten-year period. However, walks were counted as base hits, and foul balls weren't counted as strikes, thereby explaining some of the astronomical batting averages attained by players in the early days of the game. A stolen base was awarded if the runner went from first to third on a single.

By the turn of the century, during the "dead ball" era, baseball had become a game of singles, slap-hitting, speed, and base-running skills. It was usually played in large fields, where it was virtually impossible for the batters to reach the fences (if there were any fences at all). Accomplishing this feat was made even more difficult by the fact that the ball was made of string wrapped around cork and was usually covered with mud, or some other foreign substance, since the same one was used for most of the game. Pitchers were allowed to throw spitballs and could basically do whatever they wanted to the ball. Needless to say, the pitchers of the era dominated and most games were very low-scoring. Pitchers also were expected to finish any game they started, even if it lasted 14 or 15 innings, and they frequently pitched on just one or two days' rest. Some, like "Iron Man" Joe McGinnity, who pitched for John McGraw's Giants, regularly pitched both ends of a doubleheader. Also, fielders' gloves were barely larger than their hands.

Through the years, the size of the strike zone has changed several times and the pitcher's mound has been raised, then lowered again, thereby tilting the balance of power back and forth between the hitters and pitchers and helping to create a cyclical effect on the game. Furthermore, with the emergence of Babe Ruth in 1919 as the game's first great home run hitter, the lords of the game saw the kind of excitement that the home run could generate and began producing baseballs that were wound more tightly. The game changed from a low-scoring chess match to a slugfest and, really, has not been the same since. However, things have continued to go in cycles, with the hitters dominating for a number of years, the game swinging back into the control of the pitchers, things leveling off for a while, and, more recently, the hitters regaining control.

DIFFICULTIES ENCOUNTERED

WITH ALL THE CHANGES THAT THE GAME HAS UNDERGONE SINCE ITS INCEPTION, IT IS extremely difficult to compare players from one era to those from another. How do you compare someone like Christy Mathewson, who pitched during the dead ball era, to someone like Lefty Grove, who hurled during the offensive resurgence of the mid-1920s to late '30s? How do you compare a Bob Gibson or a Sandy Koufax, both of whom pitched during the pitching-dominated '60s, to a Greg Maddux or a Pedro Martinez, both of whom have excelled during the hitting-dominated era that we are in now? Or how do you compare Ty Cobb, who dominated the game during the dead ball era, to Ted Williams, who was just as dominant during the '40s and '50s?

How can the players whose careers ended prior to 1947, when the game finally was integrated and truly became "America's national pastime," be compared to the players who entered the game afterwards?

Prior to 1937, night baseball was just a thought and games were always played in daylight. The lights that were used in ballparks in the early days of night ball were not nearly as effective as those used for the past forty or so years, and made it much more difficult for the hitters to see the ball.

Prior to 1950, most relief pitchers were either washed-up starters or pitchers who were not good enough to make the starting rotation of their respective staffs. Nowadays, not only are there "closers" in the bullpen whose sole job is to finish games by getting the last two or three outs, but there are "set-up" men who usually enter the game in the seventh or eighth inning to bridge the gap between the starting pitcher and the closer.

Also, the gloves used by fielders have gotten much bigger, the dimensions of ballparks have changed, new pitches—such as the slider and split-finger fastball—have been developed, and players can now look for flaws in their mechanics by watching themselves on film.

With all the changes the game has undergone, it is clearly a difficult and daunting task to select the greatest players of all time. It is not as difficult to compare players from the same era, but in some cases even that isn't so simple. For example, whom would you choose: Christy Mathewson or Grover Cleveland Alexander? Frank Robinson or Roberto Clemente? Yogi Berra or Roy Campanella? Roger Clemens or Greg Maddux?

This book will not only attempt to select the best players from each era, but will also endeavor to rate them across the eras.

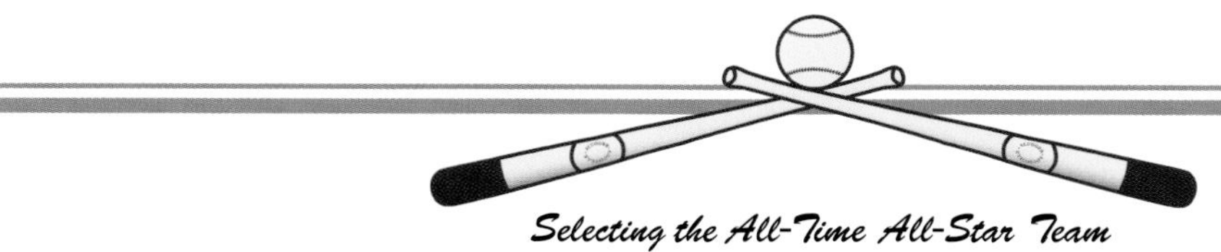

FIFTY-YEAR METHOD

I HAVE TAKEN A SLIGHTLY DIFFERENT APPROACH THAN OTHERS HAVE TO SELECTING AN All-Time All-Star Team.

First, all players entirely or predominantly from the 19th century will automatically be excluded. Since, as we saw earlier, the game was so much different during this period, the players of that time and their statistics really cannot be compared to those of later eras.

Next, prior to naming the All-Time All-Star Team, the best player at each position will be selected for the period of 1900–1950, and then for 1951–2003. This will allow us to better recognize the great players who played under different conditions, in different eras, and will give us a slightly better basis for comparison. (In fact, a truer basis for comparison would have been to rate the players for each twenty-five-year period. However, using that method, there would have been too many players whose careers would have crossed over into multiple periods. Even using my method, there are certain players whose careers overlapped—greats such as Ted Williams, Stan Musial, and Jackie Robinson. (Special mention will be given to these players later on, and an explanation will be given as to how they were dealt with.)

Finally, while many of the other all-time teams have chosen to ignore some of the great players from the old Negro Leagues because statistics are scarce, this one won't ignore them. A great player is a great player, and just because the old Negro Leaguers were not allowed to play in the majors does not mean they should be excluded from this team. In fact, when the players from the Negro Leagues competed against major leaguers in exhibition games, they won more than their fair share of the contests.

So for the first fifty-one years of the 20th century, the five greatest players at each position, including right-handed and left-handed pitcher, will be named. Then the same will be done for the period encompassing the last fifty-three years, with the top five relief pitchers and best designated hitters also being named. Then, the five best players at each position, all-time, will be selected.

STATISTICS VS. OPINION

BASEBALL, MORE THAN ANY OTHER TEAM SPORT, IS STATISTICS-ORIENTED. THIS IS probably because an individual player's performance is less dependent on the performance of his teammates than in any other team sport. In football, a running back is helped or hindered immensely by his offensive line, and it is only the great backs who excel despite playing behind a mediocre or weak line. In basketball, a scorer is immeasurably aided by having another player on the court with him who can get him the ball in the right position, at just the right time. However, in baseball, while it is true that a batter's RBI and runs scored-totals and a pitcher's win-loss record are affected by the other players around him, his other individual statistics are largely independent of the performance of his teammates.

It is for this reason that a player's performance can be judged largely by his statistics. They are there for you to see, in black and white, and they are indisputable. This is why, as was mentioned earlier, stats will be used as a measuring stick in rating the greatest players of all time. However, as was also mentioned, *too* much emphasis can be placed on stats and they can become misleading. Sometimes there are players who, every year, seem to put up outstanding numbers yet don't perform particularly well in clutch situations. There are those players who are not fundamentally sound in the field, or on the basepaths, or are too one-dimensional, or are not perceived by their teammates and coaches as being good team players. Then there are other players whose numbers don't necessarily jump out at you but who always seem to do the little things to help their team win and, as a result, are labeled "winners."

In addition, a player's statistics must be judged within the context of the era in which he played and compared to the statistics of the other players from that era. I have read other books that use complicated formulas to adjust a player's statistics based on those of the other players around him and come out with new, "adjusted" figures. Frankly, I found this to be somewhat boring and tedious and I will not subject the readers of this book to that. Rather, in judging a player's offensive performance or a pitcher's pitching performance, this book will examine how dominant they were during the era in which they played. The best way to judge this is to look at how many times during their career they were either at or near the top of their league in the various offensive or pitching categories.

For example, Ty Cobb's batting average does not need to be adjusted to that of the league average during the time in which he played. He led the American League in batting ten times during his career and finished second on five other occasions. Babe Ruth's slugging percentage and home run totals do not need to be adjusted. Over a fourteen-year stretch, beginning in 1918 and ending in 1931, he led the American League in home runs and slugging percentage twelve times. The only two times during that period he did not lead the league, he missed large portions of the season—once due to a suspension and once due to illness. His home run totals do not need to be adjusted against those of Mark McGwire because when Ruth was hitting all those home runs during the 1920s he frequently was hitting more home runs by himself than *entire teams* were hitting. Thus, even though McGwire's feat of 70 home runs was extremely impressive, it was not nearly as impressive or as dominant as what Ruth was able to accomplish.

Along the same lines, one must be careful not to be wowed by numbers that jump off the page at you because they seem to be so phenomenal. For example, during the dead ball era of the early 1900s, it was not at all unusual for pitchers to compile ERAs (i.e., Earned Run Averages) of under two runs a game. Nowadays, that seems like great pitching, but when you factor in the style of play during that period and the conditions under which the offenses had to attempt to score runs, those numbers are much more believable. Therefore, pitchers like Lefty Grove who pitched during the more offensive-minded 1920s and '30s, and Pedro Martinez who is pitching during the offensive resurgence that we have been experiencing the last several years, may actually have pitched better than their predecessors by consistently leading their respective leagues in ERA despite having higher numbers.

As for defensive statistics, they can be highly overrated as a true gauge of a fielder's ability. Fielding percentages do not give any indication of how much range a player has in the field: they just tell how many errors he made. There have been many players who had excellent fielding percentages because they didn't make many errors, but who had very little range, and therefore did not get to many of the balls that other players with more range were able to get to. Wade Boggs, in the latter stages of his career with the Yankees, won a Gold Glove award at third base one year because he made so few errors. But there were many balls he did not get to that many other third basemen would have fielded.

Then there are players who are afraid to take chances in the field, and instead prefer to make the "safe" play. An example of this type of player was Steve Garvey, first baseman for the Dodgers for many years. He was reputed to have a very weak throwing arm, and as a result would often make the safe play at first base when fielding ground balls hit to him, rather than attempt to get the lead runner at either second or third base. He also was very hesitant to charge sacrifice bunts and would usually make the sure play at first base. However, he made very few errors and always had a very high fielding percentage. Meanwhile, Keith Hernandez and Don Mattingly, probably the two finest fielding first basemen of that or maybe any era, might have had a slightly lower fielding percentage than Garvey. But they were much more aggressive in the field, took more chances, and had much more range.

So, you say, look at the fielder's number of chances, assists, and putouts to see how much range he has and how aggressive he is. While these figures come closer to determining the defensive ability of a player than does his fielding percentage, they can sometimes be misleading. For example, if an infielder plays on a team that has a pitching staff comprised mostly of strikeout and fly-ball pitchers, his opportunities to field ground balls may be somewhat limited. Meanwhile, an infielder playing on a team that has a pitching staff comprised largely of sinkerball or low-ball pitchers is likely to have far more chances. And an outfielder playing behind that staff featuring those sinkerball pitchers is likely to have fewer fly balls hit to him. Also, an outfielder with a powerful throwing arm might have fewer assists than an outfielder with a weaker arm because base runners are more hesitant to attempt to take the extra base on him.

What, then, is the answer, and how much emphasis should be given to statistics? As was suggested earlier, statistics are important and should be weighed heavily when judging a player's performance. They should not be followed blindly, however, and other factors must be considered as well. These factors include the player's reputation; the opinions of his peers and those who saw him perform regularly; and his contributions to a winning team. The emphasis here will be on statistics, but we will try to find a proper balance between them and these other factors.

OFFENSE VS. DEFENSE

THE NEXT IMPORTANT QUESTION IS HOW MUCH WEIGHT TO GIVE TO HITTING AND HOW much to defense. Statisticians have developed formulas that suggest great hitters will single-handedly win eighty to ninety games with their bats during their careers, while great defensive infielders will win only twenty to twenty-five with their gloves. While this may or may not be true, there are general perceptions held about players at different positions, and about the relative importance of offense to defense at those positions.

For example, first basemen and outfielders are generally expected to be major offensive contributors and run producers. Middle infielders (shortstops and second basemen) are perceived as being extremely important defensively; anything they can give you on offense is considered a plus.

Third basemen and catchers are thought of as being a combination of the two, with both offense and defense being equally important. In making my selections, a similar approach will be taken, with minor modifications.

At first base and in the outfield, the emphasis will be on offense, with run production being the primary prerequisite. Players who either drove in a lot of runs or were regularly on base, upsetting the opposing team's defense and scoring a lot of runs, will be given precedence. Defense will not be weighed as heavily, but the players should at least have been competent as fielders.

At the middle infield positions, defense will be weighed more heavily. However, the players should also have been solid offensively. Offense will be weighed as heavily as defense only if the player's offensive abilities were so overwhelming that they cannot be ignored.

At third base, the primary need is for someone who had some pop in his bat and was able to contribute offensively. After that, defense will be looked at closely, since the player must have been a solid defender as well.

Behind the plate, at catcher, offensive ability will be a major factor. However, just as important will be the ability to handle a pitching staff, call a good game, and be a good field general and team leader.

Finally, in judging a player's defensive ability, little emphasis will be placed on statistics since, as was mentioned earlier, figures such as fielding percentage, total chances accepted, assists and putouts can be very deceiving. Only in certain cases, where a player's numbers far exceeded those of his contemporaries, would they be a true indication of his defensive skills, and only then will the numbers be given more weight.

Nor will much emphasis be given to the number of Gold Gloves that a player won. Too often, the Gold Glove award seems to be given to players based on reputation, or because they are fairly solid offensive players (didn't Chuck Knoblauch once win a Gold Glove?). It seems that, unless a player who has previously won the Gold Glove award has a major drop-off defensively, he is almost an automatic to win it again. It also seems that a player who is a weak hitter is less likely to win one than does a decent hitter. Back in the mid-'70s, when Brooks Robinson's career was winding down and his defensive skills had eroded quite a bit, he was still awarded the Gold Glove every year. Meanwhile, there were a couple of other third basemen who had surpassed him defensively (Aurilio Rodriguez of Detroit, to name one). Therefore, the Gold Glove award is not always a true indication of a player's defensive ability. For that reason, more attention will be given to a player's reputation as a defensive player and what his peers had to say about him, than to the number of awards he won during his career.

LONGEVITY VS. SHORT-TERM BRILLIANCE

ANOTHER ISSUE TO CONSIDER WHEN SELECTING THIS ALL-TIME TEAM IS HOW MUCH importance should be placed on long-term excellence, as opposed to greatness over a shorter period of

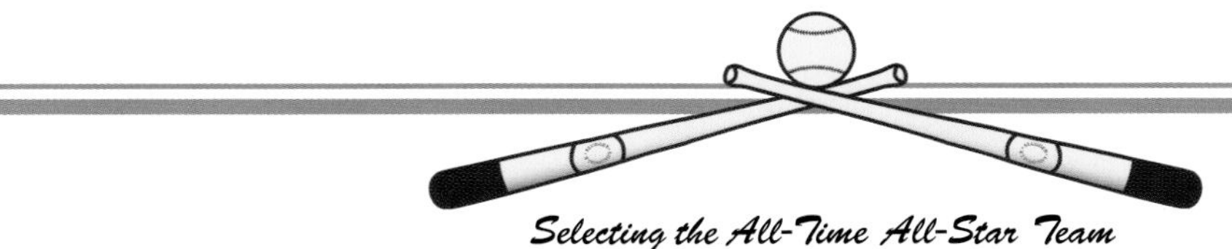

time. There have been many players who were very good for long periods of time but were never really thought of as being great, or dominant players. Some examples would be Enos Slaughter, Nellie Fox, Early Wynn, and Don Sutton, all of them players who spent over twenty years in the majors and eventually made it into the Hall of Fame. As was mentioned earlier, however, this team is for only the greatest of the great, so such players will not be given serious consideration.

There are also those players who had relatively long careers and were superb players, but who for one reason or another had only five or six seasons where they truly dominated. Examples of this would be Mickey Mantle and Chuck Klein. These players will be seriously considered, but rating Mantle over someone like Willie Mays or Hank Aaron, who were comparable to him when he was at his peak and better over a longer period of time, would be a difficult thing to do. And rating Klein over a Mel Ott, who was on a par with Klein when Klein was at his peak, but who also had many more outstanding years, would similarly be hard to do.

Then there are those players who had relatively short careers but who, for a good portion of those careers, put together some great seasons and could be considered, at their peak, dominant players. Examples would be Sandy Koufax, Dizzy Dean, and Don Mattingly. In looking at these players, my approach will be this: the player will be rated over the other top players of his period who had longer careers with better career statistics *only if,* at his peak, he exceeded the other players' performances by a *wide* margin. So in looking at Mattingly, he must be compared to Eddie Murray, the other top first baseman of his period. While Mattingly was generally considered to be the best first baseman in the game during his peak years of 1984–1988, Murray was not very far behind. And if you compare their career statistics, Mattingly's stats are dwarfed by Murray's. Therefore, Murray must be rated ahead of Mattingly.

In the case of Koufax, you would have to compare him to Warren Spahn and Whitey Ford, the other top left-handers of his era. While the career stats of both Spahn and Ford far exceed those of Koufax, you have to give the latter serious consideration because, at his peak, he was far and away the greatest pitcher in the game.

Then, there are the special cases of players like "Shoeless" Joe Jackson and Ed Cicotte, both of the infamous 1919 Chicago "Black Sox." At their peaks, Jackson and Cicotte were among the best players in baseball, but both had their careers shortened by their banishment from the game as a result of their involvement in the throwing of the 1919 World Series. Jackson's lifetime batting average of .356 ranks as the third highest all-time (behind only Ty Cobb's .367 and Rogers Hornsby's .358), and Cicotte was an exceptional right-hander who out-dueled Walter Johnson on a fairly regular basis. However, neither played more than ten or eleven years in the majors and if they hadn't been banished from the game when they were both still at or near the prime of their careers, their level of performance would have undoubtedly begun to decline: Jackson's career average certainly would have dropped a good 10 to 15 points, and Cicotte's record would have suffered as well. In these special cases, only the players' major league performance will be considered, and their career statistics will be compared to those of their contemporaries.

And finally, there are the cases of the old Negro League players who were never allowed to play in the majors. How do you compare them to the white players from the major leagues? The competition

was different, the playing conditions and number of games that were played in a season were different, and the statistics that are available for these players are sparse, at best. The philosophy that will be used in rating these players will be to listen to what the other Negro League players—and those white Major Leaguers who played against them in exhibition games—said about them. In addition, whatever statistics are available for them will be checked, and an attempt will be made to make the best possible judgment about them based on the scarcity of their records.

CHAPTER THREE The Opinions

As was mentioned earlier, factors such as a player's reputation and how his peers viewed him will weigh heavily in the selection process. One of the most direct ways to determine how others viewed a player is to look at the various opinion polls and surveys that have been conducted over the years. However, after looking at the results of some of these polls, it became obvious that there were some major discrepancies. In some cases, the differences of opinion seemed to be the result of who was being polled: the players or the sportswriters. In other instances, it seemed that the era in which the poll was conducted had a major impact on the voting results. An explanation will follow, but the one thing that seems clear is that different segments of the population at different times have different opinions. This is why, except in instances where there is complete agreement among the different factions, it is difficult to put much stock in the opinion polls.

As an example: in 1950, the general consensus was that Ty Cobb was the greatest player who ever lived, and that Babe Ruth was a distant second, or possibly even third, behind Honus Wagner. However, a few years ago, when *The Sporting News* announced its selections for the 100 greatest baseball players of the twentieth century, Ruth finished first and Cobb finished third (Willie Mays was second). In discussing the selections, Executive Editor John Rawlings admitted that there was "never any question as to who number one was going to be. It was who were going to be numbers two through one hundred." I found this intriguing since neither Cobb nor Ruth has appeared in a baseball game since 1950. That being the case, why has the Babe risen so much in stature while Cobb has fallen? It could be that Ruth's name is synonymous with the game of baseball and that he is undoubtedly the most famous player who ever lived. However, it might also be due to the fact that through the years the public's perception of what constitutes a great baseball player has changed. In 1950, many of the baseball purists were probably still clinging to the old-time style of baseball that was played during the dead ball era. Having grown up during that era, they probably felt that this slap-hitting, base-stealing style of ball was the way the game really should be played, and Cobb epitomized that style of play. However, with the influx of home run hitters such as Willie Mays, Hank Aaron, Mickey Mantle, Eddie Mathews, and Harmon Killebrew during the 1950s, the game's style of play changed even more. Later generations of fans developed a different perception of the game and how it should be played. In truth, the feats of Cobb and the other players of his era hadn't changed. They were still great players. They were just viewed a little differently.

Another example is Joe DiMaggio. In 1969, the Baseball Writers Association of America, in honor of baseball's centennial, voted DiMaggio the game's Greatest Living Player. However, when *The Sporting News* made its selections a few years ago, there were no fewer than four living players ranked ahead of him (Mays, Aaron, Ted Williams, and Stan Musial). And most polls taken these days would probably rank at least two or three of those players ahead of him. DiMaggio is still viewed as having been a truly great player, one of the greatest of all time. But why has he slipped somewhat in the public's eye? Perhaps some of the luster has been rubbed off the DiMaggio "mystique." Or perhaps some of the reverence with which he was once looked upon has been shifted to some of the other greats, like Mays and Williams. In particular, Williams seems to have grown in popularity. Perhaps this is due to the fact that the more recent generations of fans seem to appreciate his openness and his unpretentious style more than that of the always image-conscious DiMaggio. Williams is also no longer subject to the bad press that he received while he was playing. For whatever reason, the public's perception has changed here as well.

Having studied the results of these various opinion polls, however, I did find certain areas of agreement. It seems that Honus Wagner is the unanimous choice as the greatest shortstop of all time and that Babe Ruth is an almost unanimous choice to be part of the all-time outfield. While a couple of dissenters chose George Sisler or Jimmie Foxx to be the first baseman, Lou Gehrig is the overwhelming choice there. So, as a result, these three opinions will hold a great deal of weight during the selection process. The others will be given less credibility.

The annual voting for the MVP award, given annually to the outstanding performer in each league, and the Cy Young award, given to the outstanding pitcher in each league, will both be given serious consideration as well. How often did a player win one of these awards? Or, how often did he finish in the top five or ten in the voting? All of these factors will be considered. However, using this methodology can have its flaws as well, and must be done in moderation.

For one, the Cy Young award was not presented prior to 1956. Even after that, there was only one award for both major leagues, combined, until 1968. Therefore, for the first twelve years that this award was given out, it was much harder to win since a pitcher had to be considered the best pitcher in *both* leagues. This is proof of the magnificence of Sandy Koufax, since he won three Cy Youngs under those circumstances.

As for the MVP, there were certain years prior to 1930 when the award was not given out in one or both of the leagues. In fact, it was not awarded in either league for any of the 1915–1921 seasons. Babe Ruth hit 54 home runs in 1920 (to shatter the existing record of 29 that he had set the previous year), and then went on to have arguably the greatest season a hitter has ever had the next season: he hit 59 home runs, batted .378, and set all-time records for most total bases and highest slugging percentage in a single season (broken in 2001 by Barry Bonds). He most certainly would have won the MVP award in at least one of those seasons had it been presented, to go along with the one he won in 1923.

In addition, prior to 1930 it was impossible for an American League player to win the MVP award more than once. So in 1927, when Ruth hit his 60 home runs, he was not even eligible to win the award. And the following year, when both Ruth and teammate Lou Gehrig had phenomenal seasons and the Yankees won the pennant, neither was eligible (Gehrig had won it the previous year); the award was instead given to Mickey Cochrane, even though he posted relatively modest numbers in 1928.

Finally, there is one more issue to consider when contemplating how much importance can be placed on the voting for these annual awards: the favoritism shown by the sportswriters who submit the ballots. A perfect example of this is Ted Williams.

Williams won two Triple Crowns in his career, but, amazingly, did not win the MVP award in either season. The first time, in 1942, he lost out by one vote to Joe Gordon, the second baseman for the Yankees. True, the Yankees had won the pennant that year and Gordon had a very good season, but Williams had kept Boston in the pennant race for much of the season and his numbers far exceeded those of Gordon. (That year Gordon hit 18 home runs, had 103 RBI, and batted .322, while Williams hit 36 home runs, knocked in 137 runs, and batted .356). Yet, ironically, one of the Boston sportswriters neglected to give Williams even a tenth-place vote on his ballot, thereby costing him the award. Clearly, Williams was not a favorite of this Boston writer.

Five years later, in 1947, Williams won his second Triple Crown. That year, in a very close contest, the award was given to Joe DiMaggio over Williams despite the fact that DiMaggio had actually had what, for him, was considered to be a sub par year (he only hit 20 home runs, knocked in 97 runs, and batted .315, while Williams hit 32 homers, knocked in 114 runs, and batted .343).

As you can see, the judgments of the sportswriters can at times be somewhat suspect. Besides, I have always felt that it is the players and managers who are the most knowledgeable, who have the greatest understanding of the game, and whose opinions should be valued the most. Therefore, that is what I will do when weighing the opinions of others during the selection process.

PART TWO

The 1900–1950 All-Star Team

We are finally ready to take a look at the selections, position by position, for the first half of the 20th century. For each position, the choices for the five greatest players will be listed in order. Players who deserve honorable mention will also be listed. The career statistics of each player selected will be shown and then an explanation will be given as to why that player was chosen. We will begin at first base…

All-Star First Baseman

PLAYER	YEARS	*AB	HITS	RUNS	2B	3B	HR	RBI	AVG	SB	OBP	SLG PCT
1) LOU GEHRIG	1923–39	8,001	2,721	1,888	534	163	493	1,995	.340	102	.447	.632
2) JIMMIE FOXX	1925–45	8,134	2,646	1,751	458	125	534	1,922	.325	87	.428	.609
3) GEORGE SISLER	1915–30	8,267	2,812	1,284	425	164	102	1,175	.340	375	.379	.468
4) HANK GREENBERG	1933–40, 1945–47	5,193	1,628	1,051	379	71	331	1,276	.313	58	.412	.605
5) BILL TERRY	1923–36	6,428	2,193	1,120	373	112	154	1,078	.341	56	.393	.506
HONORABLE MENTION:												
BUCK LEONARD**	1933–50	1,587	514		85	33	71		.324	10		
JOHNNY MIZE	1936–42, 1946–53	6,443	2,011	1,118	367	83	359	1,337	.312	28	.397	.562
JIM BOTTOMLEY	1922–37	7,471	2,313	1,177	465	151	219	1,422	.310	58	.369	.500

* See Glossary, page 287

** Buck Leonard's statistics are from the Negro Leagues and are therefore incomplete.

1 LOU GEHRIG

IT WAS MENTIONED EARLIER THAT FIRST BASE WOULD BE A POSITION FROM WHICH RUN production would be given priority. That being said, there were only two possible choices: Lou Gehrig or Jimmie Foxx, two of the greatest sluggers and run producers the game has ever known. Using that selection criterion, you could also make a case for Hank Greenberg, but his career was too short and as a result his numbers pale by comparison to theirs.

The general consensus is that Lou Gehrig is the greatest first baseman of all time. He is probably the most famous. After all, he played in New York on those fabled Yankees teams with Babe Ruth. He appeared in seven World Series, starring in many of them. And, of course, he held the record for consecutive games played until Cal Ripken, Jr. finally broke it.

Jimmie Foxx is not as famous, and his memory has not been carried down through the years the way Gehrig's has. If you look closely at their statistics though, there is really not a great deal of difference

between them, with Gehrig holding an edge in most of the categories except for home runs. Chances are, had he not been stricken with a fatal illness when he was only thirty-six years old, Gehrig would have surpassed Foxx in that category as well.

However, this is a comparison worth making since both players had many of their peak years at right around the same time. Both played as full-time regulars in their respective lineups for eleven years from 1928 to 1938. During that period, Foxx had an edge in home runs, but Gehrig had an edge in runs batted in, batting average, and runs scored. Both were surrounded by other talented players much of the time: Gehrig had Hall of Famers Babe Ruth, Earle Combs, Tony Lazzeri, Bill Dickey, and Joe DiMaggio, at different times, while, in his years with the A's, Foxx had Hall of Famers Al Simmons and Mickey Cochrane, and later, with the Red Sox, Ted Williams and Joe Cronin.

Gehrig led the American League in home runs three times, RBI five times, batting average once, triples once, doubles twice, hits once, runs four times, on-base percentage five times, and slugging percentage twice. Foxx led the league in home runs four times (hitting 50 or more twice), RBI three times, batting average twice, runs once, on-base percentage three times, and slugging percentage five times. Each player won a Triple Crown: Gehrig in 1934, hitting 49 homers, knocking in 165 runs, and batting .363; and Foxx the previous year, hitting 48 homers, knocking in 163 runs, and batting .356. Each accomplished the remarkable feat of knocking in 100 or more runs for thirteen consecutive seasons, with Gehrig knocking in an A.L.-record 184 in 1931. Foxx won three MVP awards, Gehrig two. However, Gehrig finished in the top five in the MVP voting a total of eight times, while Foxx made it into the top five only four times. Gehrig is also tied with Hank Greenberg for the highest RBI per-game ratio in the history of baseball with a mark of .92 (Foxx's ratio is slightly lower at .83). Defensively, Gehrig was an average first baseman, while Foxx was considered to be a little stronger.

In his book, *Ted Williams' Hit List,* Williams, who did not include himself in his rankings, rated Gehrig as the second greatest hitter of all time (behind Babe Ruth) and Foxx as the third greatest. In

comparing the two, he said that the difference between them was a very close call, "an awfully tough match-up." He went on to say, "Gehrig's statistics suggest he was better than Foxx," but Williams also pointed out that ballparks in general seem to favor left-handed hitters and he added, "Foxx was definitely the most productive right-handed hitter I ever saw."

As you can see, there wasn't as much of a difference between the two players as most people would probably have thought, and you can't go wrong with either one of them. However, one must be selected, and that selection is Gehrig.

He was remarkably consistent and durable, and was a tremendous clutch performer. In addition to his incredible RBI totals, he holds the major league record for most career grand slams, with 23, and was an outstanding World Series performer. In thirty-four Series games, he hit 10 home runs, knocked in 34 runs, and batted .361. He also batted over .300 for twelve straight seasons, surpassing the .350 mark six times, and topping the .370 mark three times. He hit more than 40 homers five times, hitting 49 twice, knocked in more than 150 runs seven times, had as many as 15 triples four times, as many as 40 doubles seven times, more than 200 hits eight times, and more than 100 runs scored thirteen straight seasons. Joe DiMaggio, who played with him for three seasons, later said that Gehrig was the greatest hitter he ever saw—high praise from someone who spent many years watching Ted Williams hit.

❷ JIMMIE FOXX

AS I'VE SAID, JIMMIE FOXX IS REALLY THE only other first baseman that could be mentioned in the same breath as Lou Gehrig. Aside from his list of accomplishments that have already been touched on, he set a major league record by hitting 30 or more homers in twelve straight seasons (a record matched this past season by Barry Bonds) and came within three percentage points of winning another Triple Crown in 1932. That season, he hit 58 home runs (seriously challenging Babe Ruth's then single-season record of 60), knocked in 169 runs, and batted

.364, just missing winning the batting title. He won the MVP that year, then the following season, and again in 1938 when, playing for the Red Sox, he hit 50 homers (finishing second to Hank Greenberg's 58), and led the league in RBI, with 175, and in batting, with a .349 average. He thus became the first player in major league history to win three MVP awards and the first to hit 50 or more homers with two different teams. Foxx also hit over .300 twelve times, topping the .350 mark four times, and scored more than 100 runs eleven times.

Teammate Mickey Cochrane said of him, "I think Foxx could hit as long a ball as any of them. That even goes for Ruth."

Pitcher Willis Hudlin of the Indians said of Foxx, "He had God-given power and a quick bat. He could hit a ball out of any park."

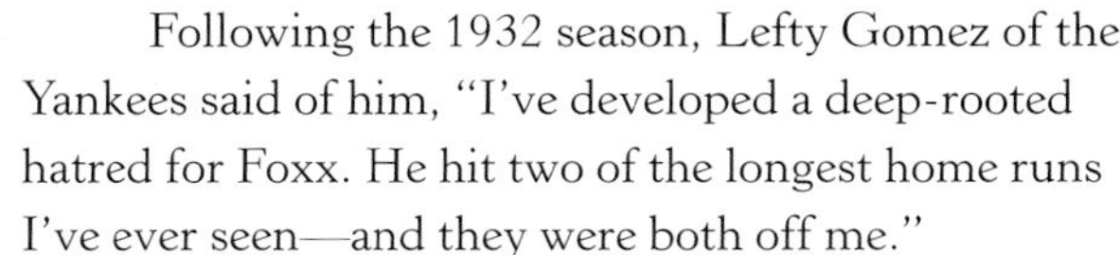

Following the 1932 season, Lefty Gomez of the Yankees said of him, "I've developed a deep-rooted hatred for Foxx. He hit two of the longest home runs I've ever seen—and they were both off me."

And speaking of his defense: sportswriter Joe Williams once said of Foxx, "No right-handed first baseman ever came in to field a bunt, turn, and throw to second or third base more quickly or more accurately."

Finally, as author Mark R. Millikin points out in his book *Jimmie Foxx, The Pride of Sudlersville,* John Steadman, sportswriter of the *Baltimore Sun* and formerly with the *Baltimore News American,* once said, "With apologies to Hank Aaron, Willie Mays, Ralph Kiner, and others, Jimmie Foxx was (and still is) the greatest right-handed slugger of all time."

❸ GEORGE SISLER

THIS WAS ANOTHER DIFFICULT CHOICE because, as was mentioned earlier, run production would be the most sought-after attribute in a first baseman. Clearly, Hank Greenberg was the next greatest run producer among the first basemen, and frankly I wouldn't have any problem slotting him into third behind Gehrig and Foxx. Since Greenberg's career was relatively short, his numbers were thereby cut down significantly. And yet, in far fewer career at-bats than George Sisler, Greenberg was still able to more than

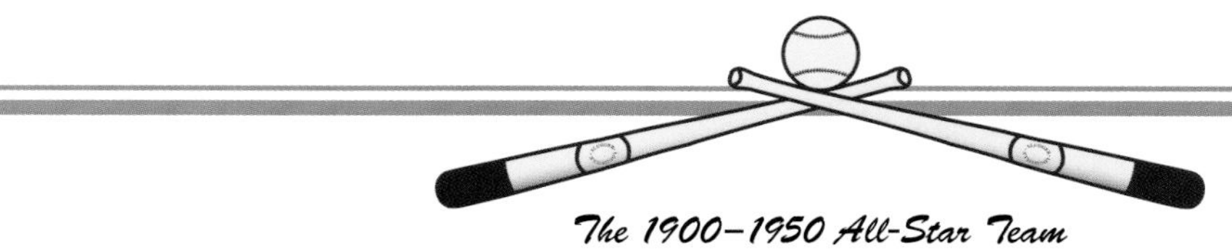

triple his home run output and accumulate more runs batted in. He also finished with a higher on-base percentage and a much higher slugging percentage, and he scored runs at a faster rate. In fact, the only categories in which Sisler holds a statistical advantage are batting average, triples, and stolen bases. Therefore, it would seem that Greenberg was far superior as an offensive player.

But was he really?

Greenberg spent virtually his entire career with the Detroit Tigers when they were perennial pennant-contenders. While he was clearly the focal point of their attack and the most dangerous hitter in their lineup, Greenberg usually had an excellent supporting cast. During most of his finest seasons, he batted right behind Hall of Fame second baseman Charlie Gehringer, who, with his .404 career on-base percentage, was on base constantly. Greenberg also played with Hall of Famers Mickey Cochrane and Goose Goslin during the mid-1930s, and later with slugging catcher/first baseman Rudy York. Having such a fine group of teammates certainly did not limit Greenberg's opportunities to both drive in and score runs.

On the other hand, Sisler spent the majority of his career with the St. Louis Browns. While the Browns did manage to make it into the first division a couple of times during Sisler's tenure there, they were, generally speaking, not a very strong team. In fact, they finished higher than fifth in only three of Sisler's twelve seasons there. Although he did receive some support in the St. Louis lineup from slugging outfielder Ken Williams (the first player in baseball history to hit 30 home runs and steal 30 bases in the same season), Sisler did not receive nearly the help from his teammates that Greenberg received from his. In addition, Sisler came up during the dead ball era, and even though his career spanned the decade of the 1920s, Sisler's best years were in the early portion of the decade, when home run totals were still generally low, and when the number of runs being scored was considerably less than it would be by the end of the decade. He also adhered more to the style of play that was prevalent during his early years and excelled more at the scientific aspects of the game, such as hitting for a high average, stealing bases, and playing exceptional defense.

So while strictly on the basis of the numbers it would appear that Greenberg was the better player, there really is a lot more to consider. He certainly was the more potent hitter and regardless of any external factors the greater run producer of the two. However, Sisler was a superb hitter in his own right and excelled at more aspects of the game. He was far superior as a base runner and fielder, and, overall, was a more complete player. For that reason, he just barely edges out Greenberg for a spot on the third team.

George Sisler was voted the American League's Most Valuable Player in 1922, when he hit an astounding .420 for the St. Louis Browns, led the league in hits, runs scored, and doubles, and kept his team in the pennant race for the entire season with his brilliant play. That year, the Browns finished a close second to the Yankees in the American League standings, making it into the second spot for the only time in Sisler's career. In 1920, he had another remarkable season, hitting .407 and totaling 257 hits—a major league record that still stands. In addition to leading the league in batting and base hits on two different occasions, Sisler also led in triples twice and finished second in home runs to Babe Ruth in 1920 by hitting 19. A marvelous base runner, he stole 42 bases that year and finished his career with 375 stolen bases and 19 steals of home. In all, Sisler knocked in over 100 runs and scored more than 100 runs four times each, batted over .350 five times, finished with as many as 15 triples five times, compiled more than 200 hits six times, stole more than 30 bases six times, and struck out only 327 times in over 8,000 career at-bats. He also was considered to be the finest defensive first baseman of his era, leading A.L. first basemen in assists seven times.

Ty Cobb called Sisler "the nearest thing to a perfect ballplayer."

❹ HANK GREENBERG

IF HANK GREENBERG HADN'T LOST ALMOST five years to military service during World War II, we might be comparing him to Gehrig and Foxx. While missing virtually all of the 1941 season (being among the first to enlist in the armed forces), the entire 1942–1944 seasons, and more than half of the 1945 campaign, Greenberg still managed to accumulate some very impressive career numbers.

His 331 home runs in just over ten full seasons in the majors indicate that, had he not missed all that time due to his stint in the military, he quite possibly would have made it to 500 for his career. He still managed to win two MVP awards, lead the league in home runs and runs batted in four times each, doubles twice, runs scored once, and slugging percentage once. Greenberg hit more than 40 homers in a season four times, knocked in more than 100 runs seven times (topping 140 four times), batted over .300 eight times, scored more than 100 runs six times, collected at least 200 hits three times, and had more than 40 doubles five times, establishing a career high with 63 in 1934.

In his first MVP season of 1935, Greenberg finished with 36 homers, 170 runs batted in, a batting average of .328, 121 runs scored, 203 hits, 16 triples, and 46 doubles, while leading the Detroit Tigers to their second consecutive pennant and a victory in the World Series. When Greenberg was named MVP a second time in 1940, he became the first player to win the award at two different positions. Playing left field for Detroit that season in order to make room at first base for young slugger Rudy York, Greenberg hit 41 homers, knocked in 150 runs, batted .340, scored 129 runs, and totaled 50 doubles to once again lead the Tigers to the pennant. In all, he played on four pennant-winning teams and two world champions in Detroit. Greenberg is also tied with Lou Gehrig for the highest RBI per-game ratio in baseball history with a mark of .92.

Greenberg seriously challenged two very famous records during his career. In 1937, he finished with 183 runs batted in, to come within one of Lou Gehrig's American League record (a record that still stands). The following season, Greenberg hit 58 home runs, to come within two of Babe Ruth's cherished then record of 60. Interestingly, Greenberg actually had 58 with several games left on the Tiger schedule, but failed to hit another. While others have said that opposing pitchers refused to give him any good pitches to hit as he drew close to 60 because they didn't want a Jewish player to break the Babe's record, Greenberg, class act that he was, refused to accept that as an excuse.

Jackie Robinson once experienced Greenberg's class first-hand. After being traded into the National League towards the end of his career, Greenberg and the Pirates were playing Robinson's Dodgers. The former had been witnessing the kind of abuse that Robinson had been taking from both fans and players, and, having experienced a great deal of anti-Semitism throughout his career, was more sympathetic than most. In a close play at first base, the two men collided, and as the hulking Greenberg helped Robinson to his feet, he offered him words of encouragement. Robinson said after the game that Greenberg "has class written all over him."

5 BILL TERRY

BILL TERRY'S NUMBERS ARE FOR THE MOST part quite similar to those of George Sisler. In fact, in approximately 1,800 fewer at-bats, Terry hit more home runs, finished with virtually the same batting average, compiled higher on-base and slugging percentages, and drove in just 100 fewer runs while scoring just 164 less. However, Terry's best years came during the late 1920s and early '30s, when offensive statistics were generally much higher than they were during Sisler's peak years. In addition, Terry spent his entire career playing in the era of the livelier ball, while Sisler's first five seasons were spent hitting in the dead ball era. Terry also had the

advantages of playing in the Polo Grounds—a great park for left-handed hitters like Terry—and of playing for the New York Giants, a pennant contender throughout most of his career. All things considered, Sisler's numbers really are more impressive.

Terry was also not nearly the run-producer that Hank Greenberg was. Therefore, he must settle for a spot on the fifth team.

Bill Terry is the last player in the National League to hit .400 in a season. After batting .372 for John McGraw's New York Giants in 1929, Terry followed that up with a mark of .401 in 1930, establishing a league record in the process by totaling 254 base hits. The lefty-swinging Terry also had outstanding seasons in both 1931 and 1932, finishing second in the league in batting both years with averages of .349 and .350, respectively. He hit .341 for his career and was also considered to be the finest defensive first baseman in the National League. In all, he hit more than 20 homers in a season three times, knocked in more than 100 runs six times, scored more than 100 seven times, had more than 200 hits six times, and batted over .350 four times. Terry finished in the top five in the league MVP voting three times, and made it into the top ten on three other occasions. Beginning in 1933, he was selected to be the National League's starting first baseman in each of the sport's first three All-Star games.

Honorable mention should be given to Buck Leonard, Johnny Mize, and Jim Bottomley:

Buck Leonard anchored first base for the Homestead Grays of the Negro Leagues for seventeen years, batting fourth behind Josh Gibson for much of his career. As a hitter, his powerful left-handed swing prompted comparisons to Lou Gehrig, while as a fielder he was frequently likened to George Sisler for his smooth style and soft hands. Leonard won two Negro National League home run titles and three batting titles, hitting .392 in 1941 and .395 in 1946. He also batted .382 in exhibition games against major leaguers. Buck O'Neill, who played and later managed in the Negro Leagues during Leonard's career, said Leonard was the best fastball hitter he ever saw.

The admiration and respect that Negro League experts had for Leonard was exhibited in 1972 when a ten-man committee appointed by then-baseball commissioner Bowie Kuhn elected him to the Hall of Fame, along with Josh Gibson. Just one year earlier, the great Satchel Paige had become the first former Negro League player to get elected to the Hall. Along with Paige and Gibson (considered by many to be the two greatest players in Negro League history), Leonard was among the very first to enter Cooperstown.

Johnny Mize led the National League in home runs four times during a career in which he hit 359 homers, despite missing three of his peak seasons due to time spent in the military during World War II. He batted a career-high .364 for the Cardinals in 1937, then won his only batting title two years later by hitting .349 for St. Louis. He hit 51 home runs for the Giants in 1947 to lead the National League, and also led the league with 138 runs batted in and 137 runs scored that year. Mize hit more than 40 home runs two other times, knocked in more than 100 runs a total of eight times, scored over 100 runs five times, and batted over .300 nine times, topping the .340 mark twice. He won three RBI titles, a batting championship, and led the league in slugging four times. Mize was selected to the All-Star team ten times and finished second in the league MVP voting twice, and third on another occasion. He ended his career as a part-time player with the Yankees from 1949 to 1953, making significant contributions to all five world championship teams.

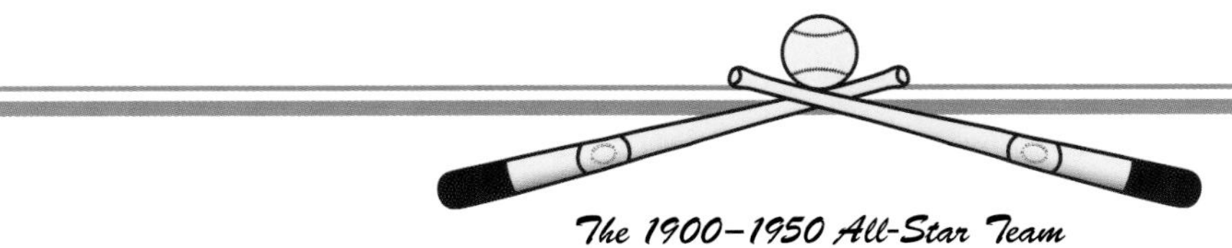

Jim Bottomley was a big run producer for the Cardinals, Reds, and St. Louis Browns during the 1920s and early 1930s, knocking in over 100 runs six consecutive seasons from 1924 to 1929 and averaging 126 per year for the Cardinals over that span. He also batted over .300 nine times, topping the .340 mark three times, and had more than 10 triples in a season nine times, reaching the 20 mark once. He led the National League in home runs once and RBI twice, and won the league's MVP award in 1928, when he hit 31 home runs, knocked in 136 runs, scored 123 others, and batted .325. He also had 20 triples and 42 doubles that year, making him one of only a handful of players to collect as many as 20 home runs, triples, and doubles in the same season.

All-Star Second Baseman

PLAYER	YEARS	AB	HITS	RUNS	2B	3B	HR	RBI	AVG	SB	OBP	SLG PCT
1) ROGERS HORNSBY	1915–37	8,137	2,930	1,579	541	169	301	1,584	.358	135	.434	.577
2) CHARLIE GEHRINGER	1924–42	8,860	2,839	1,774	574	146	184	1,427	.320	181	.404	.480
3) NAPOLEON LAJOIE	1896–1916	9,589	3,242	1,504	657	163	83	1,599	.338	380	.380	.467
4) EDDIE COLLINS	1906–30	9,949	3,312	1,821	438	186	47	1,300	.333	744	.424	.428
5) FRANKIE FRISCH	1919–37	9,112	2,880	1,532	466	138	105	1,244	.316	419	.369	.432
HONORABLE MENTION:												
BILLY HERMAN	1931–43, 1946–47	7,707	2,345	1,163	486	82	47	839	.304	67	.367	.407
BOBBY DOERR	1937–44, 1946–51	7,093	2,042	1,094	381	89	223	1,247	.288	54	.362	.461
JOE GORDON	1938–43, 1946–50	5,707	1,530	914	264	52	253	975	.268	89	.357	.466

1 ROGERS HORNSBY

As noted earlier, in the middle infield, while still looking for players who were solid offensively, more of an emphasis will be put on defense—unless, that is, there was a player whose offensive abilities were so overwhelming that they could not be ignored. Such a player was Rogers Hornsby.

While generally regarded as a mediocre fielder, Hornsby is considered to be perhaps the greatest right-handed hitter in the history of the game. His career batting average of .358 is second only to Ty Cobb's .367. Ted Williams ranked Hornsby fourth on his greatest hitters list (behind only Ruth, Gehrig, and Foxx), and with good reason.

Hornsby was the dominant player in the National League for most of the 1920s. During that period, he led the league in batting seven times, including six consecutive times from 1920 to 1925. Playing for the St. Louis Cardinals over that six-year stretch, Hornsby batted .400 or better three times, reaching a career-best .424 in 1924. From 1921 to 1925, his *overall* batting average was over

.400, making him the only player in the history of the game to maintain such a high average over a five-year period. He won two Triple Crowns, the first coming in 1922, when he hit 42 home runs, knocked in 152 runs, and batted .401, and the second coming in 1925, when he hit 39 homers, had 143 RBI, and batted .403. Hornsby was voted MVP of the league for that 1925 season, and again in 1929, as a member of the Chicago Cubs. He probably would have won the award several more times were it not for the fact that it was not presented in the National League for any of the 1915–1923 seasons. In all, Hornsby hit more than 30 homers in a season three times, knocked in more than 125 runs five times, batted over .370 eight times, collected more than 40 doubles and 200 hits seven times each, and scored more than 100 runs six times. In addition, he led the league in runs batted in, doubles, and hits four times each, runs scored five times, on-base percentage eight times, and slugging percentage ten times—all this from a *second baseman!*

❷ CHARLIE GEHRINGER

THE CHOICE FOR THE SECOND TEAM WAS A bit more difficult to make. There is very little that separates Charlie Gehringer from Nap Lajoie and Eddie Collins. All were outstanding in the field and at the bat. Defensively, Collins probably had the most range and quickness. He led American League second basemen in fielding attempts nine times. Lajoie, though not as quick, had great hands and was as steady as they come. Gehringer was also outstanding, having led A.L. second basemen in fielding six times, putouts three times, and assists seven times.

Offensively, though all were standouts, there were distinct differences in their games. Collins had very little power, having amassed only 47 home runs over twenty-five seasons and never having knocked in 100 runs in a season. However, he did hit .333 lifetime, was a terrific base-runner and stealer of bases, ranking high on the all-time stolen base list with 744, and had the highest career on-base percentage (.424) of the three.

Lajoie was probably the best pure hitter of the three. Playing his entire career in the dead ball era, he did not hit many home runs either (83). However, he was known to hit the ball as hard as anyone in his day and did accumulate 657 doubles over his career—a figure good enough to put him in the top ten all-time. He also led the league in runs batted in three times, knocking in over 100 in a season on four different occasions. He is also the only one of the three to ever win a Triple Crown, accomplishing the feat in 1901 when he hit 14 home runs, knocked in 125 runs, and batted .426, the highest single-season batting average attained since 1900. He was also a good base runner, having stolen 380 bases during his career despite not being particularly fast.

It is somewhat difficult to gauge Gehringer's offensive productivity against that of Lajoie and Collins since the former played his entire career during the more offensive-minded 1920s and '30s. However, there was a great deal of balance in Gehringer's game, as is evidenced by his career home run (184) and stolen base (181) totals. He was also a terrific run-producer, knocking in 100 or more runs on seven different occasions for the Detroit Tigers and scoring in triple digits twelve times during his career. An example of his overall excellence would be the 1929 season, when he led the league in stolen bases, doubles, triples, hits, runs scored, putouts and fielding, and hit .339. It is for this versatility that he is the choice for the second team.

Teammate Mickey Cochrane said of Gehringer: "He says hello on Opening Day and goodbye on Closing Day, and in between all he does is hit .350." Perhaps that is why he was nicknamed the "Mechanical Man."

This consistency can be seen in his numbers. Gehringer had 200 or more hits in a season seven times and hit .300 or better fourteen times. Three of his finest seasons came during the second half of his career. In 1935, he knocked in 127 runs, scored 134, had 214 hits, and batted .356. The following season, he led the league in doubles for the second time by collecting 60, and followed that up by winning the league MVP award in 1937 when he batted .371 en route to winning his only batting title. He also finished in the top five in the MVP voting two other times.

Ty Cobb said that aside from Eddie Collins, Gehringer was "the best second baseman I ever saw."

❸ NAPOLEON LAJOIE

UNFORTUNATELY FOR NAP LAJOIE, NO LEAGUE MVP award was given out until he was in the latter stages of his career; otherwise there'd be no telling how many he would have won. After all, for much of the first decade of the 20th century, he was considered to be the finest player in the American League—that league's version of Honus Wagner.

In addition to his Triple Crown season of 1901, Lajoie led the league in batting on three other occasions and also led the league in doubles five times, hits four times, runs scored once, and slugging percentage four times. In all, he batted over .350 nine times, had more than 40 doubles seven times, more than 200 hits four times, and scored more than 100 runs three times.

A fine defensive player as well, he led league second basemen in fielding six different times. Tommy Leach, another infielder who played during that era, said of Lajoie: "What a ballplayer that man was. Every play he made he executed so gracefully that it looked like it was the easiest thing in the world."

❹ EDDIE COLLINS

EDDIE COLLINS WAS THOUGHT SO HIGHLY OF AS a player that he finished in the top five in the league MVP voting on five different occasions even though no award was presented for the years 1915–1921, which were some of his peak seasons. He did win the award in 1914 when he helped lead the Philadelphia Athletics to the A.L. pennant. He also helped win two more pennants for the Chicago White Sox in 1917 and 1919. He was, in short, a winner.

Offensively, Collins hit over .340 ten times during his career, scored more than 100 runs seven times, stole more than 50 bases six times, and almost never struck out. He led the A.L. in batting and on-base percentage once, in runs scored three times, and in stolen bases four times, stealing a career-high 81 bases in 1910.

He also owns many fielding records for second basemen, including most putouts, assists, and total chances.

John McGraw once said that Collins was the best ballplayer he'd ever seen, and Connie Mack (who managed both Collins and Nap Lajoie) called Collins the best second baseman he ever saw. Mack went on to say in *Baseball's Greatest Lineup* that "no one could pick a better man for second base than Eddie Collins. He had everything. He had fighting spirit, he could hit, he could run the bases, and he was smart."

❺ FRANKIE FRISCH

WHILE HE WAS AN OUTSTANDING SECOND baseman and a fine offensive player, Frankie Frisch has to be ranked just behind Gehringer, Lajoie, and Collins. He did not have as much power as Gehringer and was not the run-producer that the Tiger great was. Playing in essentially the same era, Frisch compiled 250 more career at-bats but finished with far fewer home runs, runs batted in, and runs scored. In fact, Gehringer finished ahead of Frisch in every offensive category, except for stolen bases.

In almost the same number of at-bats, Frisch hit more home runs than Lajoie, but that was solely because of the eras in which the two men played. Lajoie's greater number of doubles and triples, as well as his higher slugging percentage, are a testament to his superior power, and he also drove in far more runs than Frisch did. The two players scored runs at approximately the same rate and stole about the same number of bases, but Lajoie was clearly the better hitter and at least Frisch's equal in the field.

Frisch had comparable power to Collins, driving in almost as many runs in approximately 800 fewer at-bats and finishing with almost the same slugging percentage. However, Collins scored runs at a faster pace and, with his higher batting average and propensity for drawing bases on balls, compiled a much higher on-base percentage. He also stole many more bases and was quite possibly the finest defensive second baseman of the first half of the twentieth century. So Frisch must settle for the fifth spot.

Frankie Frisch, nicknamed the "Fordham Flash" for his flashy style of play in the field, starred first for John McGraw's New York Giants and later for the St. Louis Cardinals, where he became one of the leaders of their famed "Gas House Gang."

Though he didn't have very much power, never hitting more than 12 home runs in any season, he was a very solid hitter and an extremely good and aggressive base runner. In spite of the fact that he played during an era in which far less emphasis was placed on stealing bases, Frisch managed to accumulate 419 stolen bases during his career.

Though Frisch is remembered more as a St. Louis Cardinal, he actually had some of his finest seasons in New York. As a member of the Giants from 1921 to 1924, he posted batting averages of .341, .327, .348, and .328, drove in more than 100 runs twice, tallied more than 200 hits twice, and scored more than 100 runs each season, leading the N.L. with 121 in 1924. The 1923 season was probably his best in New York. That year he hit 12 home runs, knocked in 111 runs, batted .348, scored 116 runs, led the league with 223 hits, and struck out just twelve times in almost 700 plate appearances. In fact, Frisch never struck out more than 28 times in any season, fanning just 272 times in almost 10,000 plate appearances.

Frisch had another outstanding season as a member of the Cardinals in 1930. That year he finished with 10 home runs, 114 runs batted in, 121 runs scored, and a .346 batting average. Even though he won the National League's MVP award in 1931, Frisch had probably his finest all-around season in St. Louis in 1927 after he was traded from the Giants to the Cardinals during the off-season for Rogers Hornsby. That year, Frisch hit .337, led the league with 48 stolen bases, handled a record 1,059 chances (including a record 641 assists), and finished runner-up to Paul Waner in the league MVP voting. Teammate Bob O'Farrell, who had won the MVP award the previous year, said: "The greatest player I ever saw in any one season was Frankie Frisch in 1927."

In all, Frisch bettered the .300 mark thirteen times, including eleven straight seasons from 1921 to 1931. He also led the N.L. in hits and runs scored once, and in stolen bases three times. He knocked in 100 or more runs three times, scored more than 100 runs seven times, and stole more than 30 bases four times.

Honorable mention should be given to Billy Herman, Bobby Doerr, and Joe Gordon:

Billy Herman played most of his career with the Chicago Cubs and was a lifetime .300-hitter, topping that mark eight times. He had more than 200 hits in a season three times and scored more than 100

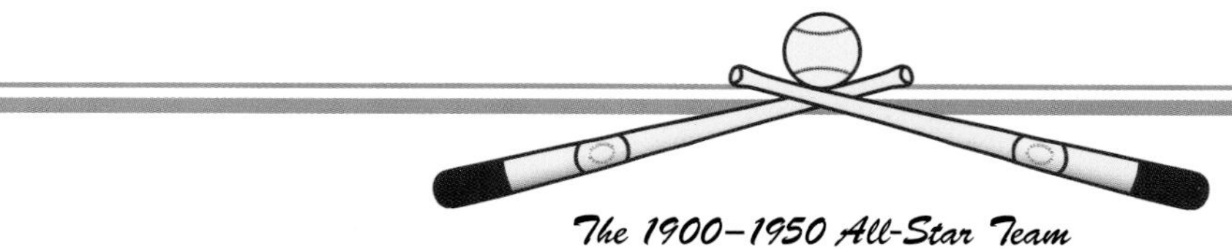

runs five times. Herman led the league in hits, doubles, and triples once, and led N.L. second basemen in assists three times. He finished in the top five of the MVP voting three times, and made it into the top ten two other times. Herman was also a perennial All-Star, having been selected to the team a total of nine times during his career.

Bobby Doerr had great power for a second baseman, hitting 223 home runs during his career with the Boston Red Sox, including three seasons with more than 20. He led the A.L. in slugging percentage in 1944 with a mark of .528, knocked in 100 or more runs in six different seasons, and batted over .300 three times. He was an excellent fielder, leading league second basemen in assists four times. Doerr was a nine-time All-Star and finished in the top ten in the league MVP voting twice. Ted Williams once said that Doerr was the one indispensable player on those Red Sox teams.

Joe Gordon was the best second baseman in baseball for much of his relatively brief eleven-year career. Replacing Tony Lazzeri as the Yankees' starting second baseman in 1938, Gordon went on to play for five pennant-winners and four world champions in his seven seasons in New York. On most of those teams, he was the second most outstanding and valuable player, behind only Joe DiMaggio. From 1939 to 1943, Gordon appeared in no fewer than 147 games (out of a possible 154) and was selected to *The Sporting News* All-Star team as the American League's top second baseman four times.

Gordon's finest seasons in New York came in 1939, 1940, and 1942. In the first of those seasons, he hit 28 home runs, knocked in 111 runs, and batted .284. The following year, he finished with 30 homers, 103 runs batted in, a batting average of .281, and a career-high 112 runs scored. In 1942, Gordon edged out Ted Williams in the A.L. MVP voting by hitting 18 home runs, driving in 103 runs, and hitting a career-best .322. His home run and RBI totals were particularly impressive when taking into account that he was a right-handed hitter playing his home games in Yankee Stadium.

After being traded to Cleveland for pitcher Allie Reynolds prior to the start of the 1947 season, Gordon had another outstanding year in 1948. Teaming with Indians shortstop Lou Boudreau to form the best double-play combination in baseball, Gordon established career-highs in home runs (32) and runs batted in (124), while batting .280 and playing a superb second base. In fact, Gordon's fielding was often overlooked because he was such a strong hitter. He was a superb defensive player who was extremely athletic and acrobatic.

Phil Rizzuto, who played alongside Gordon for three years in New York, said: "Gordon is the most acrobatic fielder I have ever played with. The plays he could make off balance, throwing in midair, or off one foot, or lying down. Unbelievable!"

As an all-around second baseman, Gordon had few equals. He surpassed the 20-homer mark seven times, topping 30 twice, knocked in more than 100 runs four times, and played on six pennant-winners and five world championship teams. He was also selected to nine All-Star teams in his eleven seasons, and finished in the top ten in the league MVP voting five times. Two years in the military while still in his prime shortened Gordon's career, prevented him from accumulating even more impressive numbers, and robbed him of any chance he may have had to challenge Frankie Frisch for the fifth spot.

All-Star Third Baseman

PLAYER	YEARS	AB	HITS	RUNS	2B	3B	HR	RBI	AVG	SB	OBP	SLG PCT
1) PIE TRAYNOR	1920–35	7,559	2,416	1,183	371	164	58	1,273	.320	158	.362	.435
2) FRANK "HOME RUN" BAKER	1908–14, 1916–22	5,984	1,838	887	315	103	96	987	.307	235	.363	.442
3) RAY DANDRIDGE*	1933–48	824	276		40	13	4		.335	1		
4) JUDY JOHNSON*	1921–38	2,692	816		125	44	19		.303	51		
5) JIMMY COLLINS	1895–1908	6,796	2,000	1,055	353	116	65	983	.294	194	.344	.409
HONORABLE MENTION:												
FRED LINDSTROM	1924–36	5,611	1,747	895	301	81	103	779	.311	84	.351	.449
STAN HACK	1932–47	7,278	2,193	1,239	363	81	57	642	.301	165	.394	.397

* Ray Dandridge's and Judy Johnson's statistics are from the Negro Leagues and are therefore incomplete.

1 PIE TRAYNOR

If Pie Traynor were to be compared to the top third basemen in the major leagues over the last fifty years he might not make it into the top five. Many more truly outstanding third basemen played in the majors during the second half of last century than during the first.

Although Frank "Home Run" Baker may have had as much overall ability as Traynor, Baker didn't have enough quality seasons, and therefore his career numbers, for the most part, do not match up well against Pie's. From all accounts, both Ray Dandridge and Judy (yes, Judy) Johnson were superior fielders to Traynor and, like Traynor, were solid line-drive hitters. However, their career statistics are extremely sketchy and too little is known about their overall offensive ability to make a clear judgment as to just how good they actually were, and whether or not they deserve to be ranked above Traynor as the top third baseman of the period. Thus Traynor is the only logical choice for the first team.

Although he never led the National League in any major offensive category, Pie Traynor is widely regarded as the finest third baseman of the first half of the century. His .320 career batting average, 1,273

runs batted in, and 164 triples top all other third basemen who played in the majors during those years.

Traynor didn't have very much home run power, hitting only 58 during his career with the Pittsburgh Pirates, but he was a very solid line-drive hitter who hit .300 or better six straight years from 1925 to 1930 and knocked in 100 or more runs five straight seasons from 1927 to 1931. His career high in RBI came in 1928 when he knocked in 124 runs, and his career high in batting average came in 1930 when he batted .366. In all, Traynor knocked in over 100 runs seven times, batted over .300 ten times, stole more than 20 bases twice, and struck out only 278 times in more than 7,500 career at-bats.

Although his reputation as a defensive third baseman has somewhat suffered through the years, he is still thought to have been a good fielder. He led N.L. third basemen in putouts seven times, chances five times, and double plays four times.

❷ FRANK "HOME RUN" BAKER

FRANK BAKER GETS THE NOD OVER RAY DANDRIDGE and Judy Johnson for second-team honors because, even though he had only six truly exceptional seasons, for those six years he was one of the very best players in baseball. In fact, during that period he was quite possibly the finest third baseman of the first half of the century.

Although Frank Baker's career home run total of only 96 would seem to belie his nickname, he did have very good power and led the American League in home runs four straight years from 1911 to 1914. Keeping in mind that this was the era of the dead ball, his home run totals of 11 and 12 during two of those years were actually quite impressive. He also led the league twice in runs batted in and once in triples, and he still holds the A.L. record for most triples by a rookie (19, in 1909). However, Baker's best season was 1912 when he led the league in home runs and RBI (with a career-high of 130) and also batted a career-best .347, a record for A.L. third basemen that stood until 1980 when George Brett batted .390. Baker also could run: he stole 235 bases during his career, including a high of 40 in 1912. In all, Baker finished in double-digits in home runs five times, knocked in over 100 runs three times, batted over .300 six times, scored more than 100 runs twice, and stole more than 20 bases five times.

Probably the only thing that prevented Baker from having an even better career and being compared more favorably to Pie Traynor was fate. Following the 1914 season, when Baker was still at the top of his game, he got into a contract dispute with team manager and owner Connie Mack. Baker sat out the entire 1915 season and was eventually traded from the A's to the Yankees. When he returned to the game a year later, he wasn't quite the same player. However, he did have two good years in New York before off-field problems sent him spiraling downward again. From that point on, he was just a part-time player.

❸ RAY DANDRIDGE

RAY DANDRIDGE AND JUDY JOHNSON WERE THE TWO finest third basemen in Negro League history. Both were exceptional fielders and outstanding contact hitters who, although not possessing a great deal of power, usually hit for a high batting average and rarely struck out. It was somewhat difficult to rank these two because of the limited availability of statistics from the Negro Leagues, but both clearly deserved to be included among the top five third basemen of this time period. Dandridge gets the higher ranking, in part because, even though the statistics for both men are incomplete, he had the higher career batting average. In addition, while Johnson was considered to be an outstanding defensive player, Dandridge was thought to be one of the best ever at the position.

Those who saw Ray Dandridge play considered him to be one of the greatest fielding third basemen in baseball history. In fact, although he played in a different era, his fielding was often compared to Brooks Robinson's—and, it is said, Dandridge had the better arm.

Hall of Famer Monte Irvin, who played against Dandridge in the Negro Leagues, said of him: "He had the quickest reflexes and the surest hands of any infielder I've ever seen. In a season, he had a bad year if he made four errors."

Dandridge was also an outstanding right-handed line-drive hitter, compiling a lifetime .335 batting average in the Negro Leagues (using the best data available), hitting a career-high .370 in 1944, and hitting .347 in exhibition games against major league pitching during the course of his career.

❹ JUDY JOHNSON

DURING HIS EIGHTEEN-YEAR NEGRO LEAGUE career, Judy Johnson played for three different teams and was often referred to as the "Black Pie Traynor." A solid line-drive hitter who drove in a lot of runs despite not hitting many home runs, Johnson was considered to be the top third baseman in the Negro Leagues for virtually all of the 1920s and the first part of the ensuing decade. He had many of his finest seasons for the Philadelphia Hilldales from 1921 to 1929, hitting a career-high .406 in 1929 and compiling averages of .391, .369, and .392 in other seasons.

In spite of his solid hitting, Johnson was actually known more for his defense and cerebral approach to the game. His fielding at third was usually described as steady or intelligent rather than spectacular.

Consider the words of Pittsburgh Crawfords outfielder Ted Page, who played with Johnson a few seasons and described him in *The Official Negro Leagues Book* as "...the smartest third baseman I ever came across. He was a scientific ballplayer who did everything with grace and poise. You talk about playing third base, heck, he was better than anybody I saw—Brooks Robinson, Mike Schmidt, or Pie Traynor."

❺ JIMMY COLLINS

THOSE WHO SAW JIMMY COLLINS PLAY CLAIMED THAT HE WAS WITHOUT EVEN A CLOSE rival. The first to charge bunts and play them barehanded, he also had excellent range. In 1899, he accepted a then-record 593 chances and the following year he set a 20th-century mark when he accumulated 251 putouts.

Collins was also a productive hitter, batting over .320 four times, knocking in more than 100 runs twice, scoring more than 100 four times, collecting more than 10 triples six times, and hitting .294 for his career. He had his first outstanding season in 1897, establishing career highs with 132 runs batted in and a batting average of .346, while also scoring 103 runs. The following season, Collins led the National League with 15 home runs while driving in 111 runs, scoring 107 others, and batting .328. He had another outstanding season in 1901, driving in 94 runs, batting .332, and setting career highs with 108 runs scored and 42 doubles—all outstanding figures for the dead ball era.

Honorable mention should be given to Fred Lindstrom and Stan Hack:

Playing most of his career with the New York Giants, Fred Lindstrom compiled a lifetime batting average of .311. Along the way, he set National League records for third basemen that still stand, batting .379 one season and accumulating 231 hits in a season twice. His two finest seasons were 1928 and 1930. In the first of those years, he hit 14 home runs, knocked in 107 runs, batted .358, and amassed 231 hits for the first time. Two years later, Lindstrom established career-highs with 22 home runs, a .379 batting average, and 127 runs scored, while driving in 106 runs and totaling 231 hits again. He batted over .300 five other times during his thirteen-year career.

The Chicago Cubs' Stan Hack was arguably the National League's best leadoff hitter for a good portion of his sixteen-year major league career. Although he possessed very little power, hitting just 57 home runs in almost 7,300 at-bats, Hack did a superb job at the top of the order. He batted over .300 six times, scored more than 100 runs seven times, drew more than 90 walks four times, compiled a lifetime batting average of .301, and finished with a career on-base percentage of .394. Extremely difficult to strike out, Hack compiled an excellent walk-to-strikeout ratio of better than 2 to 1 (1,092 walks to just 466 strikeouts). He led the league in batting average once and in hits and stolen bases twice each. A solid fielder, he also led N.L. third basemen in fielding on two different occasions.

Hack was extremely durable, missing no more than five games in any season from 1936 to 1941. During his career, he was selected to four National League All-Star teams and played for four pennant-winning teams in Chicago.

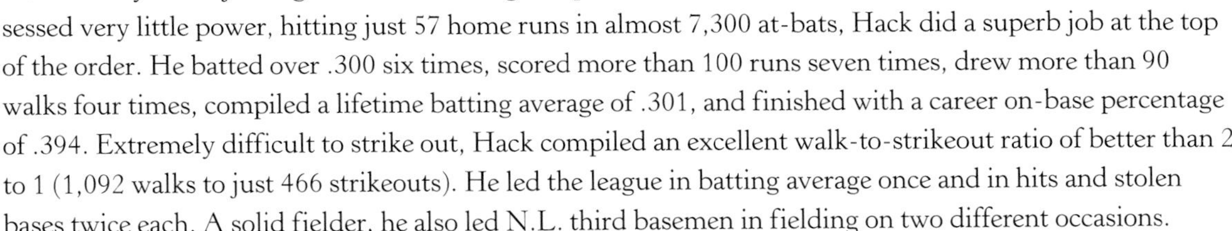

All-Star Shortstop

PLAYER	YEARS	AB	HITS	RUNS	2B	3B	HR	RBI	AVG	SB	OBP	SLG PCT
1) HONUS WAGNER	1897–1917	10,430	3,415	1,736	640	252	101	1,732	.327	722	.390	.466
2) JOHN HENRY LLOYD*	1905–32	1,769	651		90	18	26		.368	56		
3) JOE CRONIN	1926–45	7,579	2,285	1,233	515	118	170	1,424	.301	87	.390	.468
4) ARKY VAUGHAN	1932–43, 1947–48	6,622	2,103	1,173	356	128	96	926	.318	118	.406	.453
5) LUKE APPLING	1930–43, 1947–48	8,856	2,749	1,319	440	102	45	1,116	.310	179	.399	.398
HONORABLE MENTION:												
JOE SEWELL	1920–33	7,132	2,226	1,141	436	68	49	1,055	.312	74	.391	.413
LOU BOUDREAU	1938–52	6,029	1,779	861	385	66	68	789	.295	51	.380	.415
VERN STEPHENS	1941–44	6,497	1,859	1,001	307	42	247	1,174	.286	25	.355	.460

* John Henry Lloyd's statistics are from the Negro Leagues and are therefore incomplete.

❶ HONUS WAGNER

HONUS WAGNER IS UNIVERSALLY REGARDED AS NOT ONLY THE BEST SHORTSTOP OF THE first fifty years of the last century, but as the greatest shortstop in baseball history. He set the standards for the position.

When the Hall of Fame first opened in 1936, Wagner received the same number of votes as Babe Ruth, only slightly behind top vote-getter Ty Cobb. Many who saw Wagner play felt that, as an all-around player, there was never anyone better.

Ed Barrow, who managed Babe Ruth and saw a lot of Ty Cobb, said in *The Glory of Their Times*: "If I had a choice of all men who have played baseball, the first man I would select is Honus Wagner."

John McGraw, who managed the Giants for so many years, added: "I consider Wagner not only the number one shortstop, but, had he played any other position, except pitcher, he would have been equally as great."

At the very least, Wagner was without question the greatest position player in the National League during the dead ball era, dominating the first decade of the twentieth century. He won eight league batting titles and was a league leader at least twice in every major offensive department except home runs and walks. He led the league in runs batted in and stolen bases five times each, slugging percentage six times, and doubles seven times. When he retired, he had compiled more hits, runs, total bases, RBI, and stolen bases than any player to that point. He still, to this day, has more hits, doubles, triples, RBI, and stolen bases than any shortstop ever, as well as the highest career batting average. During his career, Wagner knocked in over 100 runs nine times, scored more than 100 six times, batted over .350 six times, had at least 20 triples twice, collected at least 30 doubles in twelve consecutive seasons (1899–1910), and stole more than 40 bases eight times.

Tommy Leach, who played third base for the Pirates alongside Wagner, was another who had high praise for him, calling Wagner "the greatest shortstop ever. The greatest anything ever."

❷ JOHN HENRY "POP" LLOYD

JOHN HENRY LLOYD WAS ONE OF THE GREATEST players never to have an opportunity to play in the major leagues because of the color of his skin. He played over twenty years in the black professional leagues beginning in 1905, and was frequently called "the black Honus Wagner." Wagner once commented about Lloyd: "After I saw him play, I felt honored that they should name such a great ballplayer after me."

Like Wagner, Lloyd was considered an exceptional line-drive hitter and a terrific base runner and fielder. He began to establish his reputation as a great player in 1910, when he joined Rube Foster's Chicago Leland Giants. That year, the Giants won 123 games and Lloyd hit .417. He would go on to play in the black professional leagues a total of twenty-eight seasons.

Connie Mack stated: "You could put Wagner and Lloyd in a bag together and, whichever one you pulled out, you couldn't go wrong."

With comments like that, it wasn't too difficult to make Lloyd the second choice at shortstop, behind only Wagner himself.

❸ JOE CRONIN

THE CHOICE FOR NUMBER THREE SHORTSTOP WAS A bit more difficult since Joe Cronin, Arky Vaughan, and Luke Appling were all terrific hitters, known more for their offense than their defense. However, what separated Cronin from the others was his power, having hit 170 home runs during his career.

Joe Cronin, who played with the Washington Senators and Boston Red Sox, was known for having good power for a shortstop. In addition to his 170 homers, he knocked in 100 or more runs eight times during his career, batted over .300 eight

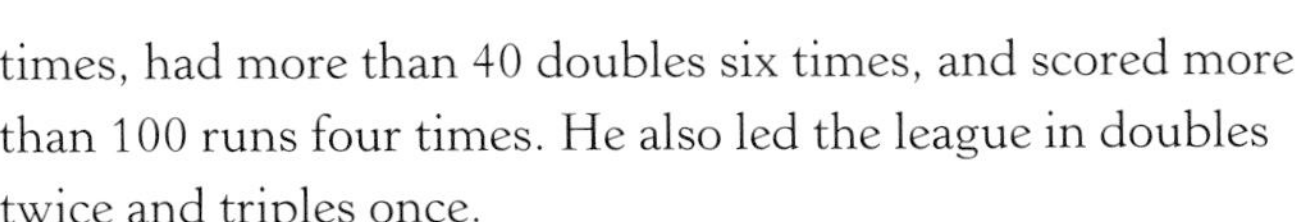

times, had more than 40 doubles six times, and scored more than 100 runs four times. He also led the league in doubles twice and triples once.

Cronin finished runner-up to Jimmie Foxx in the 1932 MVP voting after batting .318, knocking in 116 runs, collecting 43 doubles and a league-leading 18 triples, and leading American League shortstops in fielding. Cronin had his finest season two years earlier, though, when he hit .346, knocked in 126 runs, scored 127 others, collected 203 hits, stole a career-high 17 bases, and was named *The Sporting News* MVP. He was also named the outstanding major league shortstop by that same publication a total of seven times.

4 ARKY VAUGHAN

HAD HE NOT PLAYED MOST OF HIS CAREER WITH the Pittsburgh Pirates, the same team for which Honus Wagner played, Arky Vaughan's offensive accomplishments as a shortstop would probably have been better appreciated.

Though generally considered to be an above-average defensive shortstop, Vaughan was certainly not in Wagner's class as a fielder. However, he was a superb hitter who is often considered to be one of the greatest offensive shortstops in baseball history. His .318 career batting average makes him second only to Wagner among shortstops, and his .406 career on-base percentage is second to none. His .385 batting average in 1935 not only won him the N.L. batting title but set a 20th-century league record for highest average by a shortstop. In his finest season, Vaughan led the league with a .491 on-base percentage and a .607 slugging percentage, while striking out just eighteen times in almost 600 plate appearances. He also led the league three times in walks, triples, runs scored, and on-base percentage. In all, Vaughan knocked in over 90 runs four times, batted over .330 three times, had at least 10 triples eight times, and scored more than 100 runs five times. He was selected to the National League All-Star team every year from 1934 to 1942.

5 LUKE APPLING

LUKE APPLING MAY HAVE BEEN AS GOOD A PURE HITTER AS EITHER CRONIN OR Vaughan. However, he was considered to be a below-average defensive player, having led A.L.shortstops in errors no fewer than five times. His offense, though, earned him the number five spot in the rankings.

Appling won two batting titles with the Chicago White Sox, leading the league in 1936 with a career-high .388 (a major league record for shortstops), while knocking in 128 runs, scoring 111, and totaling 204 hits. He batted over .300 fourteen times during his career, compiling a lifetime mark of .310 and an outstanding career on-base percentage of .399. In spite of his defensive shortcomings, Appling was named the outstanding major league shortstop by *The Sporting News* three times.

Honorable mention should be given to Joe Sewell, Lou Boudreau, and Vern Stephens:

During his peak years with the Cleveland Indians in the mid-1920s, Joe Sewell was considered to be the best fielding shortstop in the game. His greatest claim to fame, however, was his incredible knack for almost never striking out. The holder of every major season and career record for fewest strikeouts by a batter, Sewell fanned only 114 times in fourteen seasons and 7,132 at-bats, setting a single-season record in 1932, when he struck out only three times in 503 at-bats for the Yankees. He was also a productive hitter, knocking in 100 or more runs twice, and batting over .300 nine times during his career.

Lou Boudreau was a fine-fielding shortstop and an excellent hitter. He led the A.L. in batting in 1944 with a .327 average and also led the league in doubles three times, collecting 45 two-baggers each time. Boudreau knocked in over 100 runs on two different occasions. His finest season came in 1948 when, as player-manager for the Cleveland Indians, he led his team to the pennant by reaching career highs in home runs with 18, RBI with 106, and batting with a .355 average, en route to winning the A.L. MVP award. It was as a fielder, though, that Boudreau really stood out, leading league shortstops in fielding on eight different occasions.

Vern Stephens had exceptional power for a middle infielder. Prior to moving to third base during the latter stages of his career, Stephens played shortstop for more than a decade, first for the St. Louis Browns and later for the Boston Red Sox. He led the American League in home runs once and in runs batted in three times, hit more than 20 homers six times, had more than 100 RBI four times, batted over .300 twice, and scored more than 100 runs three times during his career. He had his three finest seasons for the Boston Red Sox from 1948 to 1950. In 1948, he hit 29 homers, knocked in 137 runs, and batted .269. The following season, he hit 39 homers, knocked in a league-leading 159 runs, and batted .290. In 1950, he hit 30 homers, had 144 runs batted in, and batted .295.

NY

All-Star Catcher

PLAYER	YEARS	AB	HITS	RUNS	2B	3B	HR	RBI	AVG	SB	OBP	SLG PCT
1) JOSH GIBSON*	1930–46	1,820	644		110	45	141		.354	17		
2) BILL DICKEY	1928–43, 1946	6,300	1,969	930	343	72	202	1,209	.313	36	.382	.486
3) MICKEY COCHRANE	1925–37	5,169	1,652	1,041	333	64	119	832	.320	64	.419	.478
4) GABBY HARTNETT	1922–41	6,432	1,912	867	396	64	236	1,179	.297	28	.370	.489
5) ERNIE LOMBARDI	1931–47	5,855	1,792	601	277	27	190	990	.306	8	.358	.460

* Josh Gibson's statistics are from the Negro Leagues and are therefore incomplete.

1 JOSH GIBSON

THERE WILL UNDOUBTEDLY BE THOSE WHO QUESTION THE SELECTION OF JOSH GIBSON as the greatest catcher of the first half of the century based on the limited availability of statistical data surrounding his career. However, those who saw him play know how good he was and are aware that his incredible hitting power separated him from the other top catchers of that period. In fact, although he was never given a chance to play in the major leagues, it's very possible that Gibson was the greatest catcher in the history of the game. He is not only considered to be the greatest *catcher* in Negro League history (rated ahead of Roy Campanella, who also spent several seasons there), but quite possibly the greatest *player* in its history.

Although Negro League statistics are at best sketchy, Gibson is known to have averaged around 70 home runs a year. His career total is uncertain, but even the most conservative estimates put him ahead of Hank Aaron, with 800 to 950 career homers, albeit not against major league pitching. He is credited with being the only player to ever hit a fair ball out of Yankee Stadium.

However, Gibson was not a one-dimensional player. His lifetime batting average is the highest in Negro League history, at .354 (or .440, depending on the source). Against major league pitching, in sixteen exhibition games, he hit .424 with five home runs. Although he wasn't a great handler of pitchers or catcher of pop-ups, few base runners tried to steal on him because of his great arm.

Walter Johnson said of him: "He hits the ball a mile. Throws like a rifle. Bill Dickey isn't as good a catcher."

Roy Campanella called Gibson "not only the greatest catcher, but the greatest ballplayer I ever saw."

❷ BILL DICKEY

THE CHOICE FOR SECOND-TEAM CATCHER WAS a difficult one to make. Both Bill Dickey and Mickey Cochrane were excellent hitters and outstanding team leaders. Dickey's career batting average was .313, while Cochrane's was .320. In about 1,100 more career at-bats, Dickey had almost twice as many home runs, however, and almost 50 percent more runs batted in. Although Dickey had more power and was a better run-producer, Cochrane was considered to be a slightly better offensive player. However, Cochrane was not considered to be in Dickey's class defensively.

Charlie Gehringer, who played with Cochrane after the latter was traded from the A's to the Tigers, offered his opinion on the Dickey/Cochrane comparison when he said: "Dickey could throw a little better. Cochrane was probably a better all-around guy; he could run faster, he could do more with the bat, he could do more things to beat you. He didn't have quite the power that Dickey did, though."

However, as was stated earlier, when looking for a catcher, intangibles such as handling the pitching staff, calling a good game, and being a good field general and team leader would all be very important factors. In these areas, no one was better than Bill Dickey. That is why he is the choice for number two catcher.

An admiring sportswriter named Dan Daniel once wrote: "Dickey isn't just a catcher. He's a ball club. He isn't just a player. He's an influence."

You really can't ask for more from your catcher. And Dickey's offensive statistics weren't too shabby either. He hit over .300 eleven times in his career, topping the .330 mark four times, and in 1936 he set an all-time record for the highest batting average by a catcher with more than 400 at-bats when he batted .362. As was noted earlier, he also had good power and was a productive hitter, four times hitting more than 20 homers and knocking in better than 100 runs. Dickey's best years were 1936–1939. Over those four seasons, he averaged 26 home runs and 115 runs batted in and never failed to hit over .300. He was also durable, having caught more than 100 games for thirteen consecutive seasons, thereby setting a record that stood until broken by Johnny Bench.

Dickey's defensive credentials were just as impressive. Considered the finest defensive catcher of his time, he posted a .988 fielding percentage for his career and, when he retired, held the records for putouts and fielding average by a catcher.

❸ MICKEY COCHRANE

MICKEY COCHRANE WAS SAID TO BE THE BEST hitting catcher in baseball during his career, even though he only hit 20 homers and knocked in 100 runs once in a season. His .320 batting average and .419 on-base percentage are both career records for a catcher with more than 5,000 at-bats. He hit .300 or better nine times, establishing a career-high with a mark of .357 in 1930. Cochrane was particularly impressive during the Philadelphia Athletics' three pennant-winning seasons of 1929–1931, posting averages of .331, .357, and .349. However, his most productive year came in 1932 when he established career highs in home runs (23), runs batted in (112), and runs scored (118). In all, he batted over .330 five times and scored more than 100 runs four times. An exceptional contact hitter, the left-handed swinging Cochrane struck out only 217 times in just over 6,000 plate appearances and also possessed good running speed for a catcher. Cochrane was a two-time A.L. MVP, coming away with the award in both 1928, as a member of the Philadelphia Athletics, and again in 1934 as a member of the pennant-winning Detroit Tigers.

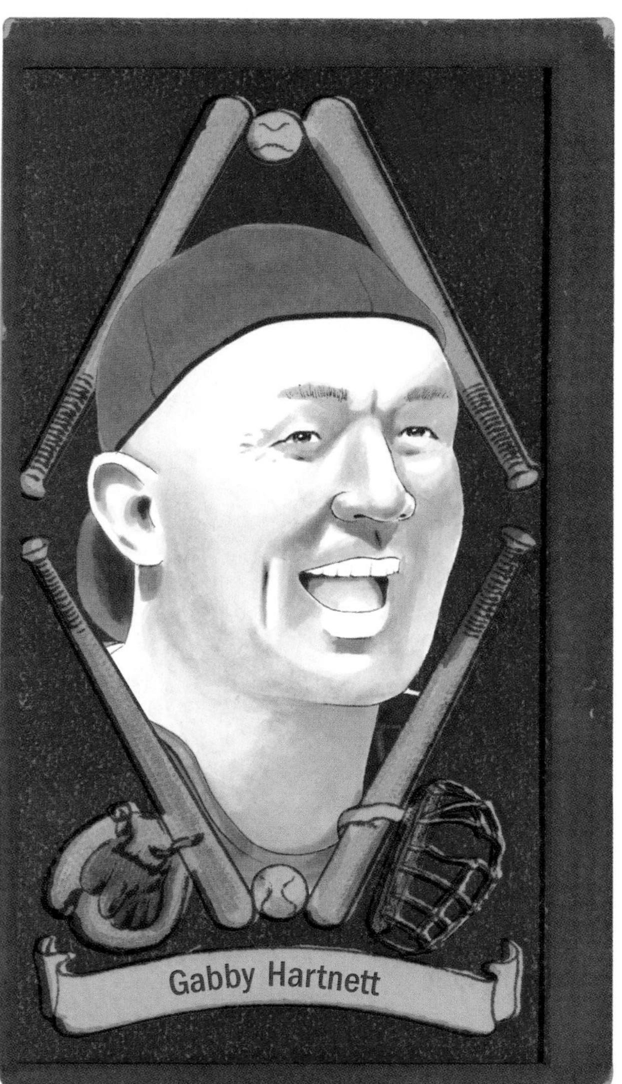

While Cochrane's offensive skills were widely praised, he was considered to be no better than average defensively. After the 1931 World Series, when the Pepper Martin–led Cardinals ran wild on the A's, Cochrane was held accountable by many. Much of the blame, however, should undoubtedly have gone to the A's pitchers, who were unable to hold the Cardinals' runners on base.

Nevertheless, Cochrane was a true team leader, as can be evidenced by the fact that, towards the end of his career, he became a player-manager for the Tigers.

4 GABBY HARTNETT

UNTIL JOHNNY BENCH CAME ALONG, GABBY Hartnett was thought by many to be the greatest catcher in National League history.

An excellent receiver who also had good power, Hartnett won the N.L. MVP award in 1935 when he batted .344 and drove in 91 runs in just 413 at-bats, while leading the Chicago Cubs to the N.L. pennant. But it was in 1930 that he had his finest season: he hit 37 home runs, had 122 RBI, and batted .339 for the Cubs. In all, Hartnett batted over .300 six times during his career, finished in the top ten in the league MVP voting four times, and was selected to the first six N.L. All-Star teams, from 1933 to 1938.

Pitcher Burleigh Grimes once said that Hartnett "had as good an arm as ever hung on a man."

Sportswriter Red Smith wrote: "Hartnett was so good that he lasted twenty years in spite of the fact that he couldn't run. All other skills were refined in him."

5 ERNIE LOMBARDI

ERNIE LOMBARDI, WHO SPENT MOST OF HIS career with the Cincinnati Reds, may have been the slowest runner ever to play major league baseball. In fact, he was so slow that opposing infielders typically played him on the outfield grass, allowing them to occasionally catch line drives off his bat that, for anyone else, would have been base hits. In spite of this, Lombardi still managed to hit .306 for his career, a testament to his ability as a hitter.

Lombardi hit .300 or better ten times during his career, leading the N.L. in batting in 1938 with a .342 average. He also won the league's MVP award that year.

All-Star Left Fielder

PLAYER	YEARS	AB	HITS	RUNS	2B	3B	HR	RBI	AVG	SB	OBP	SLG PCT
1) TY COBB	1905–28	11,434	4,189	2,246	724	295	117	1,937	.367	891	.433	.512
2) TED WILLIAMS	1939–42, 1946–60	7,706	2,654	1,798	525	71	521	1,839	.344	24	.483	.634
3) AL SIMMONS	1924–41, 1943–44	8,759	2,927	1,507	539	149	307	1,827	.334	87	.380	.535
4) JOE MEDWICK	1932–48	7,635	2,471	1,198	540	113	205	1,383	.324	42	.362	.505
5) GOOSE GOSLIN	1921–38	8,656	2,735	1,483	500	173	248	1,609	.316	175	.387	.500
HONORABLE MENTION:												
RALPH KINER	1946–55	5,205	1,451	971	216	39	369	1,015	.279	22	.398	.548

PRIOR TO DISCUSSING THE CHOICES FOR THE TOP LEFT FIELDERS OF THIS ERA, I'D LIKE TO explain how I dealt with the special circumstances surrounding the careers of some of the players under consideration.

The careers of Ted Williams, Stan Musial, and Ralph Kiner all began during the first half of the twentieth century and ended during the second half. In the case of Williams, he played nine years during the first period and ten during the second. While he was an exceptional hitter to the end and won two batting championships after 1951, he had his greatest seasons prior to that year. Therefore, he will be included with the players from the first half of the century.

In Musial's case, he played eight seasons during the first period and thirteen during the second. Even though he had some of his greatest seasons prior to 1951, he will be included with the players from the later period.

Kiner played five seasons in each period. However, his finest seasons came during the earlier period, so he will be grouped with the players from that time.

In the case of all three, however, their *entire careers* will be considered, not just the years they played prior to or after the mid-century mark.

In addition, Ty Cobb actually played more center field than left field during his career. However, he did see some action in left, especially in the latter stages of his career. While he had very good speed and

was not a bad outfielder, he certainly was not in a defensive class with either Joe DiMaggio or Tris Speaker, the two greatest defensive center fielders of this period. Since it is an imperative to be defensively strong up the middle, I chose to put Cobb in left field, in deference to DiMaggio and Speaker.

1 TY COBB

THIS WAS AN EXTREMELY DIFFICULT CHOICE, IN PART because of the greatness of both Ty Cobb and Ted Williams, but also because of the difficulty involved in comparing two great players from two such different baseball eras.

When Cobb played, the game was one of slap-hitting, speed, and base-running. There was no such thing as night baseball, and the game was still a long ways away from being integrated. By Williams's time, the sport had evolved into more of a power game. Games were often played at night—but since the lighting in most ballparks was not very good, it was more difficult for hitters to see the ball clearly than during the day. Also, for the better part of his career, Williams competed against black ballplayers as well as white players, something Cobb never did.

What, then, should be the main criteria used for making such a difficult choice? If the decision were to be based solely on who the better hitter and run-producer was, the choice would be Williams. As great a hitter as Cobb was, he didn't have nearly as much home run power as Williams, and in approximately 3,700 fewer at-bats Williams knocked in only about 100 fewer runs. However, it must also be remembered that in Cobb's era a player's power was judged more by the number of triples he hit than by his home run totals. Cobb had 295 triples for his career; Williams had only 71. Also, runs were harder to come by when Cobb played, so one would not expect his RBI totals to be on a par with Williams's. However, as hitters, the edge would have to go to Williams because of his greater power.

But there is more to offense than just hitting. Cobb was a great base runner, and his career total of 891 stolen bases dwarfs Williams's total of 24. He was a terror on the base-paths and the most feared base runner of his day. Overall, between his hitting and his base running, Cobb could beat you in more ways than Williams could. While Williams was not considered to be a great outfielder, Cobb was above average. Williams was thought to be average, at best.

In addition, while Williams was generally recognized as the greatest hitter of his time, he was not necessarily looked upon as the dominant player of his era. Joe DiMaggio and Stan Musial were both

considered to have been on his level as all-around players. When Cobb played, there were other great players such as Tris Speaker and "Shoeless" Joe Jackson. Cobb, however, was regarded as *the* dominant player in the game for almost fifteen years, until Babe Ruth came along. This was the primary consideration in selecting him over Williams as the first-team left fielder.

Cobb's record is really quite amazing. He led the American League in batting ten times over a thirteen-year period, from 1907 to 1919. During that stretch, the three times he failed to win the batting title he hit .383, .368, and .371. He batted over .400 three times during his career, hit over .300 every season from 1906 to 1928, and, at .367, has the highest career batting average of any player who ever lived. He batted over .350 16 times in his career, including eleven straight years from 1909 to 1919. He had more than 200 hits nine times, scored more than 100 runs eleven times, and stole more than 50 bases eight times. Cobb also had some power, winning the Triple Crown in 1909, knocking in over 100 runs seven times, and amassing more than 20 triples in a season four times during his career. He had probably his finest season in 1911 when he hit 8 home runs and established career highs in runs batted in (127), batting average (.420), triples (24), doubles (47), hits (248), runs scored (147), and slugging percentage (.621). Cobb won the league MVP award that year in the very first season it was presented. He also stole 83 bases that season and later set a single-season stolen-base record, with 96—a record that stood for nearly fifty years.

He also led the league in stolen bases six times, runs batted in four times, triples four times, doubles three times, hits eight times, runs five times, on-base percentage six times, and slugging percentage eight times.

Although many of his records have since been broken, when Cobb retired in 1928 he held almost every major career and single-season batting and base-running record.

2 TED WILLIAMS

TED WILLIAMS ONCE SAID THAT HE HAD A DREAM of walking down the street and having people point to him and say: "There goes Ted Williams, the greatest hitter who ever lived." He may very well have succeeded in earning that dreamed-of accolade.

In 1941, Williams batted .406; no player since has reached the .400 mark. In 1957, at the age of thirty-eight, Williams batted .388 to win the last of his seven batting championships. His career on-base percentage of .483 is the highest all-time, and his career slugging percentage of .634 is second

only to Babe Ruth's. Had he not lost almost five full years to military service, he probably would have challenged Ruth's 714 career home run total (as it is, Williams finished with 521).

Williams led the American League in home runs and runs batted in four times each, runs scored six times, on-base percentage twelve times, slugging percentage nine times, and walks eight times. He won two Triple Crowns, the first coming in 1942, when he hit 36 home runs, knocked in 137 runs, and batted .356, and the second coming in 1947, when he hit 32 homers, knocked in 114 runs, and batted .343. He also won two MVP awards, the first coming in 1946, when he hit 38 home runs, had 123 RBI and batted .342, and the second in 1949, when he hit 43 home runs, had 159 RBI, and batted .343. He also finished in the top five in the MVP voting seven other times.

During his career, Williams hit more than 30 homers eight times, knocked in over 100 runs nine times, batted over .340 eleven times, scored more than 100 runs nine times, including six seasons with at least 130, and drew more than 100 walks eleven times, including six seasons with more than 140.

Williams was never lacking in self-confidence. The story goes that when Williams was preparing to take batting practice for the first time as a rookie with the Red Sox in 1939, one of his teammates remarked to him: "Wait until you see Foxx hit!" Ted responded: "Wait until Foxx sees *me* hit!" (Jimmie Foxx was also with the Red Sox that year.)

When asked if he was ever told how to pitch to Williams, A's pitcher Bobby Shantz said: "Yes. They said he had no weaknesses, won't swing at a bad ball, had the best eyes in the business, and can kill you with one swing; he won't hit at anything bad, but don't give him anything good."

And here's what Bob Feller said in *Baseball When the Grass Was Real*: "Ted Williams? Nobody had his number. He was the best hitter I ever pitched to."

❸ AL SIMMONS

WHILE NOT QUITE ON THE SAME LEVEL AS TY COBB OR Ted Williams, Al Simmons was clearly the third greatest left fielder of the period. He was one of the game's dominant hitters for a decade, and had more power and was a greater run-producer than either Joe Medwick or Goose Goslin.

When Simmons played with Jimmie Foxx on the great A's teams of the late 1920s and early '30s, Foxx was often referred to as the A's version of Babe Ruth, while Simmons was frequently likened to Lou Gehrig.

One of the most feared batters of his day, Simmons was a tremendous hitter who stung fierce line drives to all fields. His 307 career home runs are an indication of his power, as are his 539 doubles, 149 triples, 1,827 RBI, and slugging percentage of .535. He led the league in batting in 1930 and 1931, with averages of .381 and .390, respectively. In 1929, he led the league in runs batted in, with 157. He also led the league in hits twice and runs once. Simmons knocked in 100 or more runs and batted over .300 for eleven straight seasons from 1924 to 1934. He won the league's MVP award in 1929 and finished in the top five in the voting on three other occasions.

During his career, Simmons hit more than 30 homers and knocked in more than 150 runs three times each, batted over .350 six times, including four seasons with an average in excess of .380, had more than 200 hits and scored more than 100 runs six times each, and had double-digits in triples seven times.

Though unheralded for his defense, Simmons led the league's outfielders in fielding twice. Joe Cronin once said of him: "There never was a better left fielder in hustling to the foul line to turn a double into a single."

4 JOE MEDWICK

BASED STRICTLY ON THEIR CAREER STATISTICS, A strong case could be made for putting Goose Goslin ahead of Joe Medwick and into the number four spot. After all, Goslin finished in front of Medwick in virtually every offensive category. He hit 43 more home runs, drove in more than 200 more runs, scored almost 300 more, collected 60 more triples and almost 270 more hits, stole four times as many bases, and finished with an on-base percentage that was 25 points higher. However, he also accumulated 1,000 more at-bats. Medwick actually hit home runs, knocked in runs, and scored runs at a very similar rate. Playing in slightly less of a hitter's era, he also out-hit Goslin by 8 points, finished with 40 more doubles, and compiled a slightly higher slugging percentage. Overall, the numbers would seem to indicate that the two players were very evenly matched.

There were two factors, though, that earned Medwick the higher ranking. The first was the fact that, at his peak, Medwick was a slightly more dominant player. While Goslin excelled for a longer period, driving in more than 100 runs eleven times over a thirteen-year period, he was never considered to be one of the top two or three players in the American League. However, for a four-year period beginning in 1935, Medwick was arguably the National League's best player.

Over that span, he averaged 23 home runs, 135 runs batted in, and 53 doubles, while posting batting averages of .353, .351, .374, and .322. He also collected more than 200 hits in three of those seasons and scored more than 100 runs each year. Medwick was named league MVP in 1937, when he won the Triple Crown; he finished in the top five in the MVP voting two other times during that period. Meanwhile, Goslin never finished any higher than sixth in the American League voting.

In addition, Medwick was generally considered to be an above-average outfielder for much of his career. He had a good throwing arm and committed as many as 10 errors just two times in seventeen seasons. On the other hand, Goslin occasionally had his troubles in the outfield. Although he had a strong throwing arm—posting as many as 20 assists three times—he never committed fewer than 10 errors in any of his fifteen seasons as a full-time outfielder. In fact, he totaled as many as 15 seven different times.

For his greater level of dominance during his peak seasons and for his greater ability as an outfielder, Medwick gets the nod over Goslin for the fourth team.

Joe Medwick, who played on the famed "Gas House Gang" of the Cardinals during the 1930s, is the last player to have won the Triple Crown in the National League. He accomplished the feat in 1937, when he hit 31 home runs, knocked in 154 runs and batted .374, en route to winning league MVP honors. He also led the league that year with 111 runs scored, 237 hits, 56 doubles, and a .641 slugging percentage. He'd also had a superb season the previous year when he led the league with 138 runs batted in, 223 hits, and a career-best 64 doubles, while finishing third in the N.L. with a .351 batting average.

In all, Medwick led the league in runs batted in and doubles three times each, hits twice, and triples once. He knocked in and scored over 100 runs six times each, collected more than 200 hits four times, amassed at least 10 triples and 40 doubles seven times each, and batted over .300 in fourteen of his seventeen big league seasons, bettering the .350 mark three times. He was selected to the All-Star team ten times and finished in the top ten in the league MVP voting a total of four times.

5 GOOSE GOSLIN

SPLITTING HIS TIME BETWEEN THE WASHINGTON SENATORS, ST. LOUIS BROWNS, AND Detroit Tigers, Goose Goslin batted over .300 and knocked in more than 100 runs eleven times each during his career, topping 120 RBI four times, and surpassing the .340 mark in batting three times. He also scored more than 100 runs seven times and finished in double-digits in triples nine times. In 1924, he led the American League with 129 runs batted in, and in 1928 he led the league with a .379 average, both as a member of the Senators. However, his most productive season came in 1930, after he was traded from Washington to St. Louis. That year, Goslin established career-highs with 37 home runs and 138 runs batted in, while scoring 115 runs and batting .308. A good hitter almost to the very end, Goslin had another very productive season in his final year as a full-time player in 1936. That year, as a member of the Detroit Tigers, he hit 24 home runs, drove in 125 runs, scored 122 others, and batted .315.

Although he hit more than 20 home runs only three times during his career, Goslin actually had good power, as his 173 triples will bear out. However, his home run output was hurt somewhat by the fact that he spent his first nine years in Washington, playing in a ballpark that had huge outfield dimensions. As a result,

he posted his three largest home run totals after being traded away from the Senators early during the 1930 campaign. He hit 37 home runs that season and 24 the following year, as a member of the St. Louis Browns. As was mentioned earlier, he again hit 24 in 1936 while with Detroit. Although his home run totals were adversely affected by having to play in Washington, Goslin did manage to lead the American League in triples twice while playing with the Senators. He collected 18 in 1923 and another 20 two seasons later, leading the league both times.

Honorable mention should be given to Ralph Kiner:

Ralph Kiner was unquestionably one of the greatest home-run hitters who ever lived. Although he played only ten seasons, he managed to hit 369 homers and set a major league record that still stands by leading his league in home runs for seven consecutive seasons. He hit over 50 homers in a season twice, hitting 51 in 1947 and smashing 54 in 1949. In each season from 1947 to 1951, Kiner hit more than 40 home runs, drove in more than 100 runs, and scored more than 100 others. He also batted over .300 in three of those years.

Kiner's first truly big year was 1947 when he led the National League with 51 home runs, finished second with 127 runs batted in, batted .313, and scored 118 runs. He had another great year in 1949 when he led the league with 54 home runs, 127 runs batted in, 117 bases on balls, and a .658 slugging percentage. He also batted .310 and scored 116 runs that season. In all, Kiner hit at least 35 home runs in seven of his ten big league seasons, knocked in and scored more than 100 runs six times each, batted over .300 three times, and drew more than 100 bases on balls six times. In addition to leading the league in home runs seven times, he led in runs batted in, runs scored, and on-base percentage one time each, and in bases on balls and slugging percentage three times each.

Kiner managed to accomplish all this in spite of the fact that he played on weak Pittsburgh Pirates teams for most of his career. Even though he received very little support from his teammates, Kiner was still one of the top run-producers in the game. Perhaps even more impressive is that even though the Pirates always finished in the second division, Kiner managed to finish in the top ten in the league MVP voting in every season, from 1947 to 1951, even making it into the top five twice. Had he not retired prematurely due to back problems, Kiner probably would have reached the 500-homer plateau and finished higher in the rankings.

H
NY

All-Star Center Fielder

PLAYER	YEARS	AB	HITS	RUNS	2B	3B	HR	RBI	AVG	SB	OBP	SLG PCT
1) JOE DIMAGGIO	1936–42, 1946–51	6,821	2,214	1,390	389	131	361	1,537	.325	30	.398	.579
2) TRIS SPEAKER	1907–28	10,195	3,514	1,882	792	222	117	1,529	.345	434	.428	.500
3) OSCAR CHARLESTON*	1915–42	2,992	1,069		184	63	151		.357	153		
4) COOL PAPA BELL*	1922–46	3,952	1,335		203	68	56		.338	173		
5) CHUCK KLEIN	1928–44	6,486	2,076	1,168	398	74	300	1,201	.320	79	.379	.543
HONORABLE MENTION:												
EARL AVERILL	1929–41	6,363	2,019	1,224	401	128	238	1,164	.318	70	.395	.534

* Oscar Charleston's and Cool Papa Bell's statistics are from the Negro Leagues and are therefore incomplete.

1 JOE DIMAGGIO

AT ONE TIME, TRIS SPEAKER WAS UNIVERSALLY REGARDED AS THE FINEST CENTER fielder ever to play in the major leagues. Then Joe DiMaggio came along. While Speaker was a marvelous outfielder who could do most things as well as DiMaggio, the one thing he lacked was DiMaggio's power. True, Speaker played most of his career during the dead ball era and ranks very high on the career extra-base hits list, but in approximately two-thirds the number of at-bats, DiMaggio hit more than three times as many homers and finished with 8 more runs batted in. These are the figures that earned him first-team honors over Speaker.

Joe DiMaggio may not have been the big league's first five-tool player (i.e., excelling in hitting, hitting for power, running, throwing, and fielding), but he certainly took the game to the next level. His combination of speed, power, and baseball instincts gained him general recognition as the sport's finest all-around player. In fact, the young DiMaggio of 1936–1942, prior to his years in the military and a series of nagging injuries, may have been the greatest all-around player in baseball history.

DiMaggio had his finest seasons in 1937, 1939, 1940, and 1941. In 1937 he led the American League in home runs, with 46, and runs batted in, with 167. In 1939 and 1940 he led the league in batting, with averages of .381 and .352, respectively, winning his first MVP award in 1939. In 1941 he set a major league record that still stands by hitting in 56 consecutive games, en route to batting .357 for the season and winning his second MVP award. And DiMaggio still had something left after he came out of the service. In 1947, he was selected MVP for the third time and the following year he led the American League in home runs, with 39, and runs batted in, with 155, while compiling a .320 batting average.

In all, DiMaggio led the league in home runs twice, runs batted in three times, batting average twice, slugging percentage twice, and runs scored once, and finished in the top five in the MVP voting six times. He hit more than 30 homers in a season seven times, had more than 100 RBI nine times, topping 125 seven times, scored more than 100 runs eight times, had more than 200 hits twice, and batted over .300 in eleven of his thirteen major league seasons, surpassing the .340 mark five times. He accomplished all that in spite of the fact that he was a right-handed dead pull-hitter playing half his games in Yankee Stadium, with its "Death Valley" in left and left-center field. (Let's not forget that before it was re-modeled prior to the 1976 season, Yankee Stadium's outfield fences were 402 feet away from home plate in straight-away left, 457 feet away in deepest left-center and 461 feet from home in straight-away center). DiMaggio probably hit at least 10 balls a season in that ballpark that would have been home runs anywhere else. Mickey Mantle once said that, in 1951—Mantle's first season with the Yankees and DiMaggio's last—DiMaggio must have hit at least 15 balls well over 400 feet that were caught.

Another amazing DiMaggio statistic is that he hit 361 home runs and struck out only 369 times in his career—nearly a 1 to 1 ratio that is almost unheard of! In fact, he struck out only *thirteen times* in 1941, the year he hit in 56 consecutive games.

On top of everything else, DiMaggio was a winner, having played on ten pennant winners and nine world championship teams during his thirteen-year career.

DiMaggio was also one of the finest base runners of his time, even though he stole only 30 bases during his career. The Yankees teams that he played on usually relied more on power than on speed to win games and his managers didn't want him risking injury by attempting to steal a lot of bases. But when it came to running the bases, not many were better than DiMaggio. His 131 career triples, over thirteen seasons, are an indication of the kind of speed and base-running skills he possessed.

And, finally, DiMaggio's defense should not be overlooked either. He was an outstanding and graceful center fielder, and had a very strong throwing arm. In fact, he led the league's outfielders in assists with 22 his rookie year, then had 21 and 20 the next two seasons, before players gave up trying to run on him.

Mickey Mantle once said: "As far as I'm concerned, Joe DiMaggio was probably the greatest all-around baseball player who ever lived."

❷ TRIS SPEAKER

MANY BASEBALL EXPERTS STILL CONSIDER Tris Speaker to be the finest defensive center fielder who ever played the game. He revolutionized center field play by taking advantage of his great ability to go back on a ball and playing opposing hitters shallow. He also had an excellent throwing arm, as is shown by his major league record for assists (450) and double plays (135) by an outfielder.

However, Speaker was more than just a great defensive outfielder; he was a superb hitter, as well. He led the American League in both home runs and batting average once, hitting .386 for Cleveland in 1916 to beat out Ty Cobb for the batting title. He also had other seasons where he batted .383, .388, .380, and .389, even though he failed to win the batting championship. In fact, his career average of .345 ranks among the highest all-time, and his 792 career doubles are an all-time record. He also ranks among the top ten in runs, hits, triples, and total bases. Speaker led the league in slugging twice, on-base percentage four times, doubles eight times and hits twice. He scored more than 100 runs in a season seven times during his career, had more than 200 hits four times and had more than 50 doubles five times. Speaker had perhaps his finest season for the Boston Red Sox in 1912 when he won the league's MVP award and batted .383 with 53 doubles. He is the only player ever to lead the league in doubles four straight years, topping the A.L. in that department from 1920 to 1923. In fact, in 1923 at the age of thirty-five, Speaker had his most productive season. Showing what he could do with a livelier ball, he reached career highs in home runs (17), runs batted in (130), and doubles (59), and also batted .380 with 218 hits and 133 runs scored. In his career, he batted over .300 eighteen times and had 3,514 hits.

Smoky Joe Wood roomed with Speaker in Boston and said in *The Glory of Their Times* that "Speaker played a real shallow center field and had terrific instincts...Nobody else was even in the same league with him."

Hall of Famer Joe Sewell was Speaker's teammate with the Cleveland Indians. He's quoted in *Legends of Baseball:* "I played with Tris for seven years. I've seen Joe DiMaggio and I've seen Willie Mays...and all the rest. Tris Speaker is the best center fielder I've seen."

③ OSCAR CHARLESTON

ALTHOUGH HE MAY HAVE HAD AS MUCH talent as anyone who ever played the game, Oscar Charleston never had the opportunity to prove it at the major league level. Therefore, as great as he may have been, it would be impossible to rank him above Joe DiMaggio and Tris Speaker, two of the greatest players the game has ever seen. However, Charleston was clearly good enough to be ranked just behind them in the third slot.

Oscar Charleston is considered by many to have been the greatest of all Negro League players. It diminishes Negro Leaguers to equate them with white players as the "black" this or that. However, Charleston's preeminence is such

that he is known equally as "the black Tris Speaker" for his fielding, "the black Ty Cobb" for his base-running and "the black Babe Ruth" for his hitting. He could hit for both average and power, and he had excellent speed and a strong and accurate throwing arm. Among Negro League players, only Josh Gibson could challenge Charleston's reputation as a slugger, and only Cool Papa Bell could compare as a center fielder.

Right fielder Dave Malarcher, who played alongside Charleston, said: "He could play all the outfield. I just caught foul balls. I stayed on the lines."

Former teammate Ben Taylor, a star first baseman and manager in his own right, said after the 1924 season that Charleston was the "greatest outfielder that ever lived...greatest of all colors. He can cover more ground than any man I have ever seen. His judging of fly balls borders on the uncanny."

Buck O'Neill, who played against Charleston in the Negro Leagues, said: "Willie Mays was the best *major league* player I ever saw, but Oscar Charleston was the best *baseball* player I ever saw."

4 COOL PAPA BELL

COOL PAPA BELL WAS THE FASTEST player of his time—and perhaps of any time. He was so fast that Satchel Paige once said: "He could flip off the light switch at night and be in bed before the room got dark."

A switch-hitter who hit for a very high average, Bell was considered to be, next to Oscar Charleston, the finest outfielder ever to play in the Negro Leagues. He was once credited will stealing over 170 bases in a 200-game season. Bell hit .395 in exhibition games against major league players.

Bill Veeck, owner of several major league teams, said: "Defensively, he was the equal of Tris Speaker, Joe DiMaggio, or Willie Mays."

Pro basketball pioneer and baseball scout Eddie Gottlieb said: "If he had played in the major leagues, he would have reminded people of Willie Keeler as a hitter and Ty Cobb as a base runner—and he might have exceeded both."

5 CHUCK KLEIN

ALTHOUGH HIS NAME NEVER SEEMS TO GET mentioned in discussions involving the great players of the past, Chuck Klein was a tremendous all-around player who was *the* most dominant player in the National League from 1929 to 1933. Playing for the Philadelphia Phillies during that five-year period, Klein led the league in home runs four times, runs batted in twice, batting average once, doubles twice, hits twice, runs scored three times, on-base percentage once, and slugging percentage three times. In 1930, he reached career highs in home runs (40), runs batted in (170), batting average (.386), hits (250), doubles (59), and runs scored (158). He won the league's MVP award in 1932 by leading in home runs with 38, runs scored with 152, and base hits with 226. He also knocked in 137 runs and batted .348 that year. Klein followed that up the next season by winning the Triple Crown, hitting 28 home runs, knocking in 120 runs, and batting .368. During that five-year stretch, he finished in the top five of the MVP voting every year the award was given out (it was not presented in either 1929 or 1930).

Klein was also an excellent outfielder with a very strong throwing arm. In 1930, he set a twentieth-century record for outfielders by accumulating 44 assists.

Unfortunately, for most of the remainder of his career, Klein was bothered by a series of hamstring pulls and a drinking problem that may very well have prevented him from becoming one of the truly great players of all-time.

Honorable mention should be given to Earl Averill:

Earl Averill didn't come up to the major leagues, with the Cleveland Indians, until he was already in his late twenties. However, he made the most out of his thirteen-year career. Originally a slugger, Averill

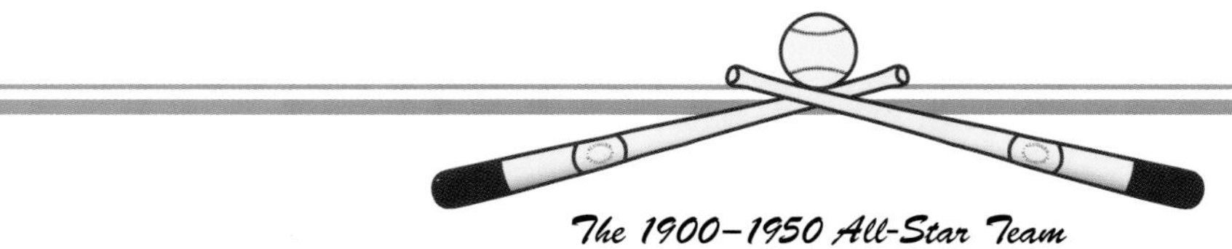

had to alter his hitting style during the latter portion of his career because of physical problems, and he became more of a "spray" hitter. Prior to that, however, he hit over 30 homers in a season three times, knocked in over 100 runs five times, and batted over .300 eight times. Averill had his finest seasons in 1931 and 1936. In 1931, he hit 32 home runs, knocked in 143 runs, and batted .333. In 1936, he hit 28 homers, had 126 RBI, batted .378, and led the league in triples with 15, and base hits with 232. Averill finished in the top five in the league MVP voting each of those seasons, and made it into the top ten two other times. He was also selected to the first six American League All-Star teams, from 1933 to 1938.

All-Star Right Fielder

PLAYER	YEARS	AB	HITS	RUNS	2B	3B	HR	RBI	AVG	SB	OBP	SLG PCT
1) BABE RUTH	1914–35	8,399	2,873	2,174	506	136	714	2,213	.342	123	.474	.690
2) JOE JACKSON	1908–20	4,981	1,772	873	307	168	54	785	.356	202	.423	.517
3) MEL OTT	1926–47	9,456	2,876	1,859	488	72	511	1,860	.304	89	.414	.533
4) HARRY HEILMANN	1914–30, 1932	7,787	2,660	1,291	542	151	183	1,539	.342	112	.410	.520
5) PAUL WANER	1926–45	9,459	3,152	1,627	605	191	113	1,309	.333	104	.404	.473
HONORABLE MENTION:												
SAM CRAWFORD	1899–1917	9,570	2,961	1,391	458	309	97	1,525	.309	366	.362	.452

1 BABE RUTH

George Herman "Babe" Ruth was, in all probability, the greatest player who ever lived. There may be those who will argue that there were a few others who were more complete players and better all-around athletes. However, few will question the fact that Ruth was the greatest offensive player of all time and that he dominated the game the way no other player ever has.

Babe was also the most colorful and charismatic player of his or any other era and the game's greatest drawing card. He almost single-handedly saved the sport and brought back its fan-base following the "Black Sox" scandal of 1919.

Nevertheless, many fans from later generations labor under a general misconception about Ruth. They picture him as being an overweight, slow-footed outfielder who was basically one-dimensional as a player and didn't do much else other than hit home runs. Nothing could be further from the truth.

First of all, prior to becoming a full-time outfielder in 1919, Ruth was a great pitcher. He had two 20-win seasons, a career ERA of 2.22, and was generally considered to be the best left-handed pitcher in the game at that time.

But the Babe made this team as an outfielder, so that's the context within which he will be judged.

While it is true that Ruth is remembered largely for his accomplishments as a home-run hitter, many of his other offensive achievements were equally amazing. In addition to leading the American League in home runs twelve times over a fourteen-year stretch from 1918 to 1931, Babe led the league in runs batted in six times, batting average once, runs scored eight times, walks eleven times, on-base percentage ten times, and slugging percentage 12 times. His career slugging percentage of .690 puts him 56 points ahead of Ted Williams, who, at .634, had the second highest percentage all-time. Ruth's single-season record for slugging percentage of .847, set in 1920, stood for more than 80 years until it was broken by Barry Bonds in 2001.

In 1921 Babe had probably the finest offensive season any player has ever had: he hit 59 homers, knocked in 171 runs, batted .378, scored 177 runs (still a record), had 204 hits (including 16 triples—obviously, he couldn't have been all *that* slow—and 44 doubles), walked 144 times, and had an on-base percentage of .512 and a slugging percentage of .846. Unfortunately for him, no league MVP award was handed out that season or he most certainly would have won it. In fact, the award wasn't presented the previous season either, when he hit 54 homers. He also wasn't eligible to win the award in either 1927 or 1928 (two of his finest seasons), since the league had yet to rescind its ridiculous rule prohibiting a player from winning the award more than once. Thus Babe's lone MVP season came in 1923 when he hit 41 homers, knocked in 131 runs, batted a career-high .393, scored 151 runs, and had 170 walks. The following season, Ruth won his only batting title when he hit .378.

In all, Babe hit more than 40 homers in a season eleven times, including four seasons of over 50, had over 150 RBI five times, over 100 RBI thirteen times, and batted over .370 six times. In addition, he never struck out 100 times in any one season and was so dominant that he frequently hit more home runs by himself in a season than *entire teams* did.

As an outfielder, Babe got mixed reviews. Rube Bressler is quoted in *The Glory of Their Times* as saying: "One of the greatest pitchers of all time, and then he became a great judge of a fly ball, never threw to the wrong base, terrific arm." In the same book, however, Harry Hooper, who played outfield with Ruth, said: "Well, Ruth might have been a natural as a pitcher and as a hitter, but he sure wasn't a born outfielder."

All things considered, Ruth was probably no better than average as an outfielder. But he was far from a defensive liability and his offense was so overwhelming that it more than compensated for any shortcomings he might have had as a fielder. Teammate Sam Jones once said: "Babe Ruth could hit a ball so hard and so far that it was sometimes impossible to believe your eyes. We used to absolutely marvel at his hits. Tremendous wallops." And writer Jimmy Austin added: "I guess when you talk about the greatest baseball player ever it has to be either the Babe, Ty Cobb, or Honus Wagner…they could beat you in so many ways."

Lou Gehrig once said: "There will never be another guy like the Babe. I get more kick out of seeing him hit one than I do from hitting one myself."

And on the day of Ruth's funeral, sportswriter Tommy Holmes said the following to Red Smith: "Some twenty years ago, I stopped talking about the Babe for the simple reason that I realized that those who had never seen him didn't believe me."

2 "SHOELESS" JOE JACKSON

CHOOSING BETWEEN JOE JACKSON, MEL OTT, and Harry Heilmann for the right field spot on the second team is difficult. Heilmann was the first to be eliminated because he was not as much of a complete player as the other two, being just an average outfielder. Also, his critics claimed that his .342 career batting average was inflated because he played during the 1920s, when astronomical batting averages were not that unusual.

The next to go was Ott. True, he had almost twice as many career at-bats as Jackson and his career totals in most categories far surpass Jackson's. But Jackson's batting average was more than 50 points higher, and he had more than twice as many triples and stolen bases than Ott. Furthermore, Jackson's on-base percentage was slightly higher, but Ott had the edge in slugging percentage, so those two pretty much negated each other. Ott was a better run-producer, driving in runs and scoring them at a slightly faster pace. However, it must be remembered that Jackson played during the dead ball era, when runs were much more difficult to come by, while Ott's career coincided with the offensive explosion of the 1920s and '30s. But probably the biggest factor in bypassing Ott was his inflated home run total. True, he hit 511 homers during his career with the Giants, as opposed to only 54 for Jackson. But the 5′7″, 160-pound Ott was assisted greatly by the ballpark he played in, New York's Polo Grounds. Ott was a left-handed, dead pull-hitter, and the right field wall in the Polo Grounds was only 258 feet from home plate. Perhaps that is why, of Ott's 511 homers, 324 were hit at home, while he managed to hit only 187 on the road. In all likelihood, had he not been able to play half his games in the friendly confines of the Polo Grounds, Ott's name would never come up in conversations regarding the great sluggers the game has seen. As a result, Mel Ott must settle for third-team honors.

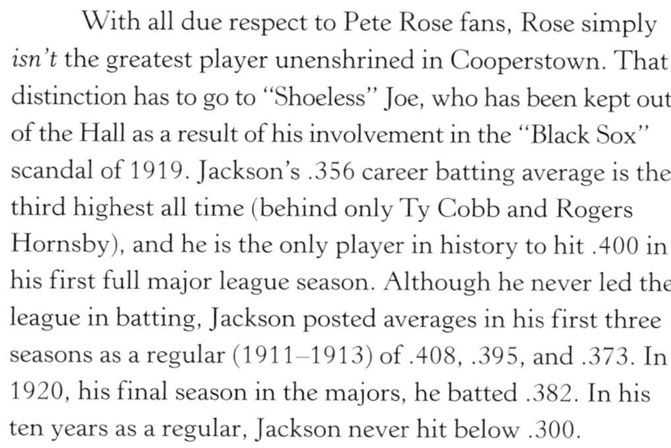

With all due respect to Pete Rose fans, Rose simply *isn't* the greatest player unenshrined in Cooperstown. That distinction has to go to "Shoeless" Joe, who has been kept out of the Hall as a result of his involvement in the "Black Sox" scandal of 1919. Jackson's .356 career batting average is the third highest all time (behind only Ty Cobb and Rogers Hornsby), and he is the only player in history to hit .400 in his first full major league season. Although he never led the league in batting, Jackson posted averages in his first three seasons as a regular (1911–1913) of .408, .395, and .373. In 1920, his final season in the majors, he batted .382. In his ten years as a regular, Jackson never hit below .300.

During the era in which Jackson played, a slugger was not measured by the number of home runs he hit, but rather by the number of triples. Therefore, even though he only hit 54 home runs during his career, Jackson was considered one of the top sluggers of his day because, in his ten full seasons, he accumulated an astounding 168 triples, leading the league three times. In 1912, he had 26 triples; in 1916, he had 21; and in 1920, he had 20. Jackson also had more than 200 hits four times, leading the league twice. Although he only knocked in more than 100 runs once, Jackson accomplished the feat in his final season. In 1920, with a livelier ball in use, he finished with 121 runs batted in.

Jackson was also an exceptional outfielder and an outstanding base runner. He stole a career-high 41 bases in 1911, then followed that up the next season with another 35.

Ty Cobb once said that Jackson was the greatest hitter he ever saw, and Babe Ruth added this: "I decided to pick out the greatest hitter to watch and study, and Jackson was good enough for me."

❸ MEL OTT

MEL OTT, THOUGH SMALL IN STATURE, WAS ONE OF THE TOP SLUGGERS OF HIS ERA. IN fact, before Willie Mays and Hank Aaron came along, Ott was thought of as the greatest slugger in National League history. When he retired in 1947, Ott held league records for most career home runs, runs batted in, runs scored, and walks. He led the N.L. in home runs six times, runs batted in once, runs scored twice, walks six times, on-base percentage four times, and slugging percentage once. Ott had his finest season in 1929 when he hit 42 homers, knocked in 151 runs, and batted .328. In all, he surpassed the 30-homer mark eight times and drove in more than 100 runs nine times. He finished in the top five in the MVP voting three times during his career. Ott was also a good outfielder, with a fine throwing arm that helped him amass as many as 20 assists in a season four times during his career.

Pie Traynor once said: "I can't name a player who has exerted as strong an influence upon so many games as Mel Ott."

❹ HARRY HEILMANN

HARRY HEILMANN EDGED OUT PAUL Waner for the fourth spot because he was the superior run producer of the two. While both men scored runs at approximately the same pace, Heilmann, in almost 1,700 fewer at-bats, knocked in more than 200 more runs. He also hit 70 more home runs and finished ahead of Waner in batting average, on-base percentage, and slugging percentage.

Harry Heilmann was the last right-handed batter in the American League to hit over .400.

Considered to be one of the finest right-handed hitters in history, Heilmann was included by Ted Williams on his list of the top twenty hitters in baseball history.

Heilmann led the A.L. in batting four times from 1921 to 1927, hitting .394 in 1921, .403 in 1923, .393 in 1925, and .398 in 1927, all for the Detroit Tigers. He also had good power, hitting at least 18 home runs four times, reaching double digits in triples nine times, collecting more than 40 doubles eight times, and knocking in more than 100 runs eight times. He also scored more than 100 runs four times and had more than 200 hits four times. From 1921 to 1927, he never hit lower than .346. Heilmann finished in the top five in the league MVP voting four times.

5 PAUL WANER

IT WAS AWFULLY CLOSE BETWEEN PAUL WANER and Sam Crawford for the fifth spot, and again the choice was made more difficult by the two men's playing in such different eras.

Crawford's career was spent entirely in the dead ball era, while Waner's best years came during the 1920s and '30s, when runs were far less difficult to come by. Crawford clearly had more power. While Waner hit slightly more home runs in approximately the same number of at-bats, he never came close to leading his league in that department. Meanwhile, Crawford led his league in that category twice and also finished with far more triples. However, Waner collected many more doubles. Crawford drove in approximately 200 more runs, but Waner scored about 200 more, so they were fairly equal as run producers, although the edge would have to go to Crawford since he played in a time when fewer runs overall were scored.

What finally tipped the scales in Waner's favor was his 42-point advantage in on-base percentage and his four batting titles. While Crawford won his fair share of home run and RBI titles, Waner was quite possibly the National League's finest hitter for batting average during his time. As a result, he was just barely able to edge out Crawford for a spot on the fifth team.

With 3,152 base hits and a career average of .333, Paul Waner was one of the great hitters of his era. Playing mostly for the Pittsburgh Pirates, he led the National

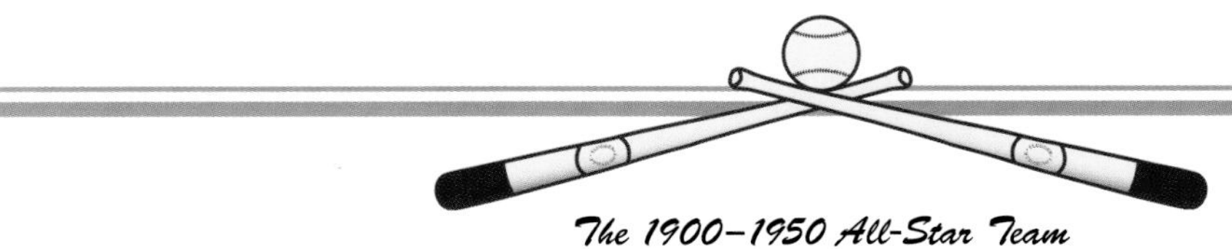

League in batting four times, runs batted in once, triples twice, doubles twice, hits twice, and runs scored twice. In fact, he led the league at one time or another in every major batting department except home runs and walks.

A veritable hit-machine, Waner surpassed the 200-hit mark eight times. His 605 career doubles ranks him high on the all-time list, with his season-high of 62 coming in 1932. Waner also knocked in over 100 runs twice. His finest season was 1927, when he was selected the National League's MVP for leading the league with 131 RBI, 237 hits, a batting average of .380, and 18 triples, while scoring 114 runs. He also finished in the top five in the MVP voting three other times. One of those times was 1928 when he batted .370, collected 223 hits and 19 triples, and led the league with 142 runs scored and 50 doubles.

Defensively, Waner was a good outfielder, possessing a strong throwing arm that enabled him to accumulate more than 20 assists three times, including a career-best 28 in 1931.

Honorable mention should be given to Sam Crawford:

Sam Crawford was one of the great sluggers and run-producers of the dead ball era. Although frequently overshadowed by Ty Cobb (Crawford played alongside Cobb in the Detroit Tiger outfield for thirteen years), Crawford was actually considered to be Cobb's superior as an extra-base hit and run producer. Crawford led the American League in runs batted in three times, surpassing the 100 mark six times, and led the league in triples six times, getting 20, or more, five times. In fact, Crawford is the all-time leader in triples, with 309. He is also one of a handful of players to have led both major leagues in home runs. Crawford finished runner-up to Eddie Collins in the 1914 MVP voting.

All-Star Utility Man

PLAYER	YEARS	AB	HITS	RUNS	2B	3B	HR	RBI	AVG	SB	OBP	SLG PCT
JACKIE ROBINSON	1947–56	4,877	1,518	947	273	54	137	734	.311	197	.410	.474

PRIOR TO DISCUSSING THE CAREER OF JACKIE ROBINSON, IT IS WORTH MENTIONING how I chose to deal with his special situation.

As another one of those players whose career overlapped the mid-century point, a valid case could be made for slotting Robinson into either time period. However, he has been included in the 1900–1950 era for a number of reasons.

First of all, even though only the statistics from Robinson's major league career are listed here, he did spend several years in the Negro Leagues prior to being signed by the Brooklyn Dodgers in 1946.

Secondly, although he had some very productive seasons after 1950, Robinson was truly at his best, and at his athletic peak, prior to 1951. In fact, there are those who consider young Jackie to have been among the greatest all-around athletes ever. A four-sport star at UCLA, Robinson excelled in football, basketball, and track and field, as well as his chosen profession. Former Dodger teammate, Duke Snider, who grew up in California and saw Robinson play college ball, is convinced that Jackie was better in football than he was in baseball.

Also, the decision was made to include Robinson on the team from the earlier time period because he exerted his greatest influence on the game prior to 1951. After all, it was in 1947 that Robinson finally integrated the major leagues.

In addition, Jackie has been added to the team as a utility player because his great athletic ability enabled him to star at four different positions for the Dodgers. At different points during his career, he was a regular at first base, second base, third base, and left field. Therefore, he is eminently qualified to fulfill such a utility role on this team.

JACKIE ROBINSON

WITH THE POSSIBLE EXCEPTION OF BABE RUTH, JACKIE ROBINSON'S HISTORICAL significance on the game of baseball is unsurpassed. We all know how he integrated the game in 1947, after being signed by Branch Rickey of the Brooklyn Dodgers. We also know that he had to deal with a tremendous amount of pressure and prejudice from fans, opposing players, and even his own teammates (especially in his first two years in the league). But what we can only try to imagine is what it made him feel like inside, how it must have saddened him, how angry and bitter it must have made him feel, and how much pressure he must have forced upon himself to perform at the highest level possible. It is this inner turmoil that caused him to age so rapidly, well beyond his years, and pass away when he was only fifty-three years of age.

We have no way of knowing to what extent this pressure affected Jackie Robinson's performance on the ball field. As it is, he was an exceptional player. But how much better would he have been if he had been allowed to just go out and play the game like everyone else? We'll never know the answer, but one thing is certain: Jackie Robinson was one helluva ballplayer.

As a member of the Kansas City Monarchs, Robinson was considered to be one of the Negro Leagues' top players. Yet, ironically, many were surprised when he became the first to sign on with a major league team. The general consensus was that Monte Irvin, who was later signed by the New York Giants, was a more gifted player. In addition, some of the older, more seasoned Negro Leaguers, such as Satchel Paige and Josh Gibson, resented the fact that Robinson was selected to be the one to integrate the majors. They felt that they deserved the chance to play in the major leagues more than he did. Nevertheless, Robinson was the choice of Brooklyn Dodger General Manager Branch Rickey because he knew that it would take a very special man—one with great character and self-control—to deal with the inevitable hardships that the first black man to play in the majors would encounter.

And deal with them Robinson did. Told by Rickey that he had to control his temper and not fight back for his first two years in the majors, Robinson absorbed the taunts and racial slurs hurled at him from fans, opposing players, and, in some instances, even his own teammates. Many of his teammates, especially those from the South, even tried to have management bar him from the team by starting a petition.

The fans of the city of Philadelphia were particularly rough on Robinson. Perhaps Jackie's worst moment came one day when they sent a black cat onto the field, near the Dodger dugout, as a reminder of how they felt about Robinson playing in the majors.

Certain individuals were also especially harsh towards Jackie. Former major league outfielder Ben Chapman was serving as an opposing team's coach in Robinson's early days in the league. Chapman was a master bench-jockey, and he took great pleasure in calling Jackie every racial epithet he could think of every time his team played the Dodgers. Having promised Branch Rickey that he would control his temper the first two years, Robinson never said a word to Chapman during that time. However, in a game during his third season, Robinson finally confronted Chapman, who had been abusing him throughout the early innings. As their paths crossed in between innings, Robinson told Chapman that he had been forced to take his crap for two whole years. However, with the handcuffs now off, the next time Chapman said anything derisive to him, Jackie would meet him in the

runway after the game and give him the worst beating of his life. Chapman never said another word to Robinson after that.

Robinson, himself, became quite adept at hurling verbal abuse at the opposition. In fact, after former Dodger manager Leo Durocher was hired by the rival New York Giants, their verbal battles became legendary. Jackie would often make remarks about Durocher's wife at the time—actress Lorraine Day. And of course, they didn't call Durocher "Leo the Lip" for nothing.

Robinson was also never at a loss for words with his own teammates. Dodger pitcher Ralph Branca said that, on those occasions when he didn't seem to be focusing properly on the opposing team's hitters, Jackie would be the first player to come to the mound and give him an earful. Branca also said that it was Robinson who comforted him after he surrendered Bobby Thomson's pennant-winning home run in the 1951 playoff game against the Giants. Seeing that Branca's spirits were very low after the game, Robinson told him that he shouldn't be too harsh on himself. Jackie told him: "Do you think they brought in our worst pitcher in that situation?…No, they brought in our best pitcher." Branca said he never forgot those words.

But it was with his playing ability and on-field presence that Robinson made his greatest contributions to the Dodgers. With the restrictions that handicapped him in his first two seasons removed by 1949, Robinson took his play to the next level. He hit 16 home runs, knocked in 124 runs, scored 122 others, collected 203 hits, and batted .342, to lead the league and win the MVP award. He had exceptional years the next four seasons as well, scoring more than 100 runs in three of those years, and batting well over .300 each season, en route to finishing his career with a .311 batting average. However, Robinson's contributions to the Dodgers cannot be measured merely by statistics. He was the finest base runner of his day, leading the league in stolen bases twice and frequently upsetting the opposing team's defense and pitcher to the point where they were far less effective than they would have been otherwise. Robinson brought the Negro Leagues' aggressive style of play to the majors, and was perhaps the fiercest competitor of his day. His competitive spirit and burning desire to win helped lead the Dodgers to six World Series and one championship in ten seasons. Cardinal second baseman Red Schoendist once said: "If it wasn't for him, the Dodgers would be in the second division."

All-Star Right-Handed Pitcher

PITCHER	YEARS	W	L	PCT	ERA	GS	CG	IP	H	BB	SO
1) WALTER JOHNSON	1907–27	416	279	.599	2.16	666	531	5,923	4,914	1,363	3,509
2) CHRISTY MATHEWSON	1900–16	373	188	.665	2.13	551	434	4,780	4,218	844	2,502
3) GROVER CLEVELAND ALEXANDER	1911–30	373	208	.642	2.56	598	437	5,189	4,868	951	2,198
4) SATCHEL PAIGE*	1926–47	123	79	.609			122	1,584	1,142	241	1,177
5) BOB FELLER	1936–41 1945–56	266	162	.621	3.25	484	279	3,827	3,271	1,764	2,581
HONORABLE MENTION:											
CY YOUNG	1890–1911	511	316	.618	2.63	815	749	7,354	7,092	1,219	2,800
ED WALSH	1904–17	195	126	.607	1.82	315	250	2,964	2,346	617	1,736
DIZZY DEAN	1930–41	150	83	.644	3.02	230	154	1,967	1,919	453	1,163
MORDECAI BROWN	1903–16	239	130	.648	2.06	332	271	3,172	2,708	673	1,375

*Satchel Paige's statistics are from the Negro Leagues and are therefore incomplete.

PRIOR TO NAMING THE SELECTIONS FOR GREATEST RIGHT-HANDED PITCHER FOR 1900–1950, special mention should be made of Cy Young. He deserves this special honorable mention since he is looked upon with such reverence, to the point that the award presented annually to the outstanding pitcher in each league was named after him. However, he has not been included with the top five right-handers because such a large portion of his career—and many of his finest seasons—occurred prior to the 20th century. While Young had several 20-win seasons after 1900, he was truly at his peak throughout much of the 1890s, when baseball was a different game, and for only a few years after the turn of the century.

❶ WALTER JOHNSON

THERE WERE MANY PITCHERS WHO EXCELLED during the pitching-dominated dead ball era. Of these, the three best were Christy Mathewson, Grover Cleveland Alexander, and Walter Johnson. All three were dominant pitchers who set the standards for others to follow. However, while Mathewson pitched for the always-contending New York Giants and Alexander's finest seasons were spent with the first-division Philadelphia Phillies, Johnson had the misfortune of spending his entire career with the lowly Washington Senators. It wasn't until the latter portion of his career, when Johnson was just a shell of his former self, that the Senators finally became a contender. In spite of this, he managed to dominate and was generally regarded as the game's finest pitcher. It is for this reason that he is the selection as the number one right-hander.

Walter Johnson's career winning percentage of .599 pitching for the Washington Senators was truly a remarkable accomplishment. Except for 1926, when he was at the end of his career, Johnson's winning percentage exceeded his team's winning percentage in every season that he worked 200 or more innings—in most cases, by well over 100 points. During his career, Johnson won 38 games by a score of 1–0, and lost 27 others by the same score. He holds the major league record for lifetime shutouts with 110, his career ERA of 2.16 is the lowest of any American League pitcher with more than 2,000 innings, and his 416 wins are the most by any 20th-century pitcher.

Johnson won over 30 games two times in his career and had 20 or more wins ten other times. During one stretch, he won at least 20 games in ten straight seasons. His ERA was below 2.00 ten times, and, in an era when batters did not strike out nearly as often as they would in later years, he struck out more than 300 batters twice. He led the American League in wins six times, in ERA five times, and in strikeouts twelve times. He led the league in all three categories, thereby capturing the pitcher's version of the Triple Crown, three times. Johnson's finest season came in 1913 when he won 36 games while losing just 7, had an ERA of 1.14, struck out 243 batters, threw 12 shutouts, and won the league's MVP award for the first of two times. The previous season, Johnson won 32 games, had an ERA of 1.39, and struck out 303.

Johnson's former teammate, Sam Crawford, once said of him: "He had such an easy motion it looked like he was just playing catch. That's what threw you off. He threw so nice and easy, and then *swoosh,* the ball was by you." He then went on to call him "easily the greatest pitcher I ever saw."

Jimmy Austin played against Johnson and said in *The Glory of Their Times* that "Lefty Grove was fast, and Sandy Koufax too. But you should have seen Walter Johnson. On a cloudy day you couldn't see the ball half the time, it came in so fast."

❷ CHRISTY MATHEWSON

THERE IS REALLY VERY LITTLE TO CHOOSE between Christy Mathewson and Grover Cleveland Alexander. Both were great pitchers. Both won 373 games during their careers. Mathewson had a slightly higher winning percentage, but that could be attributed largely to the fact that the team he played on was a little stronger than the teams Alexander pitched for. Mathewson's earned run average of 2.13 was better than Alexander's 2.56, but Mathewson pitched exclusively during the dead ball era, while Alexander's career extended into the higher-scoring 1920s. So, really, you could take your pick. And in the end Mathewson was the choice for the second team primarily because he has always been almost universally considered to be the greatest National League pitcher of the dead ball era.

Christy Mathewson won 20 or more games for twelve straight seasons, winning more than 30 in four of those seasons. He won a career-high 37 games in 1908. He led the National League in wins four times, in ERA and strikeouts five times each, and in shutouts four times. He had an ERA below 2.00 in five different seasons, with his career-best being 1.14 in 1909. Mathewson had probably his finest season in 1908, however, when he finished with a win-loss record of 37-11, an ERA of 1.43, 259 strikeouts, 390 innings pitched, 11 shutouts, and 34 complete games. He won the pitcher's Triple Crown that season—one of two times he accomplished the feat.

Mathewson also had remarkable control and over the course of his career was able to establish a strikeout-to-walk ratio of better than three-to-one. Amazingly, in 1913, he pitched 68 consecutive innings without walking a batter.

3 GROVER CLEVELAND ALEXANDER

NO PITCHER HAS EVER BEEN MORE DOMINANT for three consecutive seasons than Grover Cleveland Alexander was from 1915 to 1917. Alexander won the pitcher's Triple Crown in each of those years, the only time it has ever been done by one man three years in a row. His numbers over those three seasons: 1915—31 wins and 10 losses, with a 1.22 ERA; 1916—33 wins and 12 losses, with a 1.55 ERA; 1917—30 wins and 13 losses, with a 1.83 ERA.

Alexander won 20 or more games six other times during his career and led the National League in wins six times. He also led the league in ERA four times and in strikeouts and shutouts six times each. In 1916, he established a record by throwing 16 shutouts. He also pitched 38 complete games that year and he holds the National League record for lifetime complete games with 437. His 90 career shutouts are second only to Walter Johnson's 110, and he was able to maintain an earned run average of under 2.00 for six straight seasons, beginning in 1915.

As great as Alexander was, he probably would have been even better had he not developed a serious drinking problem during his career that hindered his performance for several seasons.

4 SATCHEL PAIGE

SATCHEL PAIGE MAY HAVE BEEN AS GOOD AS ANY PITCHER WHO EVER LIVED. HOWEVER, having played most of his career in the Negro Leagues, the statistics surrounding his remarkable achievements are extremely limited. As a result, it would be extremely difficult to rate Paige over three all-time great pitchers like Walter Johnson, Christy Mathewson, and Grover Cleveland Alexander. Therefore, Paige must settle for fourth team.

Satchel Paige pitched in the Negro Leagues for more than twenty years and is probably the most famous player to come out of them. He was such a great pitcher that when he finally got the chance to pitch in the major leagues towards the end of his career, he was quite effective, and even helped the Cleveland Indians win the pennant in 1948, even though he was already in his forties.

It was his years in the Negro Leagues that made him a legendary figure. Stories have been told of how he would sometimes tell his outfielders to sit down at the start of an inning because he planned on striking out the three hitters he would be facing—and he was usually able to back up his words. There are also stories of how he would intentionally walk the bases loaded in order to pitch to the opposing team's best hitter with the game on the line. In fact, on barnstorming tours against major league players, he was known to have walked hitters to get to Joe DiMaggio, who once said that Paige "was the best I ever faced." On those barnstorming tours, Paige regularly got the best of the likes of Dizzy Dean and Bob Feller. Indeed in one of those games, Paige struck out 22 big leaguers.

Of all the stories told about Satchel Paige, I think my favorite is one that I once heard Willie Mays tell. It seems that Willie was just a youngster, in his late teens, facing the much older Paige for the very first time in the Negro Leagues. Mays got a double his first time up. When Willie reached second base, he heard Paige tell his third baseman to let him know when "that little boy comes up again." So, the next time Mays came to bat he heard the third baseman yell to Paige "*There he is!*" Willie didn't know what was going on so he asked the catcher, who told him that Paige was going to throw him nothing but fastballs. Willie, precocious youngster that he was, said incredulously: "He's not going to throw *me* all fastballs!" As Willie tells it, the next three pitches were fastballs that Willie couldn't touch. Then Paige said to him: "Now go have a seat on the bench, son."

Cool Papa Bell, as quoted in *Baseball When the Grass Was Real,* said: "Satchel Paige was the fastest...I've seen Walter Johnson, Dizzy Dean, Bob Feller, Lefty Grove, all of them. All he threw for years was that fastball."

5 BOB FELLER

If Bob Feller hadn't gone into the military for three and a half years during the peak of his baseball career, he easily would have won well over 300 games. As it is, he finished with 266 victories against only 162 defeats. However, in the three seasons immediately preceding his stint in the service, Feller won 24, 27, and 25 games for the Cleveland Indians. In 1946, his first full year back, he had his

finest season, winning 26 games, striking out 348 batters, and finishing with an ERA of 2.18, 371 innings pitched, 36 complete games, and 10 shutouts. In 1940, he won the pitcher's Triple Crown, finishing with a record of 27-11, an ERA of 2.61, and 261 strikeouts.

In all, Feller was a 20-game winner six times, leading the league each time. He also led the league in strikeouts seven times, threw three no-hitters, 12 one-hitters, and once struck out eighteen batters in a game.

Satchel Paige said of Feller: "If anybody threw that ball any harder than Rapid Robert, then the human eye couldn't follow it."

Honorable mention should be given to Cy Young, Ed Walsh, "Three Fingered" Mordecai Brown, and Dizzy Dean:

The career of Cy Young, touched on earlier, was truly amazing. He holds several records that will never be broken. Among them are his records for most career wins (511), most innings pitched (7,354), most games started (815), and most complete games (749). He won 30 or more games five times and 20 or more games ten other times. He led the league in wins four times, in ERA, strikeouts and innings pitched two times each, and in shutouts seven times. He won the pitcher's Triple Crown in 1901, with a record of 33-10, an ERA of 1.62, and 158 strikeouts. He finished with an ERA under 2.00 six times during his career and had a perfect game to his credit. The three main keys to his success were consistency, endurance, and control.

Ed Walsh's career ERA of 1.82 is the lowest of any 20th-century pitcher. A master of the spitball (a legal pitch for much of the dead ball era), Walsh won 40 games one year and 20 or more three other times. Walsh's finest season came in 1908 when, pitching for the Chicago White Sox, he had a record of 40-15, an ERA of 1.42, 269 strikeouts, 464 innings pitched, 11 shutouts, and 42 complete games. In all, he led the American League in ERA twice, in wins once, in strikeouts twice, in innings pitched four times, in shutouts three times, and had an ERA under 2.00 five times.

"Three Fingered" Mordecai Brown, who pitched mostly for the Chicago Cubs, won 20 or more games six straight seasons, and led the National League with 27 wins in 1909. The previous season, Brown set a 20th-century record for lowest ERA, with a mark of 1.04. In fact, his career ERA of 2.06 is the third lowest ever. Brown led the league in shutouts and complete games twice each, and his career head-to-head record against the great Christy Mathewson was a very respectable 11-13. Ty Cobb said of Brown's breaking ball that "it was the most devastating pitch I ever faced. Christy Mathewson's fade-away was good, but it was nothing like that curve Three-Fingered Brown threw at you."

Along with Carl Hubbell, Dizzy Dean was the National League's most dominant pitcher during the mid-1930s. He won 20 or more games four straight years and is the last National League pitcher to win 30 games in a season, accomplishing the feat in 1934. That season, pitching for the St. Louis Cardinals, Dean won 30 games while losing only 7, had a 2.66 ERA, and led the league with 195 strike-outs and 7 shutouts, en route to winning league MVP honors. At his peak, he was so dominant that he also finished runner-up in the MVP voting in both 1935 and 1936. In all, Dean led the league in wins twice, strikeouts four times, shutouts twice, complete games three times, and innings pitched three times. Unfortunately, while pitching in the 1937 All-Star game, he was hit in the toe by a line drive off the bat of Earl Averill. The broken toe caused him to alter his pitching motion and eventually injure his right arm. If not for that, Dean may very well have gone down as one of the all-time greats.

NY

All-Star Left-Handed Pitcher

PITCHER	YEARS	W	L	PCT	ERA	GS	CG	IP	H	BB	SO
1) LEFTY GROVE	1925–41	300	141	.680	3.06	457	298	3,940	3,849	1,187	2,266
2) CARL HUBBELL	1928–43	253	154	.622	2.98	431	260	3,590	3,461	725	1,677
3) EDDIE PLANK	1901–17	326	194	.627	2.35	529	410	4,495	3,958	1,072	2,246
4) RUBE WADDELL	1899–1910	193	143	.574	2.16	340	261	2,961	2,460	803	2,316
5) LEFTY GOMEZ	1930–43	189	102	.649	3.34	320	173	2,503	2,290	1,095	1,468
HONORABLE MENTION:											
HAL NEWHOUSER	1939–55	207	150	.580	3.06	374	212	2,993	2,674	1,249	1,796

1 LEFTY GROVE

THERE ARE SOME BASEBALL HISTORIANS WHO CONSIDER LEFTY GROVE NOT ONLY TO be the finest pitcher of his era, but the greatest pitcher in the history of the game. While I won't address the validity of the second part of that statement right now, one thing is quite certain: Grove was clearly the greatest left-handed pitcher of the first fifty years of the twentieth century.

Robert Moses Grove did not begin pitching in the major leagues, for Connie Mack's Philadelphia Athletics, until he was twenty-five years old. However, he became a star almost as soon as he arrived, leading the league in strikeouts his first seven seasons. In his third season, 1927, Grove became a 20-game winner for the first time, something he would accomplish in each of the subsequent six seasons as well, and, in all, eight times during his career. In 1930, Grove won the pitcher's Triple Crown for the first time by finishing with a win-loss record of 28-5, an ERA of 2.54, and 209 strikeouts. The following season, he reached the apex of his career by having one of the finest seasons a pitcher has ever had. That year, his record was 31-4 and he finished with an ERA of 2.06 and 175 strikeouts to win the Triple

Crown again and the American League's MVP award. In all, Grove led the league in wins four times, in ERA a record nine times (including four times in a row from 1929 to 1932), and in winning percentage five times. In the six seasons from 1928 to 1933, his win-loss record was an incredible 152-41. He has the highest winning percentage of any pitcher with at least 300 victories.

Grove was so dominant that for two consecutive seasons—1930 and 1931—his earned run average was more than two runs a game below the league average. As John Thorn and Pete Palmer point out in *Total Baseball,* Grove's career ERA of 3.06, normalized for league average and adjusted for home park, is the best in baseball history.

Mickey Cochrane, who caught Grove when he was with the A's and later hit against Bob Feller, said: "Feller never saw the day when he could throw as fast as Grove. Lefty was bigger, more powerful, and had a smoother delivery."

And baseball historian Bill James asks: "What argument, if any, could be presented against the proposition that Lefty Grove was the greatest pitcher who ever lived?"

❷ CARL HUBBELL

JUST AS LEFTY GROVE WAS THE CLEAR-CUT CHOICE for number one left-hander, Carl Hubbell was the obvious choice for the second team. Along with Dizzy Dean, he was the National League's most dominant pitcher for much of the 1930s. In fact, Hubbell is one of only three pitchers in the history of baseball to win his league's MVP award twice (Walter Johnson and Hal Newhouser are the others).

In his first MVP season of 1933, Hubbell won 23 games while losing 12, his ERA was an astounding 1.66, and he also led the league with 308 innings pitched and 10 shutouts. During that season, he pitched a record 18-inning shutout against the Cardinals and won 2 games for the Giants in the World Series. In his second MVP season of 1936, he finished with a record of 26-6, an ERA of 2.31, 304 innings pitched, and 25 complete games. Hubbell won 20 or more games five consecutive seasons, from 1933 to 1937. During his career, he led the league in wins and ERA three times each, and in complete games, shutouts, and innings pitched once each.

However, Hubbell is probably remembered best for his performance in the second All-Star game, played in 1934. In that game he struck out, in order, Babe Ruth, Lou Gehrig, Jimmie Foxx, Al Simmons, and Joe Cronin, all future Hall of Famers.

3 EDDIE PLANK

WHILE RUBE WADDELL, AT HIS PEAK, MAY HAVE BEEN more dominant, Eddie Plank was far more consistent and had many more outstanding seasons. His 133 more victories are an indication of that. Therefore, it's not difficult to settle on Plank for the third team.

Although he never led the American League in any of the major pitching categories, Eddie Plank won 20 or more games eight times during his seventeen-year career. Pitching for some of Connie Mack's outstanding Philadelphia A's teams in the early 1900s, Plank was often overshadowed by Chief Bender and Rube Waddell, two of the other outstanding starters on the A's pitching staff. However, in the end, Plank turned out to be the A's best and most consistent pitcher, winning 326 games during his career.

The numbers Plank posted during his three finest seasons were particularly impressive. In 1909, he won 19 games and had an ERA of 1.76. In 1911, his record was 23-8 and his ERA was 2.10. The following season, he finished at 26-6, with a 2.22 ERA.

Plank's 326 career victories place him third on the all-time list among left-handers, behind only Warren Spahn and Steve Carlton.

❹ RUBE WADDELL

RUBE WADDELL WAS THE FIRST GREAT STRIKE-out pitcher of the 20th century. Although his career was relatively short and the number of prime years he enjoyed few, he managed to leave his mark on the record books. In 1904, Waddell struck out 349 batters, a modern single-season record that endured until 1965 when Sandy Koufax eclipsed it. The next season was Waddell's best, however. That year, he finished 27-10, with a 1.48 ERA, and 287 strikeouts to win the pitcher's Triple Crown. In all, Waddell won 20 or more games four times, led the league in strikeouts six times, and struck out more than 300 batters twice.

Unfortunately, Waddell was very irresponsible and was unable to dedicate himself to his profession the way his manager, Connie Mack, would have liked him to. For that reason, he fell out of favor with Mack and was eventually released. Otherwise, there is no telling how great he might have become.

❺ LEFTY GOMEZ

CONSIDERED TO BE THE TOP LEFT-HANDER IN the American League, next to Lefty Grove, for most of the 1930s, Lefty Gomez won 20 or more games four times for Joe McCarthy's great New York Yankees teams. Gomez won the pitcher's Triple Crown twice, the first time coming in 1934 when he finished with a record of 26-5, an ERA of 2.33, and 158 strikeouts. He accomplished the feat a second time in 1937, when he finished 21-11, had an ERA of 2.33, and struck out 194 batters. In addition to leading the league in wins and ERA twice each, and in strikeouts three times, he also led in innings pitched once and in shutouts three times. Gomez was also one of the best postseason performers in history, holding a lifetime 6-0 record in World Series competition.

Honorable mention should be given to Hal Newhouser:

Hal Newhouser was arguably baseball's best pitcher from the mid- to late 1940s. From 1944 to 1949, he won 136 games while losing only 67, had four 20-win seasons, led the American League in wins four times, and won two MVP awards, while pitching for the Detroit Tigers.

One of only three pitchers in baseball history to garner as many as two MVP awards, Newhouser's success was fleeting, but overwhelming. In 1944, he had a record of 29-9, finished with an ERA of 2.22, 312 innings pitched, and 25 complete games, and was voted league MVP for the first time. The following season, he led A.L. pitchers in every major pitching category by going 25-9, posting an ERA of 1.81, and finishing with 212 strikeouts, 313 innings pitched, 8 shutouts, and 29 complete games. He was voted league MVP again that season. In 1946, Newhouser finished runner-up in the MVP voting by going 26-9, compiling a league-leading 1.94 ERA, and totaling 275 strikeouts, 292 innings pitched, and 29 complete games. He had three more good seasons before he developed arm trouble and lost his effectiveness.

Had it not been for the fact that Newhouser had two of his greatest seasons during World War II, when many of the game's premier players were in the service, he would have received a higher ranking.

1900–1950 All-Star Lineup

NOW THAT THE SELECTIONS HAVE BEEN MADE FOR THE TOP PLAYERS AT EACH POSITION for the period of 1900–1950, it is time to make out the lineup. Although the designated hitter did not come into play until more than twenty years after the end of this period, one will be included here, since the lineup for the next period will have one. Besides, it creates a spot on the team for Ted Williams—and if ever a man was born to be a designated hitter it was Ted Williams. So here goes:

	FIRST TEAM		SECOND TEAM
1.	Ty Cobb *LF*	1.	Joe Jackson *RF*
2.	Honus Wagner *SS*	2.	Charlie Gehringer *2B*
3.	Babe Ruth *RF*	3.	Tris Speaker *CF*
4.	Lou Gehrig *1B*	4.	Jimmie Foxx *1B*
5.	Rogers Hornsby *2B*	5.	Al Simmons *LF*
6.	Ted Williams *DH*	6.	Hank Greenberg *DH*
7.	Joe DiMaggio *CF*	7.	Frank Baker *3B*
8.	Josh Gibson *C*	8.	Bill Dickey *C*
9.	Pie Traynor *3B*	9.	John Henry Lloyd *SS*
RHP	Walter Johnson	*RHP*	Christy Mathewson
LHP	Lefty Grove	*LHP*	Carl Hubbell

This lineup offers speed and base-running ability at the top of the order, with Cobb and Wagner, and power throughout the rest of the lineup. It also splits up the left-handed bats of Cobb, Ruth, Gehrig, and Williams with the right-handed bats of Wagner and Hornsby. Imagine a team where Ted Williams bats *sixth,* Joe DiMaggio *seventh,* and Josh Gibson *eighth!*

PART THREE

The Second Half of the Twentieth Century

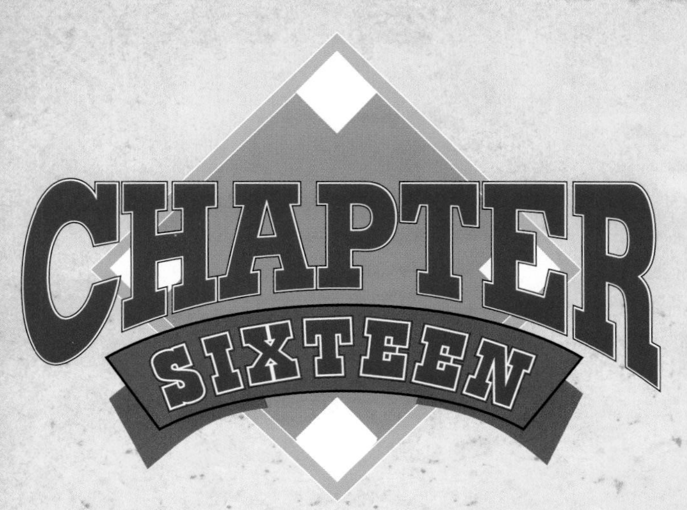

The Further Evolution of the Game

I'VE EARLIER DISCUSSED MANY OF THE CHANGES THE GAME OF BASEBALL HAS UNDERGONE through the years and, more specifically, the way it evolved during the first half of the 20th century. As the sport moved into the second half of the century, it bore a much closer resemblance to the game that we are familiar with. Yet there were still many additional changes on the horizon.

While night ball had been introduced to the major leagues in the 1930s, baseball in 1950 was still played predominantly during the day. It wouldn't be for a decade or so that night games would increasingly become the norm. The idea of having relief pitchers who were specialists, rather than starters who were either past their prime or not good enough to make the starting rotation, was still in its infancy. While there had been a few stand-out relievers up to that point, such as Joe Page, Johnny Murphy, and Jim Konstanty, the age of specialization was still a long way away, and it was not unusual for a pitcher to lead the league with as few as 14 or 15 saves. In fact, as recently as twenty years ago it wasn't unusual for a starting pitcher to have as many as 15 or 16 complete games in a season. And there certainly weren't any pitchers who specialized as "set-up" men.

In addition, baseball was much more of a "station-to-station" game in that the aggressive baserunning style that epitomized the dead ball era had been replaced largely by a "wait for the big inning" mentality. It was not uncommon for a player to lead his league in stolen bases with only 25 or 30. Jackie Robinson was one player who began to alter this style of play, and he would be followed by others such as Luis Aparicio, Willie Mays, and, later, Maury Wills and Lou Brock.

Perhaps the greatest change in the game would prove to be the emergence of black and Hispanic players during the 1950s. While still very much in the minority, they would begin to have a major impact on the game. Prior to 1951, the American League had held a decided advantage over its National League counterpart in the annual All-Star game. This edge was largely due to the junior circuit's wealth of sluggers: among them, Babe Ruth, Lou Gehrig, Jimmie Foxx, Joe DiMaggio, and Ted Williams. However, the American League would be slower to integrate than the National League, and as a result would fall behind and become the weaker of the two leagues. Starting in the late 1950s, the N.L. would begin to dominate the All-Star game and showcase the majority of the sport's most talented and exciting players. In the twelve years from 1951 to 1962, the National League's MVP award would be won by a black player ten times, while it was only in 1963 that Elston Howard became the first black player to win the award in the American League. It would take the A.L. another twenty years to recover from its shortsightedness, and once again be able to compete with the N.L. on an even playing field.

Finally, just as the game went through its cyclical changes during the first part of the century, it would again do so in the latter half. While all aspects of the game seemed to stabilize somewhat during the 1950s, pitching began to dominate once again in the following decade. This dominance reached its peak in 1968, when batting averages plummeted lower than ever before and pitchers began setting all kinds of records. Carl Yastrzemski was the only player in the American League to hit over .300 that year, winning the batting title with a mark of just .301. Bob Gibson finished with a record-setting 1.12 ERA, Denny McLain won 31 games for the Tigers, Don Drysdale broke the record for most consecutive scoreless innings pitched, and several pitchers finished the season with ERAs under 2.00. As a result, prior to the start of the 1969 season, the pitcher's mound was lowered from fifteen inches above the playing surface to ten inches and the size of the strike zone was reduced, in order to give pitchers less of an advantage. These changes stabilized things once more, until the hitters started to regain control during the 1990s.

There are many theories about what is behind the latest offensive resurgence, and there is most likely a bit of truth in all of them. Some say it is because hitters are bigger and stronger than ever before, due largely to the increasing popularity of weight training among modern players. There have even been allegations that steroid use has become rampant among current big leaguers. Some point to the dilution of pitching talent resulting from the constant expansion that has occurred during the last two decades. Others say that the ball is livelier than it ever was, while others mention the lighter bats that are being used by hitters today to give them added bat speed; a different approach to hitting that sacrifices contact for power. Many hint at the basic inability (or fear) of most pitchers to consistently pitch inside to batters, while still others blame the smaller strike zone and other rule changes that have been employed in recent years for tipping the scales in favor of the hitters.

Whatever the reason, the game is clearly geared more towards offense now than it was at any other point during the second half of the century. This must be considered when comparing the players of this generation to the players from the past three or four generations within this period. Just as a player's statistics had to be judged within the context of the era in which he played during the first half of the century, the same will have to be done now. As an example, Ken Griffey, Jr. hitting 50 or 55 home runs in a season, when weighed against the home run totals of some of his contemporaries, is really no more impressive than Hank Aaron hitting 40 or 45 when he played. Similarly, Pedro Martinez finishing the season with an ERA around 2.00 is actually comparable to what Bob Gibson accomplished in 1968. These are all things that must be taken into account when ranking the performances of the top players from this era.

However, there are other factors—some of which are very subtle—that must be considered as well. One of these involves the greater emphasis that has been placed on statistics in recent years. We are a society that has become obsessed with statistics, and far more attention is paid to individual statistics than ever before. We have also become a highlight-reel-oriented culture, with stations such as ESPN tele-

vising nightly the outstanding plays of the day. Another change involves the huge sums of money being thrown at players in recent years that has made many of them nothing more than high-priced mercenaries looking to sell themselves to the highest bidder, and in the process destroying any sense of team unity and loyalty between players and fans.

All of these factors are interrelated, and the end result has been a more individualistic approach to the game, with a "me first" mentality replacing the team concept that players of previous generations had a far greater appreciation of. With few exceptions, no longer do players put their teams ahead of themselves and sacrifice their own personal interests for the betterment of their team. Players are becoming increasingly concerned with their own statistics and are less willing to do the little things necessary to help their teams win. The sacrifice bunt has become an impoverished art, and the idea of hitting behind a runner to advance him on the bases would not even enter the minds of many batters.

Players want to hit as many home runs, drive in as many runs, and steal as many bases as possible so that when they become eligible for free agency their statistics afford them the opportunity to sign the largest contract possible. Players such as Frank Robinson and Ernie Banks hoped that a good year might garner them an additional ten or twelve thousand dollars in salary at season's end. Current stars, on the other hand, realize that an additional 10 home runs could mean millions of dollars to them on the open market. Mickey Mantle won the American League Triple Crown in 1956 by hitting 52 home runs, driving in 130 runs, and batting .353. After he batted .365 the following season, the Yankees' front office attempted to reduce his salary because he finished with "only" 34 home runs and 94 runs batted in. Times have certainly changed.

Current players are keenly aware of the emphasis that is placed on their statistics. Barry Bonds knows that by putting up prolific offensive numbers he will be viewed as one of the greatest players of all time. Sammy Sosa knows that hitting a lot of home runs will earn him a regular spot on SportsCenter and allow him to command huge sums of money. Bonds, as he should, takes great pride in being the only player in baseball history to hit more than 600 home runs and steal more than 500 bases. But the players of past generations never realized that so much emphasis would be placed on such statistics.

In 1988, after Jose Canseco became the first player to hit 40 home runs and steal 40 bases in the same season, Mickey Mantle said that he never dreamed that such a big deal would be made over something like that. He added that if he had known he would have done it himself. And there is little doubt that if players such as Willie Mays and Hank Aaron had put their minds to it they could have accomplished the feat as well. However, their focus was to help their teams win games and they would usually attempt to steal bases only when it was beneficial to their teams—not to pad their statistics.

The point here is that statistics only tell you so much about a player. Impressive numbers are nice to look at, but by themselves do not determine a player's worth. Because of the greater significance placed on statistics in recent years, they can only be used in moderation when comparing the players from this generation to those from the previous three or four. While it would be foolish to presume that players from thirty or forty years ago were not aware of the kinds of numbers they were compiling, it must be realized that they did not place as much emphasis on them. The "team concept" was generally more important to them than it is to the players of today.

Chapter Seventeen: Evaluating Active Players

ANOTHER DILEMMA THAT FACED ME DURING THE SELECTION PROCESS FOR THE SECOND half of the 20th century was how to deal with players who are currently active. For stars nearing the end of their careers who have already proven their greatness this was not a major concern. Players like Barry Bonds, Roberto Alomar, Randy Johnson, and Greg Maddux all have some good seasons left in them, but have already proven that they deserve to be included with the all-time greats.

Then there are those who are in the second half of their careers and have proven their greatness, but have not been around quite long enough to make their marks on the record books. This group would include players such as Mike Piazza, Frank Thomas, Ivan Rodriguez, Ken Griffey, Jr., and Mariano Rivera. The decision I made was to include these players in the final rankings, but only as high as their current achievements would take them. For example, "Junior" Griffey has been, with the possible exceptions of Barry Bonds and Alex Rodriguez, the finest player of his generation. If he is able to avoid the injuries that have plagued him over the last few seasons, he may yet be able to amass the kind of numbers that would permit him to be grouped with the greatest players of all time. However, to this point he has not accomplished enough to be included with the likes of Mays and Mantle. He must be viewed as a work-in-progress, someone who by the end of his career may deserve a higher ranking than he now deserves.

Frank Thomas and Jeff Bagwell, in particular, forced upon me a great deal of deliberation since they are without question two of the most dominant hitters of this era. In my youth, I saw quite a bit of Harmon Killebrew and Willie McCovey and I can say without much hesitation that both Thomas and Bagwell are superior as players. However, while both current sluggers have been able to compile much higher on-base and slugging percentages than either Killebrew or McCovey had, neither has yet been able to accumulate the home run and RBI totals that their predecessors amassed during their careers. Since, as was stated earlier, run production would be the number one priority for a first baseman, this presented quite a dilemma to me when it came to ranking these four men.

Finally, there are those players who have already shown that their talents are on a par with many of the great players that preceded them, but who are still young and appear to have many more exceptional years ahead of them. This would include the likes of Alex Rodriguez, Nomar Garciaparra, and Derek Jeter. All three have demonstrated that they're uniquely gifted all-around players. When their careers are over, it is very possible that all three will deserve to be ranked among the top five or six shortstops of all time. Rodriguez, in particular, has an incredible amount of talent that could one day have him challenging Honus Wagner for the title of World's Greatest Shortstop. However, at this stage of their careers, it is impossible to predict what will happen and to project what their numbers will look like eight or ten years from now. All too often in the past players have appeared who, for five or six years, gave every indication that they would turn out to be among the greatest who ever played. Yet, for one reason or another, they faltered and were unable to live up to the tremendous promise they showed early on. Factors such as injuries, alcohol, drugs, or just plain bad luck can curtail even the most promising career. Let's take a look at some of those players who, in their first several seasons, looked like sure Hall of Famers, but for various reasons faltered during the latter stages of their careers.

Tony Oliva was arguably the best hitter in the American League for much of the 1960s. He led the league in batting his first two full seasons, with averages of .323 and .321, and knocked in over 90 runs both seasons. He also had good power, hitting 32 home runs his first season. In all, from 1964 to 1971 he led the A.L. in batting three times, hits five times, and doubles four times, while hitting over .300 six times and knocking in more than 100 runs twice. He seemed destined to end up in Cooperstown. In 1971, however, en route to winning his third batting title, Oliva tore up his knee. He had surgery at the end of the season, and while he played another five seasons and had one or two more respectable years, was never the same player. Oliva finished his career with 220 home runs, 947 runs batted in, and a .304 batting average—hardly Hall of Fame numbers.

Dave Parker came up to the Pittsburgh Pirates in the mid-1970s and was almost immediately labeled the game's next great superstar. There was nothing he couldn't do on the ball field. He could hit, hit for power, run, and field, and he had an arm like a cannon. He batted over .300 his first five seasons in the majors and led the N.L. in batting two straight seasons. In 1977, he led the league with a .338 average and won the batting title again the following year with a .334 mark, while hitting 30 home runs and knocking in 117 runs to win the league's MVP award. He had another good season in 1979, but unfortunately everything started to fall apart for him after that. He developed a weight problem and a dependency on cocaine and was never a dominant player again. After five sub par seasons, Parker made a comeback with the Reds. In 1985, he hit 34 homers, knocked in 125 runs, and batted .312, and the following year he hit 31 more homers and knocked in 116 runs. But the damage had been done. Parker finished his career with 339 home runs, 1,493 runs batted in, and a .290 average—all very respectable numbers. However, with his ability, he should have been able to accomplish so much more.

Denny McLain won 20 or more games three times for the Detroit Tigers from 1966 to 1969. In 1968, he became the first pitcher in 34 years to win 30 games in a season. That year, his record was 31-6, his ERA was 1.96, and he struck out 280 batters. Not only did he win the American League's Cy Young award, but he was also named its Most Valuable Player. In 1969, he followed up with a 24-9 record and a 2.80 ERA that earned him his second consecutive Cy Young award. However, he was suspended for

much of the following season for his involvement with gamblers, and after he returned to the game was never an effective pitcher again.

Don Mattingly was generally considered to be the best player in baseball during the mid-1980s. In 1984, his first full season in the big leagues, he won the A.L. batting title with a .343 average. The following season, he won the league's MVP award by hitting 35 home runs, knocking in a league-leading 145 runs, and batting .324. The next year, he batted .352, had 238 hits, 53 doubles, and once again hit over 30 homers and knocked in over 100 runs. In all, from 1984 to 1989, Mattingly had five seasons with more than 100 runs batted in, three seasons with more than 200 hits, three seasons with approximately 50 doubles, and batted well over .300 each year. He was also a tremendous defensive first baseman. During the 1988 campaign, he began experiencing back problems. As a result, his offensive production and, in particular, his power numbers, began to drop off dramatically. After the 1989 season, Mattingly would never again come close to hitting 20 homers in a season. While he remained a fine fielder and a solid offensive performer, he was no longer the dominant player he had once been.

In his first two seasons, Dwight Gooden looked like a certain Hall of Famer. As a nineteen-year-old rookie in 1984, he won 17 games while losing only 9, compiled an ERA of 2.60, and set a rookie record by striking out 276 hitters. The following season, he finished 24-4, with an ERA of 1.53 and 268 strikeouts, to win the National League's Cy Young award. Gooden was already considered to be the best pitcher in baseball. However, his performance slipped somewhat the following three seasons. Though he won 17 games in 1986, 15 in 1987, and 18 in 1988, Gooden was not the dominant pitcher he had been in his first two seasons. His earned run average rose to slightly above the 3.00 mark, and his strikeout totals dropped off dramatically. It later surfaced that Gooden had developed an addiction to cocaine that was affecting his play. He had his last good season in 1990, winning 19 games, but, at the age of twenty-five, was never to be a big winner again.

So you can see that it is extremely difficult to predict how even the most promising career will turn out. This book will not attempt to do this with the likes of Rodriguez, Garciaparra, and Jeter, and, as a result, will rank them only as high as their current accomplishments take them.

One final point should be made: Since I concluded my player evaluations at the end of the 2003 regular season, any statistics subsequently compiled by players who were active as of that date will not be included here.

SPECIAL PRICES FOR DAY TRIPS
ALSO BY WEEK OR MONTH

PART FOUR

The 1951–2003 All-Star Team

All-Star First Baseman

PLAYER	YEARS	AB	HITS	RUNS	2B	3B	HR	RBI	AVG	SB	OBP	SLG PCT
1) STAN MUSIAL	1941–44, 1946–63	10,972	3,630	1,949	725	177	475	1,951	.331	78	.418	.559
2) EDDIE MURRAY	1977–97	11,336	3,255	1,627	560	35	504	1,917	.287	110	.359	.476
3) JEFF BAGWELL*	1991–2003	7,125	2,137	1,402	455	30	419	1,421	.300	196	.411	.549
4) FRANK THOMAS*	1990–2003	6,611	2,048	1,255	428	11	418	1,390	.310	32	.428	.568
5) MARK MCGWIRE	1987–2001	6,187	1,626	1,167	252	6	583	1,414	.263	12	.394	.588
HONORABLE MENTION:												
WILLIE MCCOVEY	1959–80	8,197	2,211	1,229	353	46	521	1,555	.270	26	.377	.515
HARMON KILLEBREW	1954–75	8,147	2,086	1,283	290	24	573	1,584	.256	19	.379	.509
ORLANDO CEPEDA	1958–74	7,927	2,351	1,131	417	27	379	1,365	.297	142	.353	.499
TONY PEREZ	1964–86	9,778	2,732	1,272	505	79	379	1,652	.279	49	.344	.463
RAFAEL PALMEIRO*	1986–2003	9,553	2,780	1,548	543	38	528	1,687	.291	93	.373	.522

* Indicates player is still active

As we start to take a look at the selections for the second half of the century, an explanation is in order as to why Stan Musial has been included as a first baseman. While Musial is remembered more as a left fielder than as a first baseman, he did play a lot of first base, especially during the second half of his career. For much of the 1950s and through his final season in 1963, Musial was either the Cardinals' regular first baseman, or split time with other players there. In addition, the crop of left fielders during this time period was very strong, and inserting Musial at first base would strengthen the team more.

1 STAN MUSIAL

While Eddie Murray and Mark McGwire were both great sluggers, and as Frank Thomas and Jeff Bagwell remain tremendous offensive forces, Stan Musial was the obvious selection for first-team honors at first base. Playing in an era that was only slightly more conducive to putting up big

offensive numbers than when Murray played, Musial, in approximately 350 fewer career at-bats, finished well ahead in almost every offensive category. He had far more doubles, triples, hits, and runs scored, and even knocked in slightly more runs. Murray hit almost 30 more home runs, but he finished far behind Musial in batting average, on-base percentage, and slugging percentage.

In far fewer at-bats, McGwire hit more than 100 more home runs than Musial and drove in runs at a faster pace. However, he was well behind in every other offensive category, and few would argue that Musial was a much more complete hitter and offensive player. Besides, a good portion of McGwire's numbers were compiled after the mid-1990s, at a time when big offensive numbers were quite prevalent throughout all of baseball.

Thomas and Bagwell have benefited as well from playing during this offensive-minded era, but their overall numbers compare more favorably with Musial's. Although each player has come to the plate approximately 4,000 fewer times than Musial, each has hit only about 55 fewer home runs. Both Thomas and Bagwell drive in runs at a faster pace, score them at a slightly faster rate, and have very similar on-base and slugging percentages. However, Musial collected far more doubles and triples, posted a significantly higher batting average, and with his three MVP awards and seven batting titles was a more dominant player during his playing days. Therefore, he has to be considered the obvious choice for first-team honors.

Stan Musial was the National League's best player for more than a decade, and its best hitter for even longer. He came up to the big leagues at the end of the 1941 season, and by 1943 had won the first of his three MVP awards. Musial was the league's most dominant player for the next several seasons as he also garnered MVP honors in 1946 and 1948, to become the first National League player to win the award three times. In all, he finished in the top five in the MVP voting nine times, and when he retired held league records for most hits, runs scored, doubles, runs batted in, and total bases.

During his career, Musial led the National League in batting seven times, runs batted in twice, runs scored five times, hits six times, triples five times, doubles eight times, and both on-base and slugging percentage six times. He also led the major leagues in total bases six times. Although he never led the league in home runs, Musial hit 475 for his career and bettered the 30 mark six times. He also knocked in over

100 runs ten times, batted over .300 seventeen times, had more than 200 hits six times, scored more than 100 runs eleven times, and had 20 triples twice and over 50 doubles three times. In addition, he was extremely difficult to strike out, never fanning more than 46 times in a season, and only 696 times in almost 11,000 career at-bats. Musial also batted over .350 five times in his career. His finest season came in 1948 when he hit 39 home runs, knocked in 131 runs, and batted .376 to win MVP honors and come within one home run of winning the Triple Crown. That year he also led the league with 18 triples, 46 doubles, 230 hits, 135 runs scored, an on-base percentage of .450, and a slugging percentage of .702.

Musial was an excellent performer in All-Star games. He holds records for most homers (6), extra-base hits (8), and total bases (40) in All-Star competition. Defensively, he was an above-average outfielder and an average first baseman. But as a hitter, he had few equals.

Pitcher Preacher Roe, giving advice on how to pitch to Musial, said: "I throw him four wide ones and then I try to pick him off."

Once, when asked why he always walked around with a smile on his face, Musial answered: "If you knew, at the start of the season, that you were going to end up hitting .340 or .350, you'd smile a lot also."

2 EDDIE MURRAY

THERE WILL NO DOUBT BE THOSE WHO question the selection of Eddie Murray over Mark McGwire for second-team honors. After all, in more than 4,000 fewer at-bats, McGwire hit 79 more career homers and had a considerably higher on-base percentage and slugging percentage. In addition, he had awesome seasons in 1998 and 1999, when he hit 70 and 65 homers, respectively. However, if you look at the career numbers of the two first basemen, Murray is far ahead in virtually every other category. Also, as was mentioned earlier, for the first half of his career McGwire was a totally one-dimensional player. His career batting average hovered around the .250 mark until he was finally able to raise it to a very mediocre .263 by the time he retired. It wasn't until his last few seasons that he became more patient at the plate and more of a complete hitter. Of course, it should also be remembered that the prodigious offensive numbers he was able to put up in the late 1990s coincided with the offensive explosion that was occurring throughout baseball as a whole. In addition, McGwire was never more than an adequate first baseman, defensively.

Frank Thomas has been less one-dimensional as a hitter throughout his career. He has a much higher batting average than McGwire—a higher average than Murray as well—and also has extremely high on-base and slugging percentages. However, he has always been a below-average fielder, to the point where he has even been used primarily as a designated hitter over the last several seasons. Murray, on the other hand, was an outstanding defensive first baseman. In addition, through either injuries or merely sub par performances, Thomas has had a few seasons in which he has not been the dominant force he has been throughout most of his career. Meanwhile, Murray was one of the most consistent and reliable players of his time. For his greater consistency and superior defensive ability, he deserves to be ranked higher than Thomas.

Although his career totals are generally not on a par with those of Murray due to the latter's 4,200 additional at-bats, Jeff Bagwell is another whose statistics compare quite favorably to those of Murray. He hits home runs and both drives in and scores runs at a faster pace. His batting average is 13 points higher, his on-base percentage is some 50 points higher, and his slugging percentage is 73 points higher. Bagwell is also an above average fielder who has been an extremely consistent performer for more than a decade. A legitimate case could be made for slotting him just ahead of Murray.

However, most of Murray's finest seasons came during the 1980s, at a time when it was much more difficult to post huge offensive numbers. In addition, his best years were spent hitting in Baltimore's old Memorial Stadium—not a very good park for hitters. Factoring these into the equation, along with his remarkable consistency and greater career numbers, it seemed that Murray was the best choice for the second team.

All Eddie Murray did was quietly put up impressive numbers, year after year, until people finally started to notice that he was one of the best first basemen to ever play the game. Playing most of his career prior to the mid-1990s, when offensive numbers began to climb dramatically, Murray never put up any outlandish numbers. He only led the American League in home runs and runs batted in once, but he hit more than 30 homers five times, knocked in more than 100 runs six times, batted over .300 seven times, had more than 30 doubles seven times, scored more than 100 runs three times, and was a model of consistency. Evidence of this consistency can be seen in his statistics from 1982 to 1985:

1982—32 HOMERS, 110 RBI, .316 AVERAGE
1983—33 HOMERS, 111 RBI, .306 AVERAGE
1984—29 HOMERS, 110 RBI, .306 AVERAGE
1985—31 HOMERS, 124 RBI, .297 AVERAGE

How much more consistent can someone be? In addition, Murray hit over 20 homers sixteen times during his career, accomplishing the feat thirteen times in fourteen years from 1977 to 1990. He also had 19 career grand slams, second only to Lou Gehrig's 23, and is one of only three players in baseball history (Willie Mays and Hank Aaron are the others) to reach the 500-home run and 3,000-hit plateaus. Murray finished in the top five in the MVP voting five times, and was an excellent defensive first baseman, winning the Gold Glove award three times.

Sparky Anderson once said: "Other people may disagree, but if you're asking me what player I'd want up there to win a game for me, it's Eddie Murray."

❸ JEFF BAGWELL

THERE WERE ACTUALLY SIX MEN WHO MERITED consideration for the final three spots: Willie McCovey, Harmon Killebrew, Rafael Palmeiro, Mark McGwire, Jeff Bagwell, and Frank Thomas.

McCovey and Killebrew had a few things going for them. They were both tremendous home run hitters who drove in a lot of runs during what was essentially a pitcher's era. They both spent the better part of their careers playing in ballparks that were not particularly kind to hitters. Most of McCovey's career was spent playing in windy Candlestick Park—hardly a hitter's paradise. Meanwhile, Killebrew played most of his home games in Minnesota's old Metropolitan Stadium, which was, to say the least, a fair ballpark for pitchers. Each won an MVP award, and each was selected to several All-Star teams (Killebrew, eleven times; McCovey, six times).

However, both McCovey and Killebrew were basically one-dimensional. Neither player was particularly strong in the field, and neither had any running speed. Even as hitters they were extremely limited in what they could do. While both drew a lot of walks allowing them to compile very respectable career on-base percentages, neither hit for a very high average. Killebrew never came close to batting .300, and McCovey topped .300 just a couple of times during his career. As a result, their batting averages and on-base percentages are much lower than those of both Jeff Bagwell and Frank Thomas. They also finished with much lower slugging percentages and far fewer doubles, and scored runs at a much slower pace. So McCovey and Killebrew were the first to fall out of consideration here.

Rafael Palmeiro's career statistics are perhaps the most impressive of the group. He has 110 more home runs than Bagwell and Thomas, has driven in almost 300 more runs, has scored more runs, and has a chance to become only the fourth player in major league history to hit 500 home runs and total 3,000 base hits. He has also been, throughout his career, a solid defensive first baseman.

However, it took Palmeiro far more at-bats than either Thomas or Bagwell has been able to accumulate thus far to surpass them in those categories. He has come to the plate almost 3,000 more times than Thomas, and almost 2,500 more times than Bagwell. Both players knock in and score runs at a much faster pace and hit for a higher average. Thomas's on-base percentage is 55 points higher, while Bagwell's is almost 40 points better. Thomas's slugging percentage is almost 50 points higher, and Bagwell's is almost 30 points higher.

Another factor to consider is that both Thomas and Bagwell have been far more dominant throughout their careers than Palmeiro has been in his. While the latter has made it into the top ten in the league MVP voting a total of just three times, never finishing any higher than fifth, Thomas has finished in the top ten eight times and Bagwell has made it into the top ten on six different occasions. Thomas has also won the award twice, while Bagwell was named the winner once.

In addition, while the statistics of all three players are inflated somewhat by the era in which they play, Palmeiro has the further advantage of having spent most of his career hitting in great hitters' ballparks: Chicago's Wrigley Field, Baltimore's Camden Yards, and The Ballpark at Arlington. All things considered, Palmeiro is not quite the player that Thomas or Bagwell is, and does not deserve to be ranked as high.

So that leaves Mark McGwire, Frank Thomas, and Jeff Bagwell. McGwire is the most popular of the three and would probably be the pick of most fans. After all, his home run feats are legendary and he is considered by most to be a certain Hall of Famer. Thomas and Bagwell, on the other hand, at this point in their careers, would probably be thought of as borderline Hall of Fame candidates by most. However, if one is able to look past McGwire's iconic status and view things objectively, it becomes clear that both Thomas and Bagwell are better players. Since the career statistics of Thomas and Bagwell are actually quite similar, let's use Thomas's numbers to get a clearer picture.

Playing in essentially the same era, with approximately the same number of at-bats, McGwire hit roughly 165 more home runs and finished with a higher slugging percentage. The two men knocked in runs and scored them at about the same rate. However, Thomas is well ahead in every other offensive category. His career batting average is almost 50 points higher, his on-base percentage is some 35 points higher, and he has 176 more doubles, twice as many triples, and 400 more hits. He has won two MVP awards—something McGwire never did—and even won a batting title—something McGwire never came close to doing. While it is true that Thomas is a liability in the field, McGwire was no Gold Glover himself. Even taking into consideration his defensive shortcomings, Thomas is the more complete player and deserves a higher ranking. Bagwell has the additional advantage of being both a better base runner and a better fielder. In spite of his great popularity McGwire will have to settle for a spot on the fifth team.

We are left with Frank Thomas and Jeff Bagwell. As was just mentioned, their career statistics are remarkably similar. Bagwell has approximately 500 more at-bats, but the two players have virtually the same number of home runs and runs batted in. Therefore, the slight edge there would have to be given to Thomas. However, Bagwell scores runs at a slightly faster pace, has three times as many triples, and has stolen six times as many bases. On the other hand, Thomas's batting average is 10 points higher, his on-base percentage is 17 points better, and his slugging percentage is almost 20 points higher. It would seem that Thomas is the slightly better offensive player.

Thomas also won two MVP awards, to Bagwell's one, and finished in the top ten of the voting eight times, to Bagwell's six. He would therefore have to be given the edge there as well.

However, throughout his career Thomas has been a weak fielding first baseman. As was mentioned earlier, he has been such a liability in the field that, for the better part of the last several seasons, the White Sox have frequently used him as a designated hitter. Meanwhile, after beginning his career as a third baseman Bagwell turned himself into a solid fielder at first, even winning a Gold Glove in 1994.

He is also far superior to Thomas as a base runner, having stolen as many as 30 bases twice in his career. He is a much more complete player than Frank Thomas. For that reason, Bagwell gets the nod as third-team first baseman.

Since he's played his entire career in Houston, Jeff Bagwell has never received the acclaim of some of his contemporaries. Nevertheless, he has clearly been the National League's best all-around first baseman over the last ten years. In 1994, Bagwell became only the fourth unanimous MVP selection in major league history, finishing that strike-shortened season with 39 home runs, a .368 batting average, and a league-leading 116 runs batted in, 104 runs scored, and .750 slugging percentage. Three years later, he became the first full-time first baseman in baseball history to hit more than 30 home runs and steal more than 30 bases in the same season. That year, Bagwell hit 43 homers, stole 31 bases, and drove in a career-high 135 runs for the Astros. In 1999, he duplicated his earlier feat by hitting 42 home runs and stealing 30 bases, while knocking in 126 runs, batting .304, and walking 149 times.

From 1996 to 2001, Bagwell averaged 39 home runs, 126 runs batted in, 128 runs scored, and 122 bases on balls, hitting more than 30 homers each year. He batted over .300 four times during that span. In all, he has hit more than 30 homers nine times, topping the 40-mark on three separate occasions, knocked in more than 100 runs eight times, scored more than 100 eight times, and batted over .300 six times.

4 FRANK THOMAS

FRANK THOMAS HAS BEEN, FOR MORE THAN A decade, one of the most feared hitters in the game, and also one of the most disciplined. With all his size and awesome power, "The Big Hurt" is a remarkably patient and consistent hitter. He is the only player in history to hit .300 with at least 20 homers, 100 RBI, 100 runs scored, and 100 walks in seven consecutive seasons. He is also one of only three players to drive in at least 100 runs in his first seven big league seasons.

In all, Thomas has hit more than 40 homers in a season five times, knocked in over 100 runs ten times, batted over .300 nine times, and drawn at least 100 walks nine times. He won the MVP award in

both 1993 and 1994. In 1993, he finished with 41 homers, 128 RBI, and a .317 average. In the following strike-shortened season he had 38 homers, 101 RBI, and a .353 average. He also had tremendous years in both 1996 (40 homers, 134 RBI, and a .349 average) and 2000 (43 homers, 143 RBI, and a .328 average). Thomas has led the American League in on-base percentage four times and is first among active players in that department.

❺ MARK MCGWIRE

ALL THE NEGATIVES NOTWITHSTANDING, MARK McGwire is still one of the greatest sluggers in the history of the game. He finished his career fifth on the all-time home run list with 583, and has the highest home run-to-at-bat ratio in the history of the game. We all know about his 1998 and 1999 seasons, when he hit 70 and 65 home runs, respectively, but McGwire is also one of only two players in the history of the game (Sammy Sosa is the other) to top the 50-homer mark in four straight seasons.

In all, McGwire led the majors in home runs four times, hit more than 30 homers eleven times in fifteen seasons, knocked in over 100 runs seven times, drew more than 100 bases on balls four times, and hit over .300 twice. He reached his career high in runs batted in, with 147, in both 1998 and 1999, and walked a career high 162 times in 1998.

San Diego Padres manager Bruce Bochy said of McGwire: "He's probably the strongest power hitter of all time."

Honorable mention should be given to Willie McCovey, Harmon Killebrew, Orlando Cepeda, Tony Perez, and Rafael Palmeiro:

Willie McCovey was probably the most feared hitter in baseball during the late 1960s. Although he spent a good portion of his career playing in the shadow of the great Willie Mays, McCovey, at 6´4˝ and 230 pounds, was hard to miss. His 521 career home runs tied McCovey with Ted Williams on the all-time homer list, and his 18 career grand slams place him third all-time. He led the National League in home runs three times, in runs batted in twice, and in slugging three times, leading the league in both homers and runs batted in two straight seasons (1968 and 1969). He hit more than 40 homers twice and

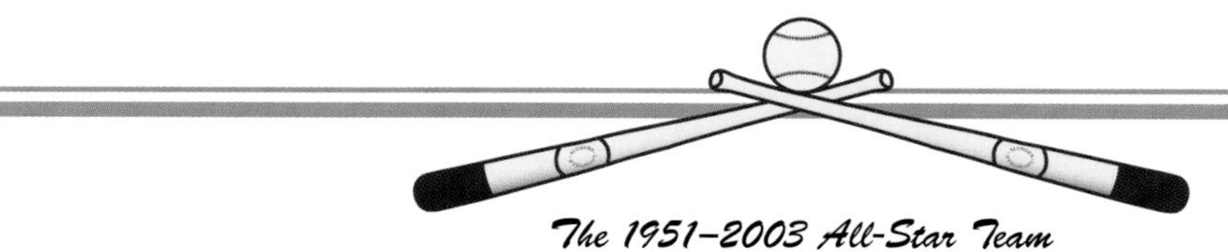

knocked in over 100 runs four times. McCovey's finest season came in 1969, when he hit 45 homers, knocked in 126 runs, batted .320, finished with a .458 on-base percentage, and led the league with a .656 slugging percentage—a performance that earned him league MVP honors that year.

Manager Gene Mauch once said of McCovey that "he's the most awesome hitter I've ever seen."

With 573 career home runs, Harmon Killebrew ranks sixth on the all-time list. He has the fourth highest home run-to-at-bat ratio in the history of the game (behind only Mark McGwire, Babe Ruth, and Ralph Kiner), and he is the top right-handed home run hitter in American League history. During his career, Killebrew led the league in home runs six times, runs batted in three times, walks four times, and slugging once. He topped the 40-homer mark eight times, knocked in more than 100 runs nine times, and drew over 100 walks seven times. He led the league in home runs three straight years, from 1962 to 1964, with totals of 48, 45, and 49. Killebrew's finest season was 1969, when he won the MVP award and led the league with 49 home runs, 140 runs batted in, and 145 walks. He also hit .276 that season.

Killebrew's contemporary, Boog Powell, once said: "Every time Harmon comes to the plate, he's dangerous. He is as good a clutch hitter as there is in the league. I have more respect for him than anyone."

Orlando Cepeda came up with the San Francisco Giants in 1958 and had several outstanding seasons before being traded to the St. Louis Cardinals prior to the 1967 season. In 1961, he led the National League with 46 home runs and 142 runs batted in, while batting .311. With St. Louis in 1967, he won the National League's MVP award by hitting 25 homers, leading the league with 111 runs batted in, and batting .325. In all, Cepeda topped the 30-homer mark five times, knocked in over 100 runs five times, and batted over .300 nine times.

Tony Perez came up to the Cincinnati Reds in 1964 as a third baseman and spent several seasons there before being moved to first base prior to the 1972 season. Although he never led the National League in any major offensive category, Perez was one of the most consistent RBI men in the league for years. He knocked in over 100 runs seven times during his career, and from 1967 to 1977 never knocked in fewer than 90 runs. He also hit over 20 homers nine times and batted over .300 twice. Perez had his two finest seasons in 1969 and 1970. In 1969, he hit 37 homers, knocked in 122 runs, and batted .294. The following season, he hit 40 homers, knocked in 129 runs, batted .317, and finished third in the league's MVP voting. Sparky Anderson once said that, with all the leaders that the Big Red Machine had in Johnny Bench, Joe Morgan, and Pete Rose, they all deferred to Perez. He was the number one leader on that team.

Rafael Palmeiro has been one of the most productive hitters in the game for the past decade. He has topped the 40-homer mark four times, hitting as many as 47 twice, knocked in over 100 runs ten times, and batted over .300 six times. From 1995 to 2003, Palmeiro has averaged 42 home runs and 121 runs batted in for Baltimore and Texas, hitting no fewer than 38 home runs in any of those years, and driving in more than 100 runs each season. His two best years with the Orioles were 1996 and 1998. In the first of those seasons, Palmeiro hit 39 home runs, drove in 142 runs, and batted .289. Two years later, he hit 43 homers, knocked in 121 runs, and batted .296. However, Palmeiro had his finest season of all for Texas in 1999 when he hit 47 homers, knocked in 148 runs, and batted .324. With 528 home runs and 2,780 base hits as of this writing, Palmeiro has a chance to become only the fourth player in major league history to compile 500 home runs and 3,000 hits. One of the most complete first basemen of his era, Palmeiro, with three Gold Gloves to his credit, is also a fine fielder.

All-Star Second Baseman

PLAYER	YEARS	AB	HITS	RUNS	2B	3B	HR	RBI	AVG	SB	OBP	SLG PCT
1) JOE MORGAN	1963–84	9,277	2,517	1,650	449	96	268	1,133	.271	689	.395	.427
2) ROBERTO ALOMAR*	1988–2003	8,902	2,697	1,490	498	78	206	1,110	.301	474	.372	.444
3) ROD CAREW	1967–85	9,315	3,053	1,424	445	112	92	1,015	.328	353	.395	.429
4) RYNE SANDBERG	1981–97	8,385	2,386	1,318	403	76	282	1,061	.285	344	.344	.452
5) PAUL MOLITOR	1978–98	10,835	3,319	1,782	605	114	234	1,307	.306	504	.369	.448
HONORABLE MENTION:												
RED SCHOENDIST	1945–63	8,479	2,449	1,223	427	78	84	773	.289	89	.338	.387
NELLIE FOX	1947–65	9,232	2,663	1,279	355	112	35	790	.288	76	.349	.363
BOBBY GRICH	1970–86	6,890	1,833	1,033	320	47	224	864	.266	104	.373	.424
JEFF KENT*	1992–2003	6,064	1,754	943	404	34	275	1,100	.289	79	.352	.503

* Indicates player is still active

1 JOE MORGAN

AN EVALUATION OF THE TOP SECOND BASEMEN OF THIS TIME PERIOD REVEALS THAT there really is not that much difference in their skill levels. A legitimate case could be made for each of the top five selections. Rod Carew and Paul Molitor were probably the best pure hitters of the bunch, but during the first half of their careers, they were each shifted to other positions, in part because of the defensive deficiencies they demonstrated at second. Ryne Sandberg was probably the steadiest and most consistent fielder of the group, but while he was a fine offensive player, he had only four or five truly outstanding offensive seasons. As a result, the choice came down to Joe Morgan and Roberto Alomar.

Defensively, Morgan was very solid and reliable. In 1977, he set a record for second basemen by making just five errors all season. However, Alomar is the more spectacular of the two, and has far greater range. Therefore, as fielders, the edge has to go to him. Offensively, it is very difficult to compare the two because of the distinct eras in which they played. Morgan played most of his career during the '60s and

'70s, when pitching was far more dominant than it has been throughout most of Alomar's career. This must be taken into consideration when comparing their offensive statistics. A look at the numbers indicates that Morgan had the edge in power, while Alomar hit for the higher average. When factoring in Morgan's 375 more career at-bats, plus the distinct eras in which they competed, the two are very close as run-producers. Alomar knocks in runs at a slightly higher rate, while Morgan had the edge in runs scored. However, Morgan was more prolific as a base-stealer and, with his penchant for drawing walks, had a higher on-base percentage. Therefore, offensively, he would have to be given the edge.

What eventually earned Morgan first-team honors was his integral role on one of the finest teams in baseball history, the "Big Red Machine." While not its only leader, Morgan was the catalyst, the one who pulled everything together. As such, he was recognized as the National League's MVP for both the 1975 and 1976 seasons. In 1975, Morgan hit 17 home runs, knocked in 94 runs, batted .327, stole 67 bases, and led the league in both walks (132) and on-base percentage (.471). The following season, he finished with 27 home runs, 111 runs batted in, an average of .320, led the league in both on-base (.453) and slugging percentage (.576), and was widely recognized as the best all-around player in the game. After his trade to Cincinnati from Houston following the 1971 season, Morgan became a true superstar. From 1972 to 1977, he averaged 21 home runs, 84 runs batted in, 60 stolen bases, batted .301, and scored more than 100 runs each year.

During his career, Morgan hit more than 20 homers four times, stole more than 40 bases nine times and more than 60 bases three times, scored more than 100 runs eight times, and drew more than 100 bases on balls eight times. He led the N.L. in on-base percentage four times and in runs scored once.

More than anything, however, Morgan was a winner. In his twenty-two big league seasons, he helped his teams win six divisional titles, four pennants, and two world championships.

❷ ROBERTO ALOMAR

ALTHOUGH HIS PERFORMANCE HAS SLIPPED somewhat the past two seasons, Roberto Alomar has been, for more than a decade, one of the finest all-around players in the game. He has been an excellent offensive player, a superb base runner, and perhaps the finest defensive second baseman in baseball history. He has excellent hands, a strong arm, and the most range of any second baseman in the game. Offensively, he has hit more than 20 homers three times, knocked in over 100 runs twice, batted over .300 nine times, scored more than 100 runs six times, and stolen more than 30 bases eight times during his career. Alomar's two finest seasons came in 1999 and 2001, both for the Cleveland Indians. In 1999, he hit 24 homers, knocked in 120 runs, and batted .323. In 2001, he hit 20 homers, had 100 RBI, and batted .336. Both seasons he finished in the top five in the league MVP voting. Earlier in his career, Alomar helped lead the Toronto Blue Jays to two consecutive world championships.

❸ ROD CAREW

THOUGH NOT NEARLY THE DEFENSIVE PLAYER that Ryne Sandberg was, Rod Carew's seven American League batting championships and .328 career average were difficult to ignore and earned him a spot on the third team, just ahead of Sandberg.

Many people remember Rod Carew as a first baseman, but he was the Minnesota Twins' regular second baseman from 1967 to 1975. Due to his erratic play there and the retirement of Harmon Killebrew, Carew was shifted to first base following the 1975 season. Once there, he became an adequate first sacker and continued his rampage against American League pitching. In winning his seven batting titles, Carew led the league in hitting four consecutive seasons, from 1972 to 1975. He also led the league in hits three times, runs scored once, triples twice, and on-base percentage four times. In all, Carew exceeded 200 hits four times, 30 stolen bases four times, and hit over .300 fifteen years in a row, from 1969 to 1983, including five seasons of .350 or better. His finest season came in 1977, when he won the American League MVP award by setting career highs in virtually every major offensive category. That year, Carew hit 14 homers, knocked in 100 runs, had a slugging percentage of .570, and led the league with a .388 average, a .452 on-base percentage, 16 triples, 239 hits, and 128 runs scored.

Carew was also a good base runner, stealing home seven times in 1969 to tie Pete Reiser's single season record. When he retired, Carew had the highest career batting average since Ted Williams of any player who had played in at least 1,000 games.

4 RYNE SANDBERG

WHILE RYNE SANDBERG HAD MORE power, hitting 60 more home runs in approximately 2,500 fewer at-bats, there is little doubt that Paul Molitor was a better all-around offensive player. He hit for a higher average, stole more bases, and finished well ahead of Sandberg in every offensive category, with the exception of home runs and slugging percentage. Molitor, though, had a longer career than Sandberg, and posted a good portion of his impressive numbers while serving as a designated hitter. He was the regular second baseman for the Milwaukee Brewers for only a few seasons before being shifted to other positions and eventually settling in to the role of DH. He was never anything more than an adequate fielder, and his extensive service as a designated hitter must be taken into consideration when comparing him to Sandberg, who was one of the finest fielding second basemen in the history of the game. Therefore, while Sandberg was a fine offensive player as well, it was his superb defense that earned him a spot on the fourth team, ahead of Molitor and—another superior offensive threat—Jeff Kent.

Ryne Sandberg's defensive resume is as impressive as that of any second baseman who has ever played the game. In addition to winning nine Gold Gloves, he is the all-time leader in fielding average among major league second basemen, with a mark of .990. From June 21, 1989 to May 17, 1990, he played 123 consecutive games and accepted 582 chances without making an error, both records for all infielders other than first basemen. During his career, Sandberg put together streaks of 30 or more errorless games fifteen times.

Sandberg also had some fine offensive seasons for the Cubs. He led the National League in runs scored three times and in home runs once. In 1990, he became only the third second baseman in major league history to hit 40 home runs in a season (Rogers Hornsby and Davey Johnson were the others). During his career, Sandberg knocked in more than 100 runs twice, scored more than 100 runs seven times, and batted over .300 four times. In 1985, he stole a career-high 54 bases. The previous year, Sandberg was voted the N.L.'s Most Valuable Player when he hit 19 home runs, knocked in 84 runs, batted .314, and led the league with 19 triples and 114 runs scored.

❺ PAUL MOLITOR

NEITHER PAUL MOLITOR NOR JEFF KENT built their reputation on their defense. As was mentioned earlier, Molitor was the Milwaukee Brewers' regular second baseman for only a few seasons before being shifted to other positions and eventually becoming a DH. Meanwhile, although not considered to be a defensive liability, Kent is merely adequate in the field, with limited range and a slightly above average .977 lifetime fielding percentage.

Offensively, Kent has more power and drives in runs at a faster pace. However, Molitor hit for a higher average, accumulated far more doubles and triples, stole many more bases, and with his superior speed and base running ability scored runs at a faster pace. Much more of a contact hitter, Molitor also struck out much less frequently than Kent does. In short, Molitor was the better all-around hitter and a more complete offensive player, and for that reason he gets the nod for fifth-team honors.

A lot of people think of Paul Molitor as anything but a second baseman. While he spent his last eight major league seasons primarily as a designated hitter, Molitor previously had stints as a first baseman, third baseman, and an outfielder. However, prior to that, he originally came up to the Milwaukee Brewers as a second baseman. He spent several seasons there before being shifted to other positions due to his erratic fielding and penchant for getting injured. As a hitter, though, Molitor was always a standout. A member of the 3,000-hit club, he batted over .300 twelve times, knocked in over

100 runs twice, scored over 100 runs five times, and had more than 200 hits four times. He also stole more than 30 bases eight times, and more than 40 four times. Molitor led the A.L. in runs scored three times, and in base hits, doubles, and triples once each. He had his finest season in 1987, when he hit .353 and led the league in both runs scored and doubles.

Honorable mention should be given to Red Schoendist, Nellie Fox, Bobby Grich, and Jeff Kent:

Red Schoendist teamed with shortstop Marty Marion during the '40s and '50s to give the St. Louis Cardinals one of baseball's best-ever double-play combinations. An excellent fielder, Schoendist also batted over .300 seven times during his career. He led the National League with 200 hits in 1957 and in doubles, with 43, in 1950. Schoendist's finest season came in 1953 when he hit 15 home runs, knocked in 79 runs, batted .342, and scored 107 runs. That same year he finished fourth in the league MVP voting.

Nellie Fox batted over .300 six times for the Chicago White Sox. He also scored more than 100 runs four times, led the A.L. in hits four times, and led league second basemen in fielding six times. Fox was voted the league's MVP in 1959 when he helped lead Chicago to the pennant, but actually had his finest season in 1954 when he established career-highs with a .319 batting average and 201 hits. Fox was a twelve-time All-Star, finished in the top ten in the league MVP voting a total of six times, and was the recipient of three Gold Glove awards during his career.

Bobby Grich was one of the finest defensive second basemen of his day. He had good range and exceptional hands, and received four Gold Gloves during his career. Grich also had outstanding power for a second baseman, leading the American League with 22 homers in the strike-shortened 1981 season. He had his finest season for the California Angels in 1979, when he hit 30 homers, knocked in 101 runs, and batted .294. Grich was selected to the league All-Star team six times and finished in the top ten in the MVP voting twice.

Jeff Kent has been the most productive second baseman in baseball over the past seven seasons. In fact, not since Rogers Hornsby was posting huge offensive numbers for the St. Louis Cardinals during the early 1920s has another second baseman produced the kind of power numbers and RBI totals that Kent did from 1997 to 2002. Over that six-year period, he averaged 29 home runs and 115 runs batted in,

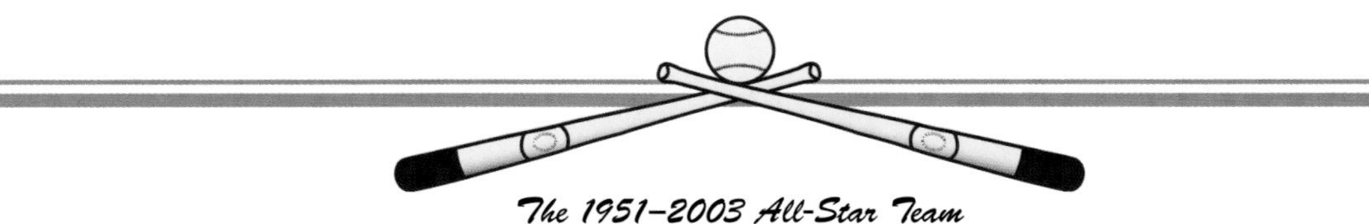

also batting over .290 five times during that stretch. Kent's finest season came in 2000 for the Giants when he was named the National League's Most Valuable Player for hitting 33 home runs, driving in 125 runs, and establishing career-highs with a .334 batting average and 114 runs scored. He has also finished in the top ten in the league MVP voting three other times and been selected to the All-Star team three times during his career. In all, Kent has topped the 30-homer mark three times, driven in more than 100 runs six times, and batted over .300 and scored more than 100 runs two times each.

a
B
P
KC

All-Star Third Baseman

PLAYER	YEARS	AB	HITS	RUNS	2B	3B	HR	RBI	AVG	SB	OBP	SLG PCT
1) MIKE SCHMIDT	1972–89	8,352	2,234	1,506	408	59	548	1,595	.267	174	.384	.527
2) GEORGE BRETT	1973–93	10,349	3,154	1,583	665	137	317	1,595	.305	201	.369	.487
3) EDDIE MATHEWS	1952–68	8,537	2,315	1,509	354	72	512	1,453	.271	68	.378	.509
4) BROOKS ROBINSON	1955–77	10,654	2,848	1,232	482	68	268	1,357	.267	28	.325	.401
5) WADE BOGGS	1982–99	9,180	3,010	1,513	578	61	118	1,014	.328	24	.415	.443
HONORABLE MENTION:												
RON SANTO	1960–74	8,143	2,254	1,138	365	67	342	1,331	.277	35	.366	.464
KEN BOYER	1955-69	7,455	2,143	1,104	318	68	282	1,141	.287	105	.351	.462

1 MIKE SCHMIDT

WITH ALL DUE RESPECT TO EDDIE MATHEWS'S 512 CAREER HOME RUNS, WADE BOGGS'S career on-base percentage of .415, and Brooks Robinson's Gold Glove, the only two men who were seriously considered for the number one slot at third base were Mike Schmidt and George Brett. They are, by a fairly wide margin, the two greatest third basemen of the past thirty years, and quite possibly of all time.

Offensively, they were two completely different types of hitter. Schmidt, with his awesome power, was a pure slugger. He hit a lot of home runs and drove in a lot of runs, but didn't hit for a particularly high average and struck out quite a bit. Brett, on the other hand, while possessing a good deal of power, was more of a gap hitter—someone who would accumulate a lot of doubles and triples, get his fair share of home runs, and hit for a very high average. Even though Schmidt was the more productive of the two, having the exact same number of RBI in approximately 2,000 fewer at-bats, Brett was probably the better all-around hitter. He was the man you would most want to see up in a clutch situation.

However, as we all know, there is more to the game than offense, and, defensively, Schmidt had a big edge over Brett. Although the latter did improve his fielding quite a bit during his career, starting out as a slightly below average third baseman and turning himself into a solid fielder, he wasn't in the same class with Schmidt, defensively. While Brett eventually was able to win a Gold Glove, Schmidt had ten to his credit and was considered to be the finest defensive third baseman in the National League in his time. For this reason, he is the choice for first-team third baseman.

Mike Schmidt is generally regarded to be the greatest all-around third baseman in major league history. His 548 career home runs put him in the top ten all-time, and his .527 slugging percentage is the highest among third basemen. Schmidt led the National League in home runs a record eight times, in runs batted in four times, in on-base percentage three times, in slugging percentage five times, and in walks four times. He hit more than 30 home runs thirteen times, including nine straight seasons from 1979 to 1987. He also knocked in more than 100 runs nine times and scored more than 100 runs seven times. Schmidt was also a three-time winner of the National League's MVP award. He won it for the first time in 1980, when he led the league in home runs, with 48, in runs batted in, with 121, and with a .624 slugging percentage, while batting .286 and leading the Phillies into the World Series. He won it again the following strike-shortened season by once again leading the league in homers with 31, runs batted in with 91, and slugging percentage with a .644 mark, and batting a career-high .316. Schmidt won his final MVP award in 1986 when he once again led the league with 37 homers and 119 RBI, while batting .290. He also finished in the top five in the MVP voting two other times.

❷ GEORGE BRETT

GEORGE BRETT WAS ONE OF THE BEST HITTERS AND VERY POSSIBLY THE GREATEST clutch hitter of the last thirty years. He seemed to be at his best when the pressure was on, and some of his greatest performances and biggest hits came during the postseason.

While not generally considered to be a home run hitter, Brett hit 317 during his career and several others in the playoffs and World Series. In particular, he seemed to enjoy hitting home runs against New York in the playoffs. There was the three-run homer he hit off Grant Jackson in the top of the eighth inning in Game 5 of the 1976 ALCS to tie the score (before Chris Chambliss won the game, and the pennant, in the bottom of the ninth with his famous home run). Then there were the three Brett hit off Catfish Hunter in Game 3 of the 1978 ALCS. And, of course, there was the one he hit off Goose Gossage in Game 3 of the 1980 ALCS to clinch the pennant for the Royals and put them into the World Series for the first time.

Those heroics notwithstanding, Brett was better known for being a high-average hitter. He is the only player to have won batting titles in three different decades, having led the league in 1976 with a mark of .333, in 1980 with a .390 average, and in 1990 with a .329 average. In all, Brett led the A.L. in hits three times, in doubles twice, in triples three times, in on-base percentage once, and in slugging three times. He batted over .300 eleven times, hit more than 20 homers eight times, knocked in more than 100 runs four times, had more than 200 hits twice, and had 20 triples once. In his MVP season of 1980, in addition to hitting .390 (the highest average by any player since Ted Williams batted .406 in 1941), Brett hit 24 homers, knocked in 118 runs, and led the league with an on-base percentage of .461 and a slugging percentage of .664. He also finished runner-up in the 1985 MVP balloting. That season, he hit 30 homers, knocked in 112 runs, and batted .335. Brett finished in the top five in the MVP voting two other times.

3 EDDIE MATHEWS

IN CHOOSING FROM AMONG THE REMAINING third basemen, priority was given to run-production and solid defense. While Wade Boggs had the highest on-base percentage and scored a lot of runs, Eddie Mathews scored almost the same number of runs in approximately 650 fewer at-bats. Also, Boggs was essentially a singles and doubles hitter and not a very big RBI man, while Mathews drove in a lot of runs. In addition, Boggs was a below-average fielder for much of his career, while Mathews was a solid defensive player, having led National League third basemen in assists three times during his career. So Boggs was the first to take a seat.

Then there was Brooks Robinson. While he clearly had the edge over Mathews as a defensive player, his career on-base percentage of .325 was very mediocre, and more than 50 points lower than that of Mathews. Also, Mathews's slugging percentage was more than 100 points higher, and in approximately 2,000 fewer career at-bats he hit almost twice as many home runs, knocked in about 100 more runs, and scored almost 300 more. As good a fielder as Robinson was, it is difficult to imagine him being able to save that many runs with his glove. Therefore, Eddie Mathews was the choice for the third team.

Probably because he played most of his career on the same team as Hank Aaron, Eddie Mathews is perhaps the most overlooked superstar in the history of the game. He teamed with Aaron to form the greatest one-two home run punch in baseball history. As Braves teammates, they accounted for 863 homers between them. Mathews is also the only Brave to play in Boston, Milwaukee, and Atlanta.

A member of the 500-home run club, Mathews led the National League in homers twice and hit 30 or more in a season ten times, including nine in a row from 1953 to 1961. He also hit over 40 homers four times, knocked in more than 100 runs five times, batted over .300 three times, and collected 100 walks five times, leading the league in that department four times. Mathews had his two finest seasons in 1953 and 1959. In 1953, he led the league in homers with 47, and also knocked in 135 runs and batted .302. In 1959, he once again led the league in homers, this time with 46, and had 114 RBI and a batting average of .306. He finished runner-up in the MVP voting both seasons.

Dodger pitcher Carl Erskine once said of him, "He swings the bat faster than anyone I ever saw. You think you've got a called strike past him, and he hits it out of the catcher's glove."

4 BROOKS ROBINSON

BROOKS ROBINSON WAS THE GREATEST FIELDING THIRD BASEMAN IN THE HISTORY OF the game.

Having said that, I immediately want to add, prior to recounting Robinson's career, that there is something that has been troubling me for quite some time and that I would now like to get off my chest.

Robinson clearly deserves his place in the Hall of Fame. Perhaps he even deserved to be elected in his first year of eligibility (which he was). However, sometimes a player's reputation for doing something extremely well causes him to become a legendary and almost mythic figure. This may very well be what happened with Robinson. I say this because there were a few other third basemen who were not too far behind him defensively, and almost as good offensively, who have never been given serious consideration for the Hall, players such as Graig Nettles and Buddy Bell. Neither was quite as good as Robinson with the glove, but they were both exceptional fielders and not that far behind. And while Robinson's career offensive numbers were slightly more impressive, Nettles and Bell were both solid hitters as well. Now, this is not to suggest that they should be in the Hall of Fame; but if Robinson made it in so easily on the first ballot, shouldn't they at least have received a little more support? And what about Ron Santo? He played in Robinson's era, was a better hitter, and was a good glove man. In approximately 2,500 fewer at-bats, he hit 74 more home runs, had almost as many RBI, and out-hit Robinson by 10 points. He is someone who very possibly should be in the Hall, but has yet to be admitted.

Enough said on that subject.

Brooks Robinson revolutionized third base play. Though slow afoot and not possessing a particularly strong throwing arm, his quickness and great reflexes allowed him to make plays that most third basemen could only dream about. He holds major league records for third basemen with highest fielding average (.971), most putouts (2,697), most assists (6,205), and most double plays (618). He led American League third basemen in fielding eleven times, and eight times in putouts and assists.

Robinson was a solid hitter. He hit over 20 homers six times, batted over .300 twice, and knocked in over 100 runs twice. He also had over 80 RBI six other times. Robinson won the A.L. MVP award in 1964 by hitting 28 homers, leading the league with 118 runs batted in, and batting a career-high .317. He finished in the top five in the MVP voting four other times.

Robinson was also an outstanding big-game player. In thirty-nine playoff and World Series games for the Orioles, he hit 5 home runs and batted .303. After Robinson won the 1970 World Series MVP

award, largely for his defensive play against the Cincinnati Reds, Johnny Bench said: "I will become a left-handed hitter to keep the ball away from that guy."

5 WADE BOGGS

WADE BOGGS'S CAREER ON-BASE PERCENTAGE of .415 ranks with the best, and his .328 batting average is the highest of any third baseman in history. His 3,010 hits place him second to George Brett among third basemen, as do his 578 doubles. Boggs led the American League in batting five times, including four straight from 1985 to 1988. In the five seasons he led the league, Boggs posted averages of .361, .368, .357, .363, and .366. He also led the league in runs scored, doubles, and walks twice each, and in on-base percentage six times. He batted over .300 fourteen times, drew over 100 walks four times, and for seven straight seasons had over 200 hits and scored more than 100 runs. He hit a career-high 24 homers in 1987. Although a weak fielder in his first few seasons with the Red Sox, Boggs worked hard at his defense and eventually became a solid third baseman.

Honorable mention should be given to Ron Santo and Ken Boyer:

Ron Santo was the finest third baseman in the National League for much of the 1960s. Playing for the Cubs, from 1964 to 1967 he hit over 30 homers each season, and he hit more than 20 homers seven other times. He also knocked in more than 100 runs and batted over .300 four times each. Santo led the league in walks four times, in on-base percentage twice, and in triples once. He had his finest seasons in 1964 and 1969. In 1964, he hit 30 homers, had 114 RBI, and batted .313. In 1969, he belted 29 homers, knocked in 123 runs, and batted .289. During his career, he finished in the top five in the league MVP voting twice.

Santo was also a fine fielder. He set a major league record by leading third basemen in total chances the most times (9), and he shares National League records for leading the most times in putouts and assists (7), and double plays (6).

Ken Boyer is one of those outstanding players who people just seem to have forgotten about. One of the best all-around third basemen to play in the big leagues, he could hit, hit for power, field

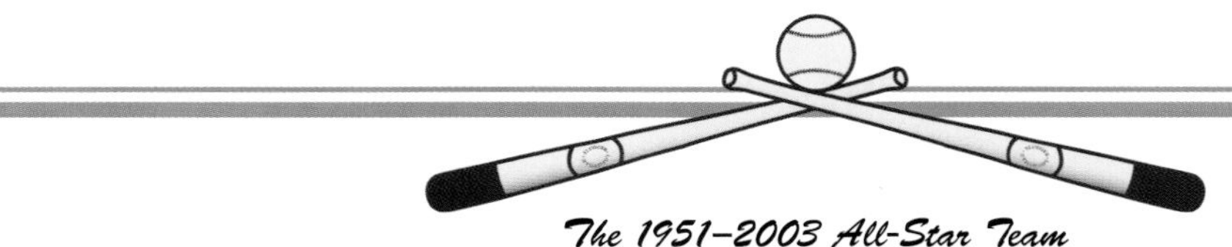

his position well, and, for a big man, run very well. During his career, Boyer hit more than 20 homers eight times, batted over .300 five times, scored over 100 runs three times, and knocked in more than 100 runs twice. He also had more than 90 RBI six other times. As an example of his speed, he stole 22 bases as a rookie in 1955, and had more than 10 triples three times. The captain of the Cardinals had his finest season in 1964, when he led his team to the World Championship and won league MVP honors by hitting 24 home runs, knocking in a league-leading 119 runs, and batting .295.

Former teammate Bill White once said that Boyer "was as good a fielder as Brooks Robinson, and a better hitter."

All-Star Shortstop

PLAYER	YEARS	AB	HITS	RUNS	2B	3B	HR	RBI	AVG	SB	OBP	SLG PCT
1) ERNIE BANKS	1953–71	9,421	2,583	1,305	407	90	512	1,636	.274	50	.333	.500
2) CAL RIPKEN, JR.	1982–2001	11,551	3,184	1,647	603	44	431	1,695	.276	36	.340	.447
3) ALEX RODRIGUEZ*	1994–2003	4,989	1,535	1,009	285	22	345	990	.308	177	.382	.581
4) OZZIE SMITH	1978–96	9,386	2,460	1,257	402	69	28	793	.262	580	.337	.328
5) ROBIN YOUNT	1974–93	11,008	3,142	1,632	583	126	251	1,406	.285	271	.342	.430
HONORABLE MENTION:												
BARRY LARKIN*	1986–2003	7,591	2,240	1,274	426	73	190	916	.295	377	.371	.446
NOMAR GARCIAPARRA*	1996–2003	3,812	1,231	685	272	47	173	669	.323	82	.370	.555
DEREK JETER*	1995–2003	4,870	1,546	926	239	41	127	615	.317	178	.389	.462

* Indicates player is still active

❶ ERNIE BANKS

THERE IS LITTLE DOUBT THAT ALEX RODRIGUEZ IS THE MOST TALENTED SHORTSTOP of the last fifty years. His combination of power, speed, and fielding excellence is in fact unmatched by any other *infielder* of the past half-century. All things being equal, by the time his career is over, there is a strong possibility he will have surpassed even the great Honus Wagner as the greatest shortstop in baseball history. However, Rodriguez, at just twenty-eight years of age, presumably still has many fine years ahead of him. Having completed in 2003 only his eighth full season in the major leagues, he is still building his legacy and has a way to go before he can be compared favorably to the all-time greats.

That being said, the only other shortstop from this period who could even be compared to Ernie Banks because of his power was Cal Ripken, Jr. However, in approximately 2,100 more career at-bats, Ripken hit 81 fewer home runs and knocked in only 59 more runs. While Banks led his league in both home runs and runs batted in twice, Ripken never led his in either category. Also, while Ripken was a more solid fielder, the difference between the two was not great enough to offset

Banks's edge as a hitter. Therefore, Banks has to be the choice for number one shortstop.

Although many people tend to think of Ernie Banks more as a first baseman, he was the Chicago Cubs' regular shortstop for the first nine years of his career. When he was moved to first base following the 1961 season it wasn't because Banks was not a good fielder, but rather because it was hoped the move would prolong his career. In fact, prior to being shifted to first, he had led National League shortstops in fielding three times.

However, it was as a power-hitting shortstop that Banks achieved his greatest fame. He is the only shortstop in National League history to win two MVP awards, and the only one in major league history to win the award in consecutive seasons. Banks won the award for the first time in 1958 by leading the league in home runs, with 47, and runs batted in, with 129, while batting .313. He also led the league that season with a .614 slugging percentage. The following season, he won the award again by hitting 45 homers, knocking in 143 runs, and batting .304. He also finished in the top five in the league MVP voting two other times—and all this with a team that consistently finished in the second division of the standings.

During his career, Banks led the N.L. in both homers and RBI twice, and in slugging percentage once. He hit over 40 homers five times, knocked in more than 100 runs eight times, and batted over .300 twice.

❷ CAL RIPKEN, JR.

WHILE CAL RIPKEN, JR. WILL ALWAYS BE REMEMBERED as the man who broke Lou Gehrig's record for most consecutive games played, it would be an injustice to him to allow this to obscure what an exceptional player he really was.

Ripken is the only shortstop in American League history to win two MVP awards. He won the award for the first time in 1983 when he hit 27 home runs, knocked in 102 runs, batted .318, and led the league in runs scored (121), hits (211), and doubles (47), all while playing exceptional shortstop and leading the Baltimore Orioles to the World Championship. He won the award again in 1991, when he set career highs in homers (34), runs batted in (114), and batting (.323). In all, Ripken hit more than 20 homers twelve times, topped the 100 RBI mark four times, and batted over .300 five times.

Defensively, though he wasn't exceptionally quick or overly spectacular, Ripken had exceptional hands and was a master at studying opposing hitters and positioning himself in the right spot in the field.

As a result, he had a very high fielding percentage and led A.L. shortstops in fielding twice.

3 ALEX RODRIGUEZ

IT GOES AGAINST THE GRAIN OF THE IDEOLOGY established earlier in this book to rank a player who is still building his legacy above others whose accomplishments are already in the record books. However, it was necessary to make an exception in the case of Alex Rodriguez. While it is true that it was Ozzie Smith's fielding, and not his hitting, that earned him a spot in the top five here, as well as a place in Cooperstown, Rodriguez's offensive superiority was just too great to overlook. In slightly more than half the number of at-bats that Smith accumulated during his career, Rodriguez has already surpassed Smith in several offensive categories. He has more than *twelve times* the number of home runs, almost 200 more runs batted in, a batting average and on-base percentage that is almost 50 points higher, and a slugging percentage that is some *250* points higher. Smith has three times as many stolen bases and triples, and is also well ahead in hits, runs scored, and doubles, but Rodriguez has been accumulating the last three at a much faster pace and should surpass him in those categories as well in the next few seasons. In addition, while Smith is generally considered to have been the greatest fielding shortstop in baseball history, Rodriguez is not that far behind. His career .977 fielding percentage is only one percentage point behind Smith's .978, and, although not as spectacular as the Cardinals great, he is exceptional in his own right, possessing excellent range, soft hands, and a strong and accurate throwing arm. In fact, Rodriguez has not made more than 10 errors in either of the last two seasons. So as great as Ozzie was in the field, Rodriguez's overwhelming offensive numbers, even at this stage of his career, merit him a higher ranking.

Robin Yount's offensive numbers compare more favorably to those of Rodriguez. In more than twice the number of at-bats, Yount finished with more than twice as many hits and doubles, and with six times as many triples. He is also still well ahead of Rodriguez in runs batted in, runs scored, and stolen bases. However, the latter has already hit almost 100 more home runs, and has a much higher batting average, on-base percentage, and slugging percentage. With the exception of triples, it is just a matter of time before Rodriguez passes Yount in the other categories as well. In addition, Rodriguez is the better fielder of the two, showing far more consistency at perhaps the most important defensive position on the diamond.

In his eight full seasons, he has committed as many as 20 errors only once, and more than 15 errors just two other times. Before being shifted to the outfield midway through his career, Yount, in his ten full seasons at shortstop, never committed fewer than 18 errors and topped the 30-mark three times. It is, therefore, no exaggeration to say that Rodriguez is a far more complete player than Yount was during his career and deserves a higher spot in the rankings.

As was mentioned earlier, Alex Rodriguez has an incredible amount of talent that could one day enable him to go down as the greatest shortstop of all time. He is one of only a handful of players to hit 40 homers and steal 40 bases in the same season. He is also the only shortstop in major league history to hit 50 home runs in a season (something he has accomplished twice already), and along with Babe Ruth is the only player in baseball history to hit more than 40 home runs in six consecutive seasons.

Rodriguez topped the 50-homer mark the first time in 2001, leading the American League with 52 while also driving in 135 runs, battting .318, and leading the league with 133 runs scored. He led the league in both home runs and runs batted in the following season, with totals of 57 and 142 respectively, while batting .300 and scoring 125 runs for Texas and also finishing second in the league MVP voting. Rodriguez also finished runner-up in the MVP voting in 1996 as a member of the Seattle Mariners. That year, he led the league with a .358 batting average, 141 runs scored, and 54 doubles, while hitting 36 home runs and knocking in 123 runs. In just eight full seasons, Rodriguez has hit more than 30 homers and driven in more than 100 runs seven times each, batted over .300 six times, scored more than 100 runs every year, and amassed more than 200 hits three times. If he stays healthy, it seems certain that Rodriguez will eventually surpass Ernie Banks as the greatest shortstop since 1950.

4 OZZIE SMITH

THIS IS ONE TIME THAT OFFENSE MUST TAKE A BACK SEAT TO DEFENSE. ALTHOUGH Robin Yount's offensive numbers were far superior to those of Ozzie Smith, we saw earlier that his fielding was, to say the least, somewhat erratic. Smith, by contrast, was a magnificent defensive player. It would have been impossible to overlook the disparity in the defensive abilities of these two players; therefore, Smith was awarded fourth-team honors.

Ozzie Smith was quite simply the greatest defensive shortstop in the history of baseball. While there have been others, such as Marty Marion, Luis Aparicio, and Omar Vizquel, who played the position exceptionally well, no one else was ever quite the acrobat and magician that the "Wizard of Oz" was. Smith often made plays that seemed like optical illusions to those who witnessed them. However, as spectacular as he was, he was also extremely consistent. In 1991, he set a record for National League shortstops by committing just 8 errors in 150 games. He won one of his N.L. record 13 Gold Gloves that year.

As great a fielder as Smith was, he proved to be quite a liability at the plate his first few seasons with the San Diego Padres, batting below .230 in three of his four seasons there. However, following his trade to the St. Louis Cardinals prior to the 1982 season, Smith gradually learned to use the artificial turf and his running speed to his advantage and turned himself into a solid hitter. He hit over .300 once and bettered the .270 mark eight other times. He was also a terrific base stealer, swiping 57 bases twice, more than 40 three other times, and a total of 580 during his career.

5 ROBIN YOUNT

DEREK JETER AND NOMAR GARCIAPARRA are both superior players to Robin Yount. Both are better hitters, with equal or more power, and are more consistent in the field. However, in their relatively brief careers, neither has yet been able to accumulate the kinds of numbers that would merit them being ranked above Yount. Therefore, the latter gets the nod for a spot on the fifth team.

Robin Yount came up to the Milwaukee Brewers as a skinny, eighteen-year-old shortstop; twenty years and 3,142 hits later, he retired as a center fielder and future Hall of Famer. He is the only player in major league history to win an MVP award at two of the most demanding positions on the diamond, shortstop and center field.

Yount won his first MVP award as a shortstop in 1982. That year, he hit 29 homers, knocked in 114 runs, batted .331, and led the American League with 46 doubles, 210 hits, and a .578 slugging percentage. After being shifted to the outfield in 1985 as a result of an injury to his throwing shoulder, Yount won the award a second time in 1989. That season he hit 21 homers, knocked in 103 runs, and batted .318. In all, Yount hit more than 20 homers four times, knocked in over 100 runs three times, scored more than 100 runs five times, and batted over .300 six times during his career.

Honorable mention should be given to Barry Larkin, Nomar Garciaparra, and Derek Jeter:

Though frequently overlooked when discussions of the top major league shortstops begin, Barry Larkin has been one of the most solid and outstanding players at the position during his eighteen-year big league career. The greatest shortstop in Cincinnati Reds' history, Larkin's career batting average of .299 is the highest among shortstops with more than 5,000 at-bats in the last fifty years. The National League 1995 MVP when he batted .319, Larkin has hit over .300 nine times, scored more than 100 runs twice, stolen 377 bases, and played an excellent shortstop. He had probably his finest season in 1996, when he hit 33 home runs, knocked in 89 runs, and batted .298.

Nomar Garciaparra has already shown that he is one of the best pure hitters in baseball. The winner of two consecutive American League batting titles, Garciaparra won his first batting crown in 1999 when he batted .357 for the Red Sox, while hitting 27 home runs and knocking in 104 runs. He led the league again the following season by hitting an astonishing .372—the highest mark by any A.L. shortstop in sixty-four years—while hitting 21 home runs and driving in 96 runs. Garciaparra's most productive season, however, came in 1998 when he hit 35 home runs, drove in 122 runs, batted .323, and finished second in the league MVP voting. Garciaparra has an excellent chance of winning the award following his outstanding 2003 campaign in which he hit 28 home runs, knocked in 105 runs, scored 120 others, batted .301, and led Boston into the playoffs as the American League's wild-card entry. He has hit more than 20 home runs in each of his six full big league seasons, topping the 30 mark twice, batted over .300 and scored more than 100 runs each year, and driven in more than 100 runs four times. While somewhat

erratic in the field, committing more than 20 errors in three of his six full seasons and compiling a rather mediocre .969 fielding average thus far, Garciaparra is extremely athletic, possessing good range and a powerful throwing arm.

Derek Jeter is another of the brilliant young shortstops in the American League. In his eight full seasons, he has hit over 20 homers twice, knocked in over 100 runs once, batted over .300 six times, scored more than 100 runs seven times, collected more than 200 hits three times, and stolen more than 20 bases five times, topping the 30 mark twice. Jeter has an excellent stolen base record, stealing 178 bases during his career, while being thrown out a total of just 47 times. His best season in that department came in 2002, when he stole 32 bases in 35 attempts. In addition to being a good base stealer, Jeter is an exceptional base runner, possessing great baseball instincts both on the basepaths and in the field. While Jeter was occasionally erratic in the field earlier in his career, committing as many as 24 errors in 2000, he has become more consistent in recent years, committing no more than 15 errors in any of the last three seasons.

Jeter had his finest overall season in 1999, when he hit 24 homers, knocked in 102 runs, batted .349, scored 134 runs, and led the American League with 219 hits. The following year, he became the first player to be named Most Valuable Player of both the All-Star game and the World Series. A five-time All-Star, he has also finished in the top ten in the league MVP voting four times. More than anything, though, Jeter is a winner and a true team leader, having been named, in 2003, the first Yankees captain since Don Mattingly. In his eight seasons with the Yankees, they have won seven division titles and will be striving to win their sixth pennant and fifth world championship this postseason. Those who have followed the shortstop regularly throughout his young career are keenly aware that the success the Yankees have experienced the last several seasons is tied closely to the arrival of Jeter in New York.

All-Star Catcher

PLAYER	YEARS	AB	HITS	RUNS	2B	3B	HR	RBI	AVG	SB	OBP	SLG PCT
1) JOHNNY BENCH	1967–83	7,658	2,048	1,091	381	24	389	1,376	.267	68	.345	.476
2) YOGI BERRA	1946–63	7,555	2,150	1,175	321	49	358	1,430	.285	30	.350	.482
3) ROY CAMPANELLA	1948–57	4,205	1,161	627	178	18	242	856	.276	25	.362	.500
4) MIKE PIAZZA*	1992–2003	5,350	1,708	888	264	6	358	1,107	.319	17	.388	.572
5) CARLTON FISK	1969–93	8,756	2,356	1,276	421	47	376	1,330	.269	128	.341	.457
HONORABLE MENTION:												
GARY CARTER	1974–92	7,971	2,092	1,025	371	31	324	1,225	.262	39	.338	.439
JOE TORRE	1960–77	7,874	2,342	996	344	59	252	1,185	.297	23	.367	.452
TED SIMMONS	1968–88	8,680	2,472	1,074	483	47	248	1,389	.285	21	.352	.437
IVAN RODRIGUEZ*	1991–2003	6,167	1,875	942	380	31	231	914	.304	90	.344	.488

* Indicates player is still active

❶ JOHNNY BENCH

JOHNNY BENCH AND YOGI BERRA WERE THE TOP TWO CANDIDATES FOR THE NUMBER one spot here. Mike Piazza is probably the best hitting catcher in major league history, but he has always been a liability in the field. Roy Campanella was a fine hitter and excellent receiver, but his major league career was too short and his hitting tended to be somewhat inconsistent. Carlton Fisk put up good numbers, but that was due more to longevity than to greatness. At no point during his career was Fisk the best catcher in the game. During his peak years in the 1970s, Bench was the best catcher in baseball and Thurman Munson was, at the very least, Fisk's equal in the American League. By the 1980s, Gary Carter had established himself as the finest catcher in the game. Therefore, Fisk could not be given serious consideration for the number one slot.

So, we are left with Bench and Berra. A look at their offensive numbers reveals a remarkable similarity. Bench hit a few more homers, while Berra drove in a few more runs and hit for a higher average. However, while Bench was plagued by injuries for much of the second half of his career, Berra was more fortunate and remained relatively healthy. Therefore, he was able to perform at a higher level for a bit longer than Bench was. Prior to the injuries taking their toll on Bench, though, he was the more dominant hitter of the two. While Berra reached the 30-homer mark twice during his career, and knocked in over 100 runs five times, he never led the league in either category. Bench reached the 40-homer plateau twice, the 100-RBI mark six times, and led the National League in home runs twice and in runs batted in three times. In addition, while Berra turned himself into a solid defensive catcher, Bench was perhaps the finest receiver in the history of the game. Taking all this into consideration, Bench was the clear-cut choice for number one.

If someone were to draw up a blueprint for the perfect catcher, it would be Johnny Bench. He was big, strong, had excellent power, great quickness behind the plate, a cannon for a throwing arm, and was an excellent handler of pitchers. After winning the National League's Rookie of the Year award in 1968, Bench only got better. After an excellent season the following year, he reached his zenith in 1970. That year, Bench won the first of his two MVP awards by leading the league in homers, with 45, and runs batted in, with 148, and batting a career-high .293. He won the award again in 1972, when he once again led the league in homers (40) and runs batted in (125), while batting .270. Bench would finish in the top five in the MVP voting two other times and hit more than 20 homers eleven times during his career.

Bench also had a flair for the dramatic. In 1972, with the Reds trailing the Pirates by a run in the ninth inning of the final league championship game, he hit a homer off Pittsburgh's ace reliever Dave Giusti to tie the score and, eventually, help the Reds get into the World Series. In 1976, he batted over .500 and hit two homers to win the World Series MVP award in the Reds' four-game sweep of the Yankees.

Defensively, Bench had no peer. He popularized catching one-handed, keeping his throwing hand behind his back to protect it from foul tips. He also possessed great quickness and such a powerful throwing arm that opposing base runners were often too intimidated to even attempt stealing against him. His ten Gold Gloves are a record for catchers.

❷ YOGI BERRA

YOGI BERRA WAS ONE OF THE BEST CLUTCH HITTERS of his era. Although his career batting average was only .285, Mickey Mantle once said that, from the seventh inning on, he was certain that Berra's average was much higher than that. Perhaps that is why he won the American League MVP award three times, and finished in the top five in the voting four other times.

In addition to his five 100-RBI seasons, Berra hit over .300 three times and hit more than 20 homers eleven times, including ten in a row from 1949 to 1958. Yogi won the MVP award in 1951 and 1955, in spite of the fact that, statistically, they were not even among his best seasons. His finest seasons were actually 1950 and 1954. In 1950, he hit 28 homers, knocked in 124 runs, and batted .322. In 1954, he hit 22 homers, had 125 RBI, batted 307, and won the MVP award.

Berra was also extremely difficult to strike out. In 7,555 career at-bats, he struck out only 414 times, and in 1950, in 597 at-bats, he fanned only 12 times.

Behind the plate, Yogi turned himself into a fine catcher. Though clumsy and very raw when he first came to the big leagues, Berra was tutored by former Yankees great Bill Dickey and eventually became so solid defensively that he accepted 950 errorless chances from July 28, 1957 to May 10, 1959. He led A.L. catchers in putouts eight times, assists and fielding average three times each, and was an excellent handler of pitchers.

Perhaps Berra's greatest legacy, however, was that of a winner. In the seventeen full seasons he spent with the Yankees, they won fourteen pennants and ten World Series, and, if you were to ask the players on those teams, most would say that Yogi was as much a contributor to that success as anyone.

❸ ROY CAMPANELLA

THIS WAS A FAIRLY CLOSE CALL. WHEN YOU LOOK AT THE NUMBERS, MIKE PIAZZA, IN approximately 1,000 more career at-bats, is well ahead of Roy Campanella in virtually every offensive category. Piazza is clearly the better hitter of the two. However, Campanella won three MVP awards as the cornerstone of those great Dodger teams of the 1950s. Also, while Piazza has a difficult time throwing anybody out at second base, Campanella was a terrific receiver who had a strong throwing arm, and was also an excellent handler of pitchers. In addition, Campanella did not come to the Dodgers until he was already twenty-seven years old, having spent several seasons in the Negro Leagues (where he was a three-time All Star) prior to that. When you consider that some of his best seasons were already behind him by then, Campanella moves ahead of Piazza into third place.

In his ten seasons with the Dodgers, Roy Campanella helped lead them to five pennants and one world championship. He hit more than 20 homers seven times, and reached the 30 mark four times. He also knocked in more than 100 runs three times and batted over .300 three times. Campanella was named National League MVP three times. He won the award the first time in 1951 when he hit 33 homers, knocked in 108 runs, and batted .325. He won it again in 1953, when he hit 41 homers, led the league with 142 runs batted in, and batted .312 while leading the Dodgers to the N.L. pennant. Campanella came away with his final MVP trophy in 1955. That season, he hit 32 homers, knocked in 107 runs, and batted .318 while helping the Dodgers to their only world championship in Brooklyn.

Defensively, Campanella was the finest catcher of his time. Possessing a strong and accurate throwing arm and an extremely quick release, he threw out (often from a kneeling position) two of every three runners who tried to steal on him. He was also a tremendous handler of pitchers and led National League catchers in putouts six times.

4 MIKE PIAZZA

BEFORE HIS CAREER IS OVER, MIKE PIAZZA WILL quite possibly go down as the greatest hitting catcher in baseball history. His career batting average of .319 is second only to Mickey Cochrane among major league catchers. In his ten full seasons, Piazza has hit more than 30 homers nine times, knocked in more than 100 runs six times, and batted over .300 nine times. He has had some truly remarkable seasons, not just for a catcher, but for anyone. In 1993, with the Dodgers, he hit 35 homers, knocked in 112 runs, and batted .318. In 1997, he hit 40 homers, had 124 runs batted in, and hit a career-best .362. With the Mets, in 1999, he once again hit 40 homers and

knocked in 124 runs, while batting .303. The following season, he hit 38 homers, had 113 RBI, and batted .324.

Defensively, Piazza's reputation has suffered because of his inability to throw runners out at second base. However, in every other phase of the game he is solid. He's an adequate receiver and a good handler of pitchers. Nevertheless, it appears that any further damage Piazza does with the bat may come as a first baseman since his poor throwing and a desire to prevent his offensive productivity from declining more rapidly seem destined to have him spend his remaining time in the big leagues at first base. This should prevent Piazza from moving up any higher on the list of catchers than he already is.

5 CARLTON FISK

CARLTON FISK HOLDS THE RECORD FOR MOST career home runs by a catcher (350), most stolen bases, and most games caught. He is one of only three catchers, along with Johnny Bench and Yogi Berra, to hit 300 home runs, and both score and drive in 1,000 runs. During his career, he hit over 20 homers eight times, knocked in more than 100 runs twice, and batted over .300 twice. He had his finest season in 1977 for the Red Sox, when he hit 26 home runs, knocked in 102 runs, and batted .315. In 1985, while with the White Sox, he reached career highs in home runs (37) and RBI (107). Defensively, Fisk had a strong arm, was a fine receiver, and called a good game. He finished in the top five in the MVP voting twice.

Honorable mention should be given to Gary Carter, Joe Torre, Ted Simmons, and Ivan Rodriguez:

Gary Carter followed Johnny Bench as the National League's best catcher. From the late 1970s to the mid-1980s, Carter was baseball's finest receiver and one of its best all-round players. He hit over 20 homers nine times, including two seasons with more than 30, and he knocked in over 100 runs four times, leading the league with 106 in 1984. That season, playing for the Montreal Expos, he also hit 27 home runs and batted .294. The following season, with the New York Mets, he hit 32 homers, knocked in 100 runs, and batted .281.

Defensively, Carter was very strong. He won three Gold Gloves, and led the league five times in assists and six straight years in putouts. He finished in the top five in the MVP voting twice.

Many people don't think of Joe Torre as a catcher, but prior to becoming a regular at both first base and third base for the St. Louis Cardinals, he was primarily a catcher for the Braves in nine of his first ten seasons. Playing that position for Atlanta in 1966, he had one of his finest seasons, hitting 36 home runs, knocking in 101 runs, and batting .315. Following the 1968 season, however, he was traded to the Cardinals for Orlando Cepeda. He caught for one more season, was moved to first base the next year, and finally became the Cardinals' regular third baseman in 1971. There, he had his greatest season. In 1971, Torre won the N.L. MVP award by hitting 24 homers and leading the league with 137 runs batted in, a .363 batting average, and 230 hits. In all, he hit over 20 homers six times, knocked in more than 100 runs five times, and batted over .300 four times.

For some reason, Ted Simmons is rarely mentioned with the top catchers of the last thirty years. Perhaps this is because he played in Johnny Bench's shadow for much of his career. However, once Bench's productivity began to decline somewhat during the mid-1970s, Simmons became the most offensively productive catcher in the National League. He batted over .300 each year, from 1971 to 1973, and had his two finest seasons in 1975 and 1977. In 1975, he hit 18 homers, knocked in 100 runs, and batted .332. In 1977, he hit 21 homers, had 95 RBI, and batted .318. During his career, he hit at least 20 homers six times, drove in more than 100 runs three times, topping 90 five other times, and batted over .300 seven times. However, while far from a defensive liability, Simmons was never considered to be particularly strong behind the plate. Had he been, he might have been able to break into the top five.

If anyone is ever going to replace Johnny Bench as the greatest defensive catcher in the history of the game, it will be Ivan Rodriguez. He has great quickness and a powerful throwing arm that, like Bench's, intimidates opposing base runners.

Offensively, Rodriguez is also very solid. After being more of a line-drive hitter during the first half of his career, he began to improve his power numbers during the late 1990s. Always a consistent hitter, he

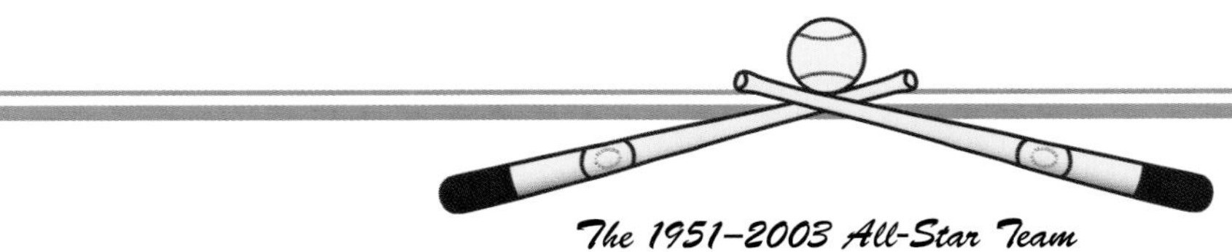

became more of a slugger in 1999 when he won the American League MVP award by hitting 35 homers, knocking in 113 runs, batting .332, and stealing 25 bases. The following year, picking up right where he left off, Rodriguez appeared to be on his way to establishing career-highs in several offensive categories. In just 363 at-bats over 91 games, he had compiled 27 home runs, 83 runs batted in, and a .347 batting average. However, an injury ended his season prematurely and ended his bid to surpass Mike Piazza as the most productive hitting catcher in baseball. Injuries also cut into his playing time significantly in each of the two subsequent seasons, although Rodriguez managed to hit over .300 each year. After leaving the Texas Rangers and signing with the Florida Marlins as a free agent after the 2002 season, Rodriguez had another solid year, falling just three points shy of reaching the .300 mark for what would have been the ninth consecutive time. However, his power numbers dropped off somewhat, perhaps indicating that the injuries he has sustained over the past few seasons have begun to take their toll. That being the case, it is questionable whether or not he will ever be able to break into the top five.

All-Star Left Fielder

PLAYER	YEARS	AB	HITS	RUNS	2B	3B	HR	RB	AVG	SB	OBP	SLG PCT
1) HANK AARON	1954-76	12,364	3,771	2,174	624	98	755	2,297	.305	240	.377	.555
2) BARRY BONDS*	1986-2003	8,725	2,595	1,941	536	74	658	1,742	.297	500	.433	.602
3) RICKEY HENDERSON*	1979-2003	10,961	3,055	2,295	510	66	297	1,115	.279	1,406	.401	.419
4) CARL YASTRZEMSKI	1961-83	11,988	3,419	1,816	646	59	452	1,844	.285	168	.382	.462
5) LOU BROCK	1961-79	10,332	3,023	1,610	486	141	149	900	.293	938	.344	.410
HONORABLE MENTION:												
WILLIE STARGELL	1962-82	7,927	2,232	1,195	423	55	475	1,540	.282	17	.363	.529
BILLY WILLIAMS	1959-76	9,350	2,711	1,410	434	88	426	1,475	.290	90	.364	.492

* Indicates player is still active

BEFORE WE TAKE A LOOK AT THE TOP LEFT FIELDERS, LET ME EXPLAIN WHY HANK AARON was included here. While Aaron spent his first several seasons playing center field for the Braves, and probably is remembered even more as a right fielder, he did spend some time in left as well. He is being inserted here in left field primarily because of my desire to have Frank Robinson on the team as the right fielder. This does mean relegating Barry Bonds to the second team, but so be it. Even though, based strictly on statistics, Bonds is clearly deserving of first-team honors, Robinson possessed certain intangibles that Bonds somewhat lacks.

To begin with, in addition to being a great player in his own right, Robinson was one of the greatest competitors the game has ever seen, and, unlike Bonds, he seemed to be at his best when the pressure was on. He hit two home runs for the Orioles in the 1966 World Series against the Dodgers, leading Baltimore to a four-game sweep and being named Series MVP in the process. He also performed admirably in the 1961 Series as a member of the Cincinnati Reds, and in both the 1970 and 1971 Series with Baltimore. In 26 games over five World Series, Robinson hit 8 home runs and drove in 14 runs. Meanwhile, Bonds, except for his outstanding performance in the 2002 postseason, has faltered when the stakes were high. Prior to 2002, in 97 postseason at-bats, covering 27 contests, Bonds had 1 home run, 6 runs batted in, and a .196 batting average. Even with his excellent 2002 postseason, Bonds has a career batting average of just .246, with 9 home runs, 22 runs batted in, and 27 strikeouts in 142 playoff and World Series at-bats.

Just as important, though, were several other attributes that Robinson possessed. He was a superb team leader, always did the little things to help his team win, and was admired and respected by all of his teammates. The same cannot be said about Bonds, who, in this era of self-absorbed athletes, is right at the top of the list. He frequently does not hustle, is too concerned with his own numbers to ever take on the role of team leader, and is not well-liked by most of his teammates. In contrast, Robinson's presence and leadership had a huge impact on his teammates. In his six seasons with the Baltimore Orioles, they won four pennants and two world championships. After he was traded at the end of the 1971 season, it would be another eight years before the Orioles would make another appearance in the World Series.

And so, while acknowledging Barry Bonds' greatness, I felt it was only proper to treat Hank Aaron as a left fielder in order to make room on the team for Frank Robinson in right.

❶ HANK AARON

BARRY BONDS IS A TRULY GREAT PLAYER—THE greatest of his generation and one of the greatest of all-time. In fact, over the last three seasons, he has played at a level that very few players have ever reached. During that time, he has raised his level of dominance to a point that even Hank Aaron might have envied. Bonds has been so dominant that it has become somewhat fashionable for many members of the media to compare him to Babe Ruth and suggest that he is quite possibly the greatest player in the history of the game. Forgive me, however, if I'm not quite prepared to raise him to that rank. The feeling here is that he is indeed among the ten or twelve greatest players of all-time, but that several factors need to be considered before ranking him ahead of Hank Aaron as the greatest left fielder of the last fifty years.

The first thing to consider is that just a few short years ago, when the MLB All-Century Team was announced, Barry Bonds was not a member. Even though he'd already won three MVP awards and had been performing at an extremely high level for more than a dozen years, Bonds was not among the ten outfielders named to the team. Ken Griffey, Jr. was. So was Pete Rose. This is not to suggest

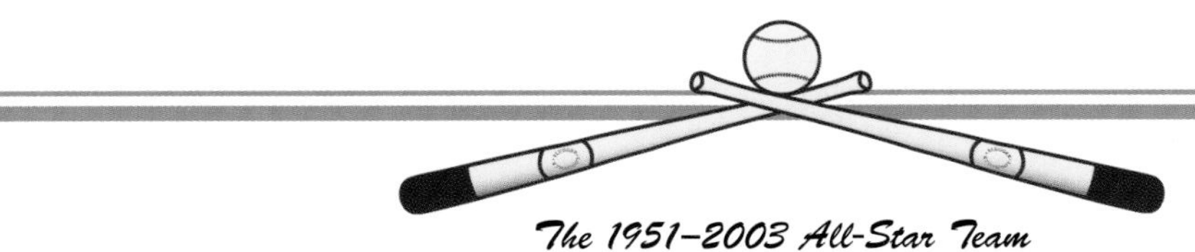

that the selections made were the correct ones. Frankly, Bonds's omission was an oversight, as was Frank Robinson's. They both should have been selected to the team instead of Griffey and Rose. The point is, however, that no one really made a fuss back then about Bonds being excluded. Those same members of the media who now refer to him as the greatest player ever didn't even seem to notice that he wasn't picked for the team. This accentuates how far Bonds has risen in stature in just a few short years. The truth is that, prior to the last three seasons, during which Bonds has put up some amazing numbers, he was always considered to be a very, very good player—but not, by any means, in a league with Hank Aaron.

Perhaps the reason for this lies in the fact that, prior to 2001, Bonds simply was not the dominant player that Aaron was during his career. Up until then, Bonds had hit as many as 40 home runs just four times in his first fifteen seasons. Aaron, by comparison, accomplished this eight times during his career. Bonds had driven in more than 100 runs eight times to Aaron's eleven, and he had batted over .300 just seven times to Aaron's fourteen. True, Bonds had hit more than 30 home runs and stolen more than 30 bases in a season five times to Aaron's one, but when the latter played, little emphasis was placed on statistics such as this. Bonds had led the league in home runs, runs batted in, and runs scored just one time each. Meanwhile, Aaron led the league in both home runs and runs batted in four times, in runs scored three times, and in batting average twice.

Another point in Aaron's favor is that, unlike Bonds, he had an outstanding postseason record. While Bonds's struggles in the postseason have already been mentioned, Aaron's numbers were extremely impressive. In two World Series and one NLCS, covering 17 postseason games and 69 at-bats, he hit 6 home runs, knocked in 16 runs, and batted .362.

But what of Bonds's three MVP awards as of 2000, compared to the one that Aaron won during his career? Isn't that an indication of the former's greater degree of dominance? There is no question that Bonds has been the National League's top player for much of his career. However, over the last twenty years or so, the game has become far more homogenized than it was during Aaron's playing days. For one thing, through free agency, players now switch leagues so frequently that it is becoming increasingly difficult for either circuit to maintain an identity of its own. In addition, the distribution of African-American and Latin players throughout baseball is wider now than it was forty, or even thirty years ago. For much of Aaron's career, the National League was superior to the American League because of its greater willingness to integrate. As a result, most of the game's top players resided in the N.L. Therefore, while Aaron won only one MVP award, it was more difficult for him to win it due to the greater level of competition in the National League at that time. It was actually quite an accomplishment for him to finish in the top five in the voting seven other times. It is particularly impressive when one considers that some of the players he lost out to were Willie Mays, Ernie Banks, Frank Robinson, Sandy Koufax, and Roberto Clemente. Let's compare the statistics of Bonds in his first three MVP seasons to those of Aaron in some of his better years to determine how much more difficult it was for the latter to come away with the award. In Bonds's first three MVP seasons, these were the numbers he posted:

1990—33 HRs, 114 RBI, .301 AVERAGE, 104 RUNS SCORED
1992—34 HRs, 103 RBI, .311 AVERAGE, 109 RUNS SCORED
1993—46 HRs, 123 RBI, .336 AVERAGE, 129 RUNS SCORED

Those are impressive numbers. However, Aaron put up comparable numbers in eight different seasons in which he *failed* to win the MVP award. Let's look at his numbers in just a few of those seasons:

1959—39 HRs, 123 RBI, .355 AVERAGE, 116 RUNS SCORED
1961—34 HRs, 120 RBI, .327 AVERAGE, 115 RUNS SCORED
1963—44 HRs, 130 RBI, .319 AVERAGE, 121 RUNS SCORED
1966—44 HRs, 127 RBI, .279 AVERAGE, 117 RUNS SCORED

Standing in the way of Aaron winning the award in each of those years was a pretty fair player: Ernie Banks in 1959, Frank Robinson in 1961, Sandy Koufax in 1963, and Roberto Clemente in 1966. This is not to diminish in any way what Bonds has been able to accomplish. Winning the MVP award as often as he has is an outstanding achievement. However, with talent now more evenly dispersed throughout both leagues, he hasn't had to face the same kind of competition that Aaron did. While Bonds did lose out to Jeff Bagwell in the 1994 voting and to Sammy Sosa in the 1998 balloting, he has also been outpolled by Terry Pendleton, Barry Larkin, and Ken Caminiti in other years—all fine players, of course, but hardly Frank Robinson or Roberto Clemente.

More than anything, though, it should be considered that whatever numbers Aaron was able to compile, he put up during an era that was much more difficult for hitters. His career spanned the years 1954 to 1976. While a proper balance was struck between hitting and pitching during the 1950s and 1970s, pitchers dominated for much of the 1960s. Pitchers were particularly dominant from 1963 to 1968, after the size of the strike zone was increased at the end of the 1962 season and before the mound was lowered prior to the start of the 1969 campaign. These were among Aaron's prime years. He regularly had to face the likes of Sandy Koufax, Juan Marichal, Bob Gibson, Don Drysdale, Ferguson Jenkins, Steve Carlton, Tom Seaver, and Gaylord Perry. Gibson and Drysdale were particularly imposing because they would knock you down as soon as look at you. Yet, in spite of the plethora of outstanding pitchers who performed during his time, Aaron managed to compile some truly magnificent seasons and demonstrate a consistency that, to this day, has not been matched by any other player.

Still, Barry Bonds is the greatest player of his era. However, while pitchers dominated the game for a good portion of Aaron's career, hitters have ruled for much of Bonds's. They have been particularly in command since the mid-1990s, when various factors began to contribute to the astronomical rise in offensive statistics. With further expansion, pitching talent has been increasingly diluted, and the number of below-average pitchers wearing major league uniforms is now greater than ever before. Whereas many of the teams that Aaron faced were typically able to throw at least two, or in some cases even three or four solid pitchers at him, most of the teams that Bonds faces are fortunate if they have even one. The only truly dominant pitchers that Bonds has had to hit against throughout much of his career are Greg Maddux, Tom Glavine, John Smoltz, and, over the last few seasons, Randy Johnson and Curt Schilling.

The game is now geared towards offense. Ballparks are smaller, the ball is livelier, the strike zone is smaller, and pitchers are afraid to throw inside. These days, if a pitcher hits a batter and the opposing hurler retaliates, a warning is issued to both pitchers and managers: if another batter is hit, both the pitcher and his manager will be ejected from the game. With that feeling of security, hitters are now able

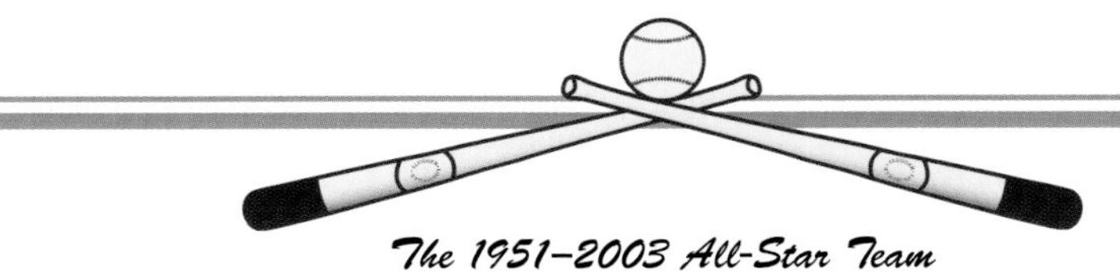

to dig in deeper in the batter's box and look for pitches they can drive out of the ballpark. Bonds, in particular, has the additional advantage of striding to the plate wearing thick padding on his right arm to protect him against any inside pitches. One can only imagine what either Drysdale or Gibson would have done if a batter tried that against them.

Throughout all of baseball, offensive numbers have been on the rise over the last decade. The increase has been particularly noticeable since 1996, when it became rather commonplace for the top sluggers in each league to surpass the 50-homer mark. Prior to that, Bonds had been an outstanding player in his first ten seasons. However, he had hit more than 40 home runs only once (something Aaron accomplished *eight* times during his career), while topping 30 four other times. Since 1996, though, Bonds has never failed to hit more than 30 homers and has surpassed 40 four times.

Bonds's numbers really took a quantum leap in 2001, when he set a new single-season home run mark with 73. That was *24* more than he had ever hit previously in his career. He established several records that year en route to winning his fourth MVP award. He won the award a record fifth time the following year by leading the league in batting for the first time in his career, with an average of .370, and establishing a new single-season record with 198 walks. Bonds also had another outstanding year in 2003 that could possibly earn him his sixth MVP award.

Earlier, when comparing Bonds's achievements to those of Aaron, the intent was not to ignore the last three incredible seasons Bonds has had, but rather to put them into perspective. Prior to these three seasons, Bonds was an exceptional player, but was not as dominant as Aaron had been during his playing days. However, since 2001, he has reached a level of dominance that Aaron never knew. In 2001, Bonds was thirty-seven years old. He is now thirty-nine. It is a fact that, no matter how well conditioned an athlete is, his skills begin to diminish when he reaches his mid-30s. His reflexes start to slow up, and in the case of a hitter, so does his bat speed. Yet, in the case of Bonds, the opposite seems to be happening. His bat speed seems to have gotten faster, and he has become even more proficient at the plate than he was previously. As he approaches what should be the twilight of his career, his numbers are on the rise. Is this the result of his superb physical conditioning? Has he perhaps enhanced his performance in some other way? Or is it merely just a part of the overall trend that seems to have developed in baseball? Whatever the reason, it seems unnatural that a man should have, by far, his greatest seasons after the age of thirty-seven. As a result, Bonds's performance over the last few seasons must be viewed with a certain amount of skepticism and given somewhat less credibility. He must therefore be ranked behind Hank Aaron on the list of left fielders.

"Hammerin' Hank" Aaron is, in all likelihood, one of the five greatest players in baseball history. His name appears all over the record books: first all-time in home runs, runs batted in, and total bases; third in runs scored and base hits; ninth in doubles. He led the National League in home runs, runs batted in, doubles, and slugging percentage four times each, in runs scored three times, and in both batting average and base hits twice. Although he never hit 50 homers in a season, Aaron hit over 40 eight times, and hit more than 20 a record twenty consecutive seasons. He also drove in more than 100 runs eleven times, batted over .300 fourteen times, had 200 hits three times, and scored more than 100 runs fifteen times, including thirteen consecutive seasons from 1955 to 1967.

Aaron won the National League's MVP award in 1957, when he led the Braves to the world championship by leading the league in homers (44), runs batted in (132), and runs scored (118), while batting

.322. He finished in the top five in the MVP voting seven other times. Aaron won the second of his two batting championships in 1959 by hitting a career-high .355. A look at Aaron's numbers for the five-year period of 1959–1963 gives you an idea of his remarkable consistency:

1959—39 HRs, 123 RBI, .355 AVERAGE
1960—40 HRs, 126 RBI, .292 AVERAGE
1961—34 HRs, 120 RBI, .327 AVERAGE
1962—45 HRs, 128 RBI, .323 AVERAGE
1963—44 HRs, 130 RBI, .319 AVERAGE

In 1971, at the age of thirty-seven, Aaron hit 47 homers, knocked in 118 runs, and batted .327. Perhaps no other player in history sustained such a high level of performance over such a long period of time.

However, Aaron was more than just a great hitter. He was an excellent base runner, stealing more than 20 bases six times in his career. And he was a fine outfielder: although not as flashy as his contemporary, Willie Mays, Aaron had fine speed, excellent range, and a strong throwing arm. He won three Gold Gloves and led N.L. outfielders in double plays three times.

Mickey Mantle once said that Hank Aaron "was to my time what Joe DiMaggio was to the era when he played."

❷ BARRY BONDS

BARRY BONDS IS WITHOUT QUESTION THE GREATEST all-around player in the game over the last quarter-century. There's nothing on a ball field that he can't do. In his youth, he was a superb outfielder with a good arm and excellent speed, a great base runner, and he remains one of the greatest home run hitters ever. He was the first man to hit 400 homers and steal 400 bases, the first to hit 500 and steal 400, and the first to hit 600 and steal 500. He is one of just a handful of players to hit 40 homers and steal 40 bases in a season.

As of this writing, Bonds is fourth on the all-time home run list, with 658, and he is coming off another magnificent season in 2003 in which he hit 45 home runs in just 390 official at-bats, while batting .341 and scoring 111 runs. His greatest year, though, came in 2001 when he broke the all-time single season records for home runs (73) and slugging percentage

(.863). Prior to that, he had never hit 50 homers in a season, but he had hit more than 40 homers four times, something he has done twice more since. He also has knocked in over 100 runs eleven times, scored more than 100 eleven times, batted over .300 ten times, and stolen more than 40 bases three times. He has led the N.L. in homers twice, runs batted in, batting average, and runs scored once each, on-base percentage seven times, and slugging percentage five times.

Bonds is also the only player in major league history to win the MVP award five times. He won it for the first time in 1990 when, playing for the Pirates, he hit 33 homers, knocked in 114 runs, and batted .301. He won it again in 1992 by hitting 34 homers, knocking in 103 runs, batting .311, and leading the league in runs scored, on-base percentage and slugging percentage. The following season, playing for the Giants, he won it for the third time by hitting 46 homers, leading the league with 123 runs batted in, and batting .336. Bonds' record-shattering 2001 season earned him his fourth MVP award. In addition to his 73 homers and .863 slugging percentage, he had 137 RBI, an average of .328, and an on-base percentage of .515. He won the fifth MVP award of his career in 2002 by hitting 46 home runs, knocking in 110 runs, leading the league with a career-high .370 batting average, scoring 117 runs, and establishing a new major league record with 198 walks.

It appears that the only two things left for Bonds to accomplish are winning the World Series and breaking Hank Aaron's career home run record, something he seems to have a very good chance of doing.

❸ RICKEY HENDERSON

RICKEY HENDERSON IS PROBABLY THE GREATEST leadoff hitter ever. One of the other players on this list, Lou Brock, was also excellent at the top of the line-up, but Henderson had more power and was more adept at getting himself on base via the walk, as his career on-base percentage of .400, versus Brock's .344, indicates.

The qualities you look for in a great leadoff hitter are the ability to get on base, upset the opposing team's defense, and score runs. Henderson has done all these things better than anyone else who ever played the game. He is the all-time leader in stolen bases (1,406), runs scored (2,295), and walks (2,190). He led the league in stolen bases twelve times, in runs scored five times, in walks three times, and in both on-base percentage and hits once. He holds the all-time single-season stolen base record, with 130, set in 1982, and stole more than 100 bases three times. He stole more than 80 bases six times, and more than 50 bases thirteen times. He scored more than 100 runs eleven times, and batted over .300 seven times.

Henderson was voted the A.L. MVP in 1990 when, for the A's, he hit 28 homers, knocked in 61 runs, batted .325, and led the league with 119 runs scored, 65 stolen bases, and a .441 on-base percentage. He finished in the top five in the MVP voting two other times. One of those times was 1985 when, playing for the Yankees, he hit 24 homers, knocked in 72 runs, batted .314, and scored 146 runs—the highest total since Ted Williams scored 150 in 1949. Henderson also holds the career record for most home runs leading off a game.

❹ CARL YASTRZEMSKI

"YAZ" WAS THE CHOICE OVER LOU BROCK FOR fourth place because, even though Brock was a bit more consistent, Yastrzemski was, at his best, a more dominant player and a better left fielder.

Carl Yastrzemski is the only American League player to hit 400 home runs and get 3,000 hits. He led the league in home runs and runs batted in once, in batting average, doubles, runs scored, and slugging percentage three times each, in hits twice, and in on-base percentage five times. He hit over 40 homers three times, drove in more than 100 runs five times, and batted over .300 six times.

In 1967, Yastrzemski had one of the finest seasons a player has ever had. That year, he was selected league MVP and won the Triple Crown by hitting 44 homers, knocking in 121 runs, and batting .326. He also led the league with 112 runs scored, 189 hits, an on-base percentage of .421, and a slugging percentage of .622, and played a superb left field. He batted .522, with 5 homers and 22 RBI in the final two weeks of the season to lead the Boston Red Sox into the World Series. Once there, he continued his brilliant play by hitting .400 with 3 home runs. Teammate George Scott once said of Yastrzemski's performance that season that, of Yaz's 44 home runs, "probably 43 either tied the game or put us in the lead." Those who saw him that year insist that, for that one season, he was as good an all-around player as anyone who ever played.

Yastrzemski followed that up in 1968 by winning his final batting title with an average of .301, finishing the season as the only American League regular with a .300 average. He had another outstanding season in 1970 when he hit hit 40 homers, knocked in 102 runs, batted .329, led the league with 125 runs scored, an on-base percentage of .453, and a slugging percentage of .592, and finished fourth in the MVP voting.

As a left fielder, Yastrzemski gave it everything he had, always going full tilt and playing Fenway Park's "Green Monster" to perfection. After being moved to first base for much of the 1975 season, he was shifted back to left field just prior to the playoff series against the three-time defending champion A's. In one of those games, Reggie Jackson lined one down the left field line that looked like a certain double. But Yaz got to the ball quickly, backhanded it, and made a perfect throw to nail Jackson at second on a very close play. Jackson said after the game that Yastrzemski was the "only man in the world who could have made that play."

5 LOU BROCK

IT IS ALMOST IMPOSSIBLE TO COMPARE LOU Brock and Willie Stargell as players since their styles were so dissimilar. One was a great leadoff hitter and base-stealer while the other was a great slugger. Brock was given the higher ranking for two reasons. First, he was one of the two or three greatest leadoff hitters in the history of the game. In addition, he had more of an impact on the game of baseball than did Stargell. Being, along with Maury Wills, the first truly great base-stealer since the dead ball era, he helped to change the game and establish a trend that would affect future generations of players. Therefore, he was given the nod over the harder-hitting Stargell.

Until Rickey Henderson came along, Lou Brock was considered by some to have been the game's greatest leadoff hitter. A member of the 3,000-hit club, Brock once held both the career (938) and single-season (118) stolen base records (both were eventually broken by Henderson). During a nine-year stretch, from 1966 to 1974, Brock led the National League in stolen bases eight times. He established a major league record by stealing 50 or more bases in twelve consecutive seasons from 1965 to 1976. He also led the league in runs scored twice, and in both triples and doubles once.

Brock's great ability as a base-stealer sometimes obscures the fact that he was a fine all-around player. He batted over .300 eight times, scored more than 100 runs seven times, and had over 200 hits four times. He had probably his finest all-around season in 1967, when he reached career highs in homers (21) and runs batted in (76), batted .299, stole 52 bases, rapped out 206 hits, and led the N.L. with 113 runs scored. The following season, he led the league in doubles, triples, and steals, becoming the first N.L. player to accomplish the feat since Honus Wagner did it sixty years earlier.

When Brock stole 118 bases in 1974, at the age of thirty-five, not only did he finish runner-up to Steve Garvey in the MVP voting, but he was named "Man of the Year" by *The Sporting News.*

Brock was also an exceptional postseason performer for the Cardinals. In the 1967 World Series, he batted .414, had 12 hits, and established a Series record by stealing 7 bases. The following year, he batted .464, banged out 13 hits, and equaled his own Series record by stealing another 7 bases.

Although not thought of as a power hitter, Brock actually had excellent power. When he was a youngster with the Chicago Cubs, he became only the second player to hit a ball into the center field stands in the Polo Grounds, almost 500 feet from home plate. However, being a consummate team player, Brock knew that he would be able to help his team the most by turning himself into an exceptional lead-off hitter, someone who could get on base and upset the opposing team's defense. He accomplished that and became one of the best ever.

Honorable mention should be given to Willie Stargell and Billy Williams:

As impressive as Willie Stargell's career numbers were, it would be an injustice to him to judge him solely on his stats. He was a true team leader, a great influence on his Pirate teammates, and one of the classiest men the game has ever known.

Although Stargell hit 475 home runs during his career, he probably would have hit many more had he not spent his first seven seasons playing in Pittsburgh's cavernous Forbes Field. Although he had some fine seasons there, his home run production rose markedly when the Pirates moved to Three Rivers Stadium prior to the 1970 season. It was there that he had his most productive seasons. In 1971, he led the National League with 48 homers, knocked in 125 runs, batted .295, and finished runner-up to Joe Torre in the MVP voting. The following season, he hit 33 homers, had 112 RBI, batted .293, and finished third in the MVP voting. In 1973, he led the league with 44 homers, 119 RBI, 43 doubles, and a slugging percentage of .646, while batting .299 and finishing second in the MVP voting once more, this time to Pete Rose. Stargell finally got his MVP award in 1979. That season, even though he was nearing the end of his career, he hit 32 homers and was the inspirational leader on the Pirates team that won the World Series. He shared the award that season with Keith Hernandez.

In all, Stargell hit over 40 homers twice, and hit more than 30 four other times. He also knocked in over 100 runs five times and batted over .300 three times. He will always be remembered most for his tremendous power, though. In sixty-one years, only 18 balls were hit out of Forbes Field, and 7 of those were hit by Stargell. He is the only player to hit a ball completely out of Dodger Stadium—and he did that twice. He also hit a homer in Montreal's Olympic Stadium that was measured at 535 feet.

Stargell's former manager Harry Walker once said of him: "I never have seen a batter who hits the ball any harder. For sheer crash of bat meeting ball, Stargell simply is the best."

Billy Williams had one of the sweetest swings in baseball. Willie Stargell once called it "poetry in motion." That swing helped Williams become one of the game's most consistent hitters. Spending most of his career with the Chicago Cubs, he had more than 20 homers and 80 RBI thirteen straight seasons.

In all, he hit over 30 homers five times, knocked in more than 100 runs three times, and batted over .300 five times.

Williams had his two finest seasons in 1970 and 1972. In 1970, he hit 42 homers, knocked in 129 runs, batted .322, and led the N.L. with 205 hits and 137 runs scored. Two years later, he hit 37 homers, had 122 RBI, and led the league with a .333 batting average and .606 slugging percentage. He finished runner-up to Johnny Bench both times in the MVP voting.

Williams was also extremely durable. He played in a National League record 1,117 consecutive games.

All-Star Center Fielder

PLAYER	YEARS	AB	HITS	RUNS	2B	3B	HR	RB	AVG	SB	OBP	SLG PCT
1) WILLIE MAYS	1951–52, 1954–73	10,881	3,283	2,062	523	140	660	1,903	.302	338	.387	.557
2) MICKEY MANTLE	1951–68	8,102	2,415	1,677	344	72	536	1,509	.298	153	.423	.557
3) KEN GRIFFEY, JR.*	1989–2003	7,079	2,080	1,271	382	36	481	1,384	.294	177	.379	.562
4) DUKE SNIDER	1947–64	7,161	2,116	1,259	358	85	407	1,333	.295	99	.381	.540
5) DALE MURPHY	1976–93	7,960	2,111	1,197	350	39	398	1,266	.265	161	.346	.469
HONORABLE MENTION:												
KIRBY PUCKETT	1984–95	7,244	2,304	1,071	414	57	207	1,085	.318	134	.360	.477
ANDRE DAWSON	1976–96	9,927	2,774	1,373	503	98	438	1,591	.279	314	.323	.482

* Indicates player is still active

1 WILLIE MAYS

For quite a few years, a legitimate case could have been made that Mickey Mantle was just as good as Willie Mays. Prior to 1962, in approximately the same number of at-bats, Mantle was slightly ahead in home runs and runs batted in, and was well ahead in runs scored and on-base percentage. Mays had significantly more doubles and triples, and had stolen more bases. Their batting averages were almost identical. Mays was the better outfielder, but overall the two were very close. However, it was during 1962—his last MVP season—that Mantle's injuries started to get the better of him. Mickey missed a good portion of '62, most of '63, and came back to have one more good year in '64. However, from that point on, he was merely a shell of his former self and was no longer the great player he'd once been. Meanwhile, Mays remained an exceptional player for several more seasons. He had outstanding years from 1962 to 1964, and then in 1965 he hit 52 home runs and won the National League MVP award for the second time. He had one more big year in 1966 and remained a solid player for the remainder of the decade, before time finally started to catch up with him. Hall of Famer and current baseball analyst Joe Morgan once said during an interview that, had Mantle not suffered through all the injuries, he probably would have been "just as good as, or maybe even better than, Willie Mays." However, as we all know, that is not what happened. Mantle himself once said that for a long time he was keeping up with Mays, but after a while, "he just sort of passed me by, like I was standing still." So, Willie is really the only logical choice for first-team center fielder.

Willie Mays was one of the most colorful, exciting, and charismatic players in the history of baseball. The first man to hit 300 home runs and steal 300 bases, Mays is third all-time in home runs and total bases, seventh in runs batted in, sixth in runs scored, and tenth in base hits. He led the National League in homers four times, in batting average once, in triples three times, in slugging percentage five times, in runs scored and on-base percentage two times each, and in stolen bases four consecutive seasons, from 1956 to 1959. He hit more than 50 homers in a season twice, more than 40 four other times, and more than 20 for fifteen consecutive seasons, beginning in 1954. Mays also knocked in more than 100 runs and batted over .300 ten times, bettering the .330 mark three times. He had 20 triples one season and scored more than 100 runs in twelve straight years from 1954 to 1965.

Mays won the MVP award for the first time in 1954. That year, he hit 41 homers, knocked in 110 runs, scored 119 more, and led the league with a .345 average, .667 slugging percentage, and 13 triples, while leading the Giants to the world championship. The following season, Mays hit 51 homers, knocked in 127 runs, batted .319, and finished fourth in the MVP voting. He had another great year in 1962 when he led the league with 49 homers, and knocked in 141 runs, while batting .304, scoring 130 runs, and finishing runner-up to Maury Wills in the MVP voting. Mays won his second MVP award in 1965, when he hit a league-leading 52 homers, knocked in 112 runs, batted .317, and led the league with a .399 on-base and .645 slugging percentage. In all, he finished in the top five in the MVP voting nine times during his career. He also hit over 30 homers and stole over 30 bases in the same season twice.

A great base runner, Mays often scored from second base on infield groundouts. He was also an extremely cerebral player. He once confided in an interview that there were times when he could have

stretched base hits into doubles but chose, instead, to stay at first. He did this because he knew that if first base was unoccupied, the opposing team's pitcher would have intentionally walked the next hitter, Willie McCovey, and Mays didn't want to take the bat out of the slugger's hands.

Mays was also a big-game player. A two-time All-Star Game MVP, he holds records for most career hits (23) and stolen bases (6) in All-Star competition. As an outfielder, Mays had few, if any, peers. The winner of eleven Gold Gloves, he set records for career putouts and total chances.

Perhaps his biggest fan was his first major league manager, Leo Durocher, who once said: "What can I say about Willie Mays after I say he's the greatest player any of us has ever seen?" "Leo the Lip" went on to say: "If somebody came up and hit .450, stole 100 bases, and performed a miracle on the field every day, I'd still look you in the eye and say Willie was better."

2 MICKEY MANTLE

SOME MIGHT ARGUE THAT KEN GRIFFEY, JR. has shown that he is as good an all-around player as Mickey Mantle was. However, Mantle didn't have the advantages that Griffey has had during his career. Mantle played during the 1950s and 1960s, when pitching was much more dominant than it has been throughout most of Griffey's career, and when the ball was not as lively as it is today. Mantle played in the "old" Yankee Stadium, which truly was a pitcher's ballpark. Never a dead pull-hitter, Mickey lost several home runs each year playing in the Stadium, with its exceptionally deep center field and power alleys. Meanwhile, before moving on to Cincinnati, Griffey spent several seasons swinging for the much closer fences of Seattle's Kingdome, a hitter's paradise. In addition, Griffey's productivity has been drastically reduced by injuries the last few seasons, while playing for the Reds. A brilliant career and what appeared to be an eventual run at Hank Aaron's all-time home run record have been derailed, and it is no longer a certainty that Griffey will even make it to 600 home runs. When his career is over, his accomplishments will have to be re-evaluated. For now, Mantle is still firmly entrenched at number two.

The greatest switch-hitter in history, Mickey Mantle also possessed what is probably the greatest combination of speed and power the game has ever seen. He could hit a ball 500 feet from either side of the plate and, in his early years, run like a deer.

Donald Honig wrote in *Baseball America:* "Right handed, [Mantle] could drive the ball as far as Foxx, and left handed, as far as Ruth. And he had running speed like you never saw. And an arm like a cannon."

As good as Mantle was, he would have been even better had he not suffered through so many debilitating injuries, and had he taken better care of himself. Nevertheless, he was able to accomplish quite a bit during his eighteen-year major league career, and, at his best, was one of the most devastating players the game has seen.

Mantle is tenth all-time in home runs and walks. He led the American League in home runs four times, in runs batted in once, in batting average once, in runs scored six times, in on-base percentage three times, in slugging percentage four times, and in walks five times. He hit more than 50 homers twice, more than 40 two other times, and more than 30 five other times. He knocked in more than 100 runs four times, batted over .300 ten times, topping the .350 mark twice, and scored more than 100 runs nine straight seasons, from 1953 to 1961.

Mickey had his greatest season, and one of the best any player has ever had, in 1956, when he won the first of his three MVP awards. That year, he won the Triple Crown and led not only the American League but also the majors in home runs (52), runs batted in (130), batting average (.353), runs scored (132), and slugging percentage (.705). He became only the second player (Jimmie Foxx was the other) to hit 50 homers and win a batting title in the same season. Mickey won the MVP award again the following year by hitting 34 homers, knocking in 94 runs, batting .365, and walking 146 times. Although he finished runner-up to teammate Roger Maris in the 1961 MVP voting, Mantle had one of his finest seasons. That year, he hit 54 homers, knocked in 128 runs, and batted .317. He was such a feared hitter that Maris did not receive one intentional walk that season, despite hitting 61 homers himself, because he had Mantle batting behind him. Mickey won his final MVP award the following season, even though he had only 377 official at-bats (roughly two-thirds of a full season). That year, he hit 30 homers, had 89 RBI, batted .321, and walked 122 times. Mantle finished in the top five in the MVP voting five other times.

Mickey was famous for his tape-measure home runs, and was credited with hitting the longest ever in a major league game. That one came on April 17, 1953, when he hit a ball that was measured at 565 feet off Washington Senator left-hander Chuck Stobbs at Washington's Griffith Stadium. He also hit one, about ten years later, batting left-handed, at Yankee Stadium that came within two feet of going completely out of the ballpark. That one was a line drive that was still rising when it hit off the façade of the stadium's upper deck in right field and, according to Mantle, was probably the hardest ball he ever hit.

Hall of Famer Charlie Gehringer once said: "Mantle hits the longest ball in the game. He can belt it as far as Babe Ruth or Ted Williams, maybe farther."

Mantle's great power obscured the fact that he was also an excellent base runner. Although he never stole more than 21 bases in any season, primarily because the Yankee teams he played on relied more on power than on speed, he was thrown out only 38 times in almost 200 stolen base attempts during his career, for a phenomenal success rate of 80 percent.

Mickey also holds World Series records for most home runs (18), runs batted in (40), runs scored (42), and total bases (123). In his first fourteen seasons, the Yankees appeared in twelve World Series and won seven world championships.

❸ KEN GRIFFEY, JR.

WHILE HIS CAREER IS FAR FROM OVER, KEN Griffey, Jr. has already accomplished enough to earn a spot on the third team. Although slowed by injuries the last few seasons, Griffey, while playing for the Seattle Mariners, hit more than 40 homers seven times, knocked in more than 100 runs eight times, topping 130 four times, batted over .300 seven times, and scored more than 100 runs six times. He became only the second American League player (Babe Ruth was the other) to hit more than 50 home runs in consecutive seasons, accomplishing the feat in 1997 and 1998. He also won the American League's MVP award in 1997 by hitting 56 homers, driving in 147 runs, and batting .304. The following season, he once again hit 56 homers and knocked in 146 runs, while batting .284.

Griffey is an exceptional outfielder with fine speed and a good throwing arm. During his career, he has won ten Gold Glove awards. Griffey has also been selected to eleven All-Star teams and finished in the top ten in the league MVP voting a total of seven times. It will be difficult for him to move past Mickey Mantle in the rankings, but Griffey has the kind of talent that may enable him to do so. However, he will have to stay healthy, something he has been unable to do the past three seasons. The injuries he has sustained have seriously cut into his playing time and greatly reduced his offensive productivity.

❹ DUKE SNIDER

ALTHOUGH HE USUALLY CAME OUT THIRD-BEST IN COMPARISONS TO WILLIE MAYS AND Mickey Mantle when all three were playing in New York, Duke Snider hit more home runs (326) than

any other player during the 1950s. Perhaps the best all-around player on those great Dodger teams of the '50s, Snider hit more than 40 home runs five consecutive seasons from 1953 to 1957. He also knocked in more than 100 runs six times, batted over .300 seven times, and scored more than 100 runs six times. He led the National League in homers, RBI, and on-base percentage once each, in runs scored three times, and in slugging percentage twice. From 1953 to 1956, there wasn't a more dangerous hitter in the game. These are the numbers he compiled those four seasons:

1953–42 HRS, 126 RBI, .336 AVG., 132 RUNS (LED N.L.)
1954–40 HRS, 130 RBI, .341 AVG., 120 RUNS (LED N.L.)
1955–42 HRS, 136 RBI, .309 AVG., 126 RUNS (LED N.L.)
1956–43 HRS (LED N.L.), 101 RBI, .292 AVG., 112 RUNS

In 1955, Snider was named *The Sporting News* "Player of the Year," and he finished in the top five in the league MVP voting in each of the 1953 to 1955 seasons.

Snider also excelled in the World Series. He hit 4 homers in both the 1952 and 1955 fall classic to become the only man to accomplish the feat twice. He also holds N.L. records for career World Series home runs (11) and RBI (26).

Although often overlooked, Snider's defense was also very solid. Ralph Kiner once commented on Snider's fielding: "I'd say Duke covers more ground, wastes less motion, and is more consistent than anyone since DiMaggio."

5 DALE MURPHY

THERE WILL, NO DOUBT, BE THOSE WHO DISAGREE WITH THE SELECTION OF DALE MURPHY over either Kirby Puckett or Andre Dawson for fifth place on the list of center fielders.

After all, when you look at the numbers, Dawson is well ahead of Murphy in almost every offensive category. However, Dawson also had almost 2,000 more career at-bats. Also, while Dawson was a

very good player for many years, he really had only one dominant season during his entire career, while Murphy had several.

In the case of Puckett, there will be those who argue that he out-hit Murphy by more than 50 points and was voted into the Hall of Fame, while Murphy has yet to be voted in. Regarding the first point: yes, Puckett's career batting average was 53 points higher than Murphy's. However, other factors must be taken into consideration. First, Puckett played half his games in Minnesota's Metro-dome (also known as the "Homer-dome"), with its artificial surface and shallow fences. Playing in that ballpark helped to raise his batting average a good 20 points. Secondly, Puckett hardly ever walked. As a result, his career on-base percentage of .360 is only 14 points higher than Murphy's. Also, while Murphy's career batting average of .265 is not particularly impressive, he failed to bat over .252 in any of his last six seasons. As a result, his average dropped from the .280 it had been up to that point to its final mark of .265.

In addition, in approximately 650 more career at-bats, Murphy hit almost twice as many home runs and drove in almost 200 more runs. He also won two MVP awards, while Puckett failed to win any.

As far as Puckett being in the Hall of Fame and Murphy not, there are several players who have been voted into the Hall who really shouldn't be there, and there are several other more-deserving players who have not been voted in. Players such as Rick Ferrell and Bill Mazeroski were good players but made it into the Hall largely because they had friends on the Veterans Committee. And if Pee Wee Reese and Phil Rizzuto were elected, why hasn't Vern Stephens been voted in yet?

Now, this is not to say that Puckett should not be in the Hall of Fame. However, his election does not automatically make him a great player, nor does it necessarily make him a better player than someone who isn't in. Frankly, I was surprised when he made it in on the first vote, since I thought that honor was always reserved for the true greats. It seemed that Puckett's credentials should have made him more of a borderline case, rather than an automatic, first-ballot selection. If he was elected in his first time on the ballot, then why hasn't Don Mattingly—whose career statistics are almost identical to Puckett's—

been voted in yet? Puckett may have had more good years than Mattingly, but the latter, in his prime, was the more dominant player. And Tony Oliva, who played in Minnesota a generation before Puckett, has not even come close to being elected. Yet in fewer career at-bats and without having the advantage of playing in the Metro-dome, Oliva put up numbers that were not far behind those of Puckett. And, with three batting titles, Oliva was actually a more dominant player than Puckett was when he played.

This shouldn't be interpreted as a "bash Kirby Puckett" diatribe, because he was an excellent player—one of the finest of his time. But his being a Hall of Famer should not necessarily carry much weight in his comparison to Murphy.

Having said all that, let's get back to the rankings.

From 1982 to 1985, Dale Murphy was the best all-around player in the National League, and maybe in all of baseball. He won the league's MVP award in both 1982 and 1983, despite getting very little support from his Braves' teammates. These are his numbers for the four-year period beginning in 1982:

1982—36 HOMERS, 109 RBI (LED N.L.), .281 AVERAGE
1983—36 HOMERS, 121 RBI (LED N.L.), .302 AVERAGE
1984—36 HOMERS, 100 RBI, .290 AVERAGE
1985—37 HOMERS, 111 RBI, .300 AVERAGE

He had another outstanding year in 1987 when he hit 44 homers, knocked in 105 runs, and batted .295. In all, Murphy hit more than 30 homers six times, knocked in more than 100 runs five times, batted over .300 twice, scored more than 100 runs four times, and hit more than 30 homers and stole more than 30 bases in the same season once. He led the N.L. in homers, RBI, and slugging twice each, and in runs scored once. He was also an excellent outfielder, having won five Gold Gloves during his career.

In 1982, Nolan Ryan said: "I can't imagine Joe DiMaggio was a better all-around player than Dale Murphy."

Honorable mention should be given to Kirby Puckett and Andre Dawson:

In his twelve big league seasons, Kirby Puckett batted over .300 eight times and had more than 200 hits five times. He also hit more than 20 homers six times, knocked in over 100 runs and scored more than 100 runs three times each, and had more than 40 doubles three times. He won a batting title and led the American League in hits four times. His two finest seasons came in 1988 and 1989. In 1988, he hit 24 homers, knocked in 121 runs, batted a career-high .356, and led the league with 234 hits. The following year, he led the league with a .339 average. Puckett finished in the top five in the league MVP voting three times.

Andre Dawson was one of the best all-around players in baseball for most of the 1980s. He hit more than 20 homers and stole more than 20 bases in the same season five times. During his career, he

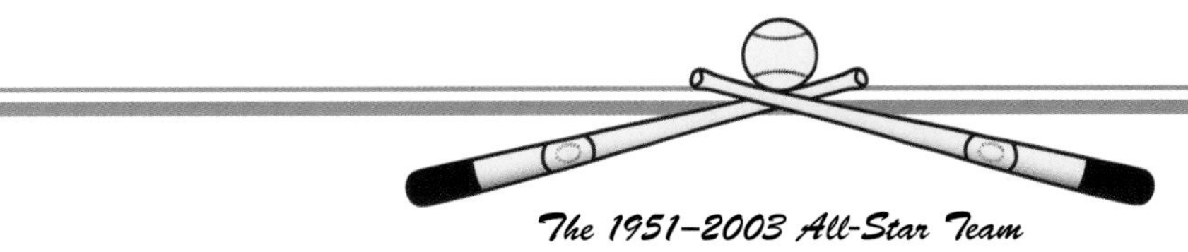

hit more than 30 homers three times, knocked in over 100 runs four times, batted over .300 five times, scored more than 100 runs twice, and stole more than 30 bases three times.

His greatest season came in 1987, after he had left the Montreal Expos and gone to the Chicago Cubs via free agency. That year, he led the National League with 49 home runs and 137 runs batted in, batted .287, and was voted league MVP.

All-Star Right Fielder

PLAYER	YEARS	AB	HITS	RUNS	2B	3B	HR	RBI	AVG	SB	OBP	SLG PCT
1) FRANK ROBINSON	1956–76	10,006	2,943	1,829	528	72	586	1,812	.294	204	.392	.537
2) ROBERTO CLEMENTE	1955–72	9,454	3,000	1,416	440	166	240	1,305	.317	83	.362	.475
3) SAMMY SOSA*	1989–2003	7,543	2,099	1,314	319	43	539	1,450	.278	233	.349	.546
4) TONY GWYNN	1982–2001	9,288	3,141	1,383	543	85	135	1,138	.338	319	.388	.459
5) REGGIE JACKSON	1967–87	9,864	2,584	1,551	463	49	563	1,702	.262	228	.358	.490
HONORABLE MENTION:												
AL KALINE	1953–74	10,116	3,007	1,622	498	75	399	1,583	.297	137	.379	.480
DAVE WINFIELD	1973–95	11,003	3,110	1,669	540	88	465	1,833	.283	223	.353	.475

* Indicates player is still active

1 FRANK ROBINSON

SOME MIGHT ARGUE THAT ROBERTO CLEMENTE WAS THE GREATEST RIGHT FIELDER OF the last fifty years. After all, he was a phenomenal outfielder, possessing one of the strongest throwing arms in baseball history. In addition, he was a great hitter, whose .317 career batting average was 23 points higher than Frank Robinson's. However, while Robinson was not the outfielder that Clemente was, he was very solid and was also one of the finest base runners of his day. More importantly, in only about 550 more career at-bats, Robinson more than doubled Clemente's home run output, knocked in approximately 500 more runs, scored over 400 more runs, stole more than twice as many bases, and finished with an on-base percentage that was 30 points higher and a slugging percentage that was 60 points higher. So as great as Clemente was, he was not the offensive player that Robinson was.

Sammy Sosa's power numbers and run-production compare more favorably to Robinson's. In approximately 75 percent the number of at-bats, Sosa has only about 50 fewer home runs. He will undoubtedly surpass Robinson in that department before his career is over. He also drives in runs at a slightly faster pace and may yet catch Robinson in that category as well. However, Robinson scored runs at a slightly faster rate and finished well ahead of Sosa in most other offensive categories. While Sosa has stolen about 30 more bases and

has a slightly higher slugging percentage, Robinson's batting average was 15 points higher, his on-base percentage was more than 40 points higher, he finished with almost twice as many triples, and he collected 200 more doubles. Factoring in the era in which he played and how much more difficult it was for hitters back then, Robinson's numbers are actually far more impressive than Sosa's. In addition, he had those intangibles that were mentioned earlier. So it really wasn't even close: Robinson is the clear-cut choice for the first team.

Tommy Lasorda said that when Major League Baseball announced its All-Century Team a couple of years ago, "it was a joke that Frank Robinson wasn't on it."

Mike Schmidt, who grew up in the Cincinnati area as a Reds' fan—and as a Frank Robinson fan in particular—once said: "Of all the players who have ever played this game, Frank Robinson may well be the most underrated."

Even though he is fifth on the all-time home run list, with 586, and also ranks in the top ten in total bases, Frank Robinson never, for some reason, seems to get the credit he deserves as one of the greatest players in baseball history.

That won't happen here.

One of the fiercest competitors the game has ever known, Frank Robinson remains the only player in baseball history to win the Most Valuable Player award in each league. He won the award for the first time in 1961, when, playing for the Cincinnati Reds, he hit 37 homers, knocked in 124 runs, batted .323, and led his team to the National League pennant. The following season, Robinson's numbers were even more impressive. That year, he hit 39 homers, knocked in 136 runs, batted .342, and led the league with 51 doubles, 134 runs scored, an on-base percentage of .424, and a slugging percentage of .624. He stayed in Cincinnati three more years but was traded to the Baltimore Orioles at the end of the 1965 campaign. At the time, Reds' management attempted to justify the deal by referring to Robinson as "an old thirty," when, in reality, they made the deal because they were uncomfortable having an outspoken black man on the team.

The trade only lit a fire under Robinson and gave him something to prove. In 1966, with the Orioles, he showed the baseball world just how "old" he was by winning the American League's MVP award. All he did that year was lead the league in home runs (49), runs batted in (122), and batting average (.316), thereby capturing the Triple Crown. He also led the league with 122 runs scored, an on-base percentage of .415, and a slugging percentage of .637, and led the Orioles into the World Series, where they swept the Dodgers in four straight games. In the Series, Robinson hit two more home runs and was voted Series MVP. He also finished in the top five in the league MVP voting four other times during his career.

In all, Robinson hit more than 30 homers eleven times, knocked in over 100 runs six times, batted over .300 nine times, and scored more than 100 runs eight times. He also stole more than 20 bases three times and was only thrown out 77 times in 281 career attempts. As a base runner, however, Robinson was best known for his aggressive style and his ability to break up the double play, a testament to his competitive nature and leadership abilities. Robinson's abilities as a leader were best exemplified by the effect he had on Baltimore. In his six seasons there, the Orioles won four pennants and two World Series. After he was traded, following the 1971 season, it would be another eight years before they would make another appearance in the World Series.

Maury Wills, in discussing Robinson, had this to say: "Although he was often overlooked in favor of Willie Mays, Hank Aaron, and Roberto Clemente, Frank Robinson could do everything any one of them could do…and some things better."

2 ROBERTO CLEMENTE

WITH THE EXCEPTION OF FRANK ROBINSON, Roberto Clemente was clearly the greatest right fielder of the past fifty years. Tony Gwynn was a great hitter—one of the best pure hitters in the history of the game. In fact, his .338 career average is 21 points higher than Clemente's. However, Gywnn played in an era that was far more hitter-friendly, had only slightly more than half the number of home runs that Clemente had (in almost the same number of at-bats), had almost 200 fewer runs batted in, and wasn't nearly as good an outfielder. There is no question that Clemente was the better player of the two.

However, based purely on statistics, a case could be made for ranking Sammy Sosa ahead of Clemente. In almost 2,000 fewer at-bats, he has hit more than twice as many home runs, driven in approximately 150 more runs, and scored only about 100 less. He has also stolen almost three times as many bases and compiled a slugging percentage that is almost 75 points higher. Clemente's on-base

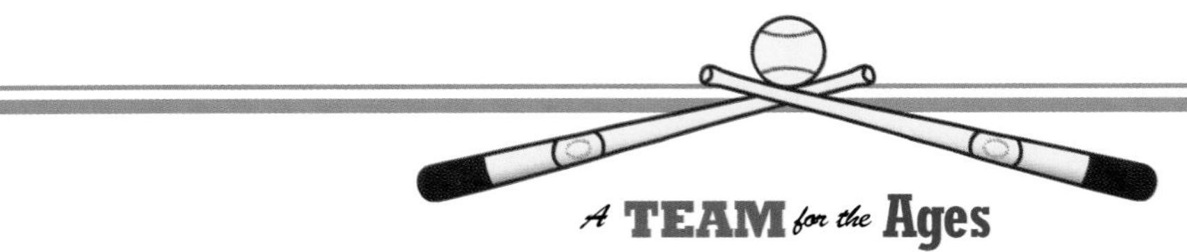

percentage was slightly better, his batting average was almost 40 points higher, and he finished with almost four times as many triples and more than 100 more doubles but, statistically the edge would seem to go to Sosa.

However, stats don't tell the whole story. They do not tell how much more difficult it was for Clemente to hit during the 1960s and early 1970s, when pitching was far more dominant than it has been throughout Sosa's career. Nor do they take into account the ballparks that both men played in. While Sosa has spent most of his career hitting in Chicago's Wrigley Field, a notoriously good park for hitters, Clemente spent the majority of his career in spacious Forbes Field, a much tougher park for hitters. Statistics also do not reflect how difficult it was for Clemente, the first truly great Latin player, to adjust to American culture. More than anything, though, statistics do not give a true indication of just how great a ballplayer Clemente really was. Whether he was running the bases with a fury rarely seen, making a fabulous throw from deep in the right field corner, or just intimidating an opposing base runner with his mere presence, you had to see Clemente to fully appreciate him and to realize how special he actually was. It was this unique blend of talents that earned him a spot on the second team, ahead of Sammy Sosa.

In addition to having to deal with the bigotry that other dark-skinned players experienced during the 1950s, Roberto Clemente, as the first true Latin star to play in the major leagues, had the added pressure of learning a new culture and a new language. On top of that, he was plagued by back injuries throughout his career, a result of an arthritic spine caused by an automobile accident. The combination of these factors would make his adjustment to the big leagues a difficult one. As a result, although he came up to the Pittsburgh Pirates in 1955, it wasn't until 1961, when he won the first of his four batting titles, that he began settling in as one of the game's greatest players.

Once established, however, Clemente never looked back. He posted the highest batting average of any player for the decade of the 1960s, with a mark of .328. During his career, Clemente batted over .300 fourteen times, topping .340 five times and .350 three times. He amassed 3,000 hits, leading the league in that department twice, and collected more than 200 hits in a season on four occasions. He also hit more than 20 homers three times, knocked in more than 100 runs twice, and scored more than 100 three times.

Although not thought of as a power hitter, Clemente had excellent power. He just had the misfortune of playing most of his career in spacious Forbes Field, with its power alleys of 457 feet in left-center and 416 feet in right-center, and its distant center field wall, 435 feet from home plate. Needless to say, this cut down considerably on his home run production and caused him to become more of a line-drive hitter. Nevertheless, Clemente did still have a few seasons where his home run and RBI totals were quite impressive. Two of those seasons were 1966 and 1967. In 1966, Clemente hit 29 homers, knocked in 119 runs, batted .317, scored 105 runs, had 202 hits, and was voted the National League's Most Valuable Player. The following season, he hit 23 homers, knocked in 110 runs, batted .357, scored 103 runs, and had 209 hits. He finished in the top five in the MVP voting that season also, and two other times during his career.

However, as great a hitter as Clemente was, he might have been even better as a fielder. The winner of twelve straight Gold Gloves, he had a powerful and accurate throwing arm, and was arguably the greatest defensive right fielder in the history of the game. In 1958, he threw out 22 runners to win the first of an N.L. record five assists titles. He also had excellent speed, great instincts, and played right field with the same flair with which Willie Mays patrolled center.

Clemente was also a great clutch performer. Appearing in the 1960 and 1971 World Series, he hit safely in each of the fourteen Series games in which he played. In the 1971 Series against the Orioles, he hit 2 homers, batted .414, had 12 hits, and was voted Series MVP.

3 SAMMY SOSA

IT WAS EXTREMELY DIFFICULT COMPARING Sammy Sosa to Tony Gwynn because of the differences in their games. Sosa is a great slugger and Gwynn was the purest hitter of his time. There was also the fact that Gwynn arrived in the big leagues in 1982, seven years earlier than Sosa. He, therefore, did not have, at least for the first half of his career, the advantage of hitting in this era of inflated numbers.

Another factor that made this choice so difficult was that Gwynn was an outstanding player for a longer period of time. From the time he won his first batting title in 1984 with an average of .351, to the time he won his eighth and final crown with a mark of .372 in 1997, Gwynn was an exceptional player. In fact, he was a great hitter to the very end, hitting well over .300 in each of the final four seasons of his career, which ended in 2001. That's eighteen years of brilliance. Meanwhile, Sosa posted solid numbers for the Cubs in 1993 and 1994, but didn't become a true impact player until 1995. Thus he has actually been performing at an extremely high level for nine years now, or half as long as Gwynn did.

In the end, though, it was impossible to overlook Sosa's superiority as a run-producer. In approximately 1,700 fewer at-bats, he has driven in approximately 300 more runs and scored only about 60 less than Gwynn did during his career. His slugging percentage is also some 90 points higher, due mostly to the fact that he has hit four times as many home runs. Gwynn has a decided advantage in batting average, on-base percentage, triples, and doubles, but the game is all about scoring runs, and in that area there really is no comparison. Even in Gwynn's two most productive seasons, he never drove in, or scored, more than 119 runs. Sosa has knocked in at least that many runs six times and scored more than that number three times as well. So for his greater ability as a run-producer, Sosa was selected over Gwynn.

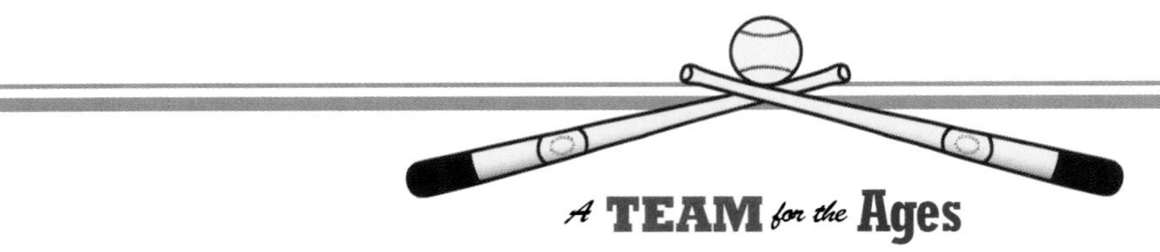

On the other hand, Reggie Jackson drove in approximately 250 more runs than Sosa has thus far, and also scored about 230 more. However, Jackson also had about 2,300 more at-bats. Jackson is also slightly ahead in on-base percentage, home runs, and triples, and well ahead in doubles, but Sosa has a much higher slugging percentage and there is little doubt that he will surpass Jackson in home runs, runs batted in, and runs scored within the next few seasons. As a result, Sosa merits a higher ranking because of his tremendous run-production and earns a spot on the third team.

Even if you take into consideration the overall inflation of power numbers throughout baseball the last several years, Sammy Sosa's accomplishments should not be taken lightly. He is one of only two players in major league history to hit more than 50 homers in four straight seasons, and he is the only one to top 60 three times. Sosa accomplished the feat the first time in 1998. That year, in his epic battle with Mark McGwire for home run supremacy, Sosa hit 66 homers, led the league with 158 runs batted in, batted .308, and was named National League MVP. The following season, he hit 63 homers, knocked in 141 runs, and batted .288. In 2000, he led the N.L. with 50 homers, had 138 RBI, and batted .320. Although overshadowed by Barry Bonds's incredible performance, Sosa had perhaps his finest season in 2001. That year, he hit 64 home runs, knocked in a league-leading 160 runs, and batted a career-high .328. Even when you consider that 50 or 60 homers in a season do not hold the same significance they once did, very few players in the history of the game have ever put together four consecutive seasons even close to the ones Sosa had from 1998 to 2001.

After another solid season in 2002, in which he hit 49 home runs and drove in 108 runs, Sosa struggled somewhat during the first half of the 2003 season. However, he finished strong to top the 40-homer and 100-RBI marks for the sixth consecutive year.

In all, Sosa has hit more than 40 home runs seven times, knocked in at least 100 runs nine times, scored more than 100 runs five times, and batted over .300 four times.

4 TONY GWYNN

THIS WAS ANOTHER INSTANCE WHERE TONY GWYNN WAS PITTED AGAINST A GREAT slugger. Reggie Jackson was far superior to Gwynn as a home run-hitter and run-producer. In approximately 600 more at-bats, he out-homered Gwynn four-to-one, finished with almost 600 more runs batted in, and scored runs at a slightly faster pace. His slugging percentage was also 30 points higher. However, Gwynn finished well ahead in every other offensive category. His batting average was 76 points higher than Jackson's, his on-base percentage was 30 points better, and he finished with far more doubles, triples, base hits, and stolen bases. Gwynn was also a better outfielder and base runner. In short, he was the more complete player of the two.

Still, there is that run-production issue. Jackson scored almost 200 more runs, but he also had almost 600 more at-bats, so this disparity is really just a minor one. When one considers that Jackson played on better teams throughout most of his career and therefore usually had better hitters batting behind him, the difference in runs scored loses all significance. The difference in runs batted in, however, is a far greater one. Part of that could also be attributed to the superior teams that Jackson played for. Another reason is that he drove himself in via the home run 428 more times than Gwynn did. However, another factor was that Jackson usually batted in the middle of his team's lineup, in either the third, fourth, or fifth spot. While Gwynn did hit third in some seasons, he spent the majority of his time in either the leadoff or number two position, spots in the order far less conducive to driving in runs. When this is taken into account, the disparity in their RBI totals also loses some of its significance. While Jackson was still the better run-producer of the two, Gwynn's superiority in the other aspects of the game is enough to make up the difference. He therefore edges out Jackson for a spot on the fourth team.

Tony Gwynn's .338 career batting average is the highest of any player whose career began in the last fifty years, and the highest since Ted Williams retired with a mark of .344. A member of the 3,000-hit club, he led the National League in batting eight times, hits seven times, and runs scored once. He had more than 200 hits in a season five times, scored more than 100 runs twice, had more than 10 triples four times, and stole more than 30 bases four times, swiping a career-high 56 in 1987. One of the most difficult players in the game to strike out, Gwynn fanned only 434 times in over 9,000 career at-bats. In 1984, he struck out only 23 times in 606 official at-bats, and in 1995 he struck out only fifteen times in 535 at-bats.

Amazingly, during his twenty-year major league career Gwynn batted over .300 nineteen straight seasons. He also hit over .350 six times, batting .370 in 1987, .358 in 1993, .394 in the strike-shortened 1994 season, and .368 in 1995. However, his finest and most productive season came in 1997, when he reached career-highs in home runs (17) and RBI (119), and batted .372.

Gwynn was also a good outfielder and base runner. During his career, he won five Gold Gloves and stole 319 bases.

5 REGGIE JACKSON

Both Al Kaline and Dave Winfield were far superior to Reggie Jackson as outfielders. In fact, they may have been better all-around players. However, Jackson was able to edge both players out for the number five spot because of his 563 career home runs (which place him eighth on the all-time list), outstanding run production, and ability to perform under pressure.

Jackson led the American League in home runs four times, in slugging percentage three times, and in runs scored twice. He hit more than 40 homers twice and topped 30 five other times during his career. He also knocked in over 100 runs six times and stole more than 20 bases four times. He had his first outstanding season with the Oakland Athletics, in 1969. That year he hit 47 homers, knocked in 118 runs, batted .275, and led the league with 123 runs scored and a .608 slugging percentage. He won the league MVP award in 1973 when he hit 32 homers, knocked in a league-leading 117 runs, batted .293, and led the league, once again, in both runs scored and slugging percentage. Jackson had another big year for the Yankees in 1980 when he led the league with 41 homers, knocked in 111 runs, batted .300 for the only time in his career, and finished runner-up to George Brett in the MVP voting. He also finished in the top five in the league MVP voting three other times.

However, it was his postseason performances that defined his career and earned him his "Mr. October" nickname. He is the only player to have been named MVP in two World Series, having led the A's to the world championship in 1973 and the Yankees to the title in 1977. In that 1977 Series against the Dodgers, Jackson set World Series records for home runs (5), slugging percentage (.755), runs scored (10), total bases (25), and became only the second player to hit 3 home runs in one Series game (Babe Ruth did it twice).

As an outfielder, although Jackson was fast and had a strong throwing arm, he was extremely erratic. In 1968, his first full season, he led A.L. outfielders in assists with 14, but also in errors with 12. This would prove to be the first of five times during his career that he would lead the league in errors.

Honorable mention should be given to Al Kaline and Dave Winfield:

Al Kaline finished 1 home run short of becoming only the second American League player to finish his career with 400 home runs and 3,000 base hits. Coming to the Detroit Tigers directly out of high school, and never having played minor league ball, Kaline, ironically, had his two finest seasons prior to

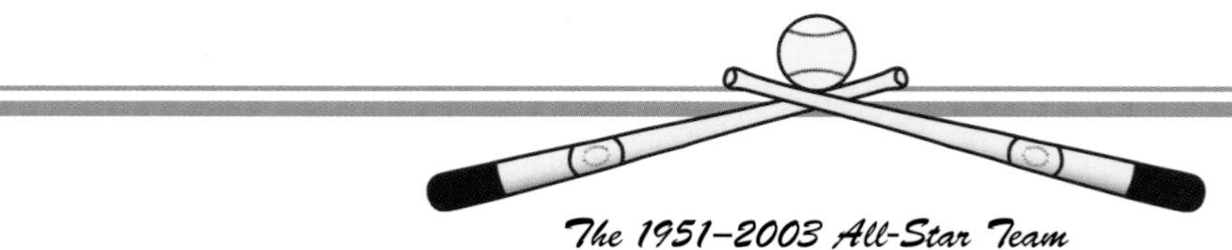

celebrating his twenty-second birthday. In 1955, at the tender age of twenty, he hit 27 home runs, knocked in 102 runs, scored 121 others, and led the league with a .340 batting average and 200 base hits. Although he finished behind Yogi Berra in the MVP voting that season, he was named the A.L. "Player of the Year" by *The Sporting News*. The following season, he once again finished in the top five in the MVP voting by hitting 27 homers, knocking in a career-high 128 runs, and batting .314. He would finish in the top five in the MVP voting two other times. Although Kaline never hit 30 homers in a season, he topped the 20 mark nine times, knocked in 100 runs three times, and batted over .300 nine times.

As an outfielder, Kaline was the closest thing the American League had to Roberto Clemente. He won ten Gold Gloves and in 1971, at the age of thirty-six, played the entire season errorless, as part of a 242-game streak without a miscue. Like Clemente, he had a powerful and accurate throwing arm. In one game, Kaline once threw out runners at second base, third base, and home plate in successive innings.

Dave Winfield is one of just three players to have amassed at least 3,000 hits, 450 home runs, and 200 stolen bases. He hit more than 30 homers three times and topped the 20 mark twelve other times. He also knocked in over 100 runs eight times, batted over .300 four times, scored more than 100 runs three times, and stole more than 20 bases four times. He had perhaps his finest season for the San Diego Padres in 1979, when he hit 34 homers, led the National League with 118 runs batted in, and batted .308.

Winfield also had several outstanding seasons for the New York Yankees. In 1982, he hit 37 homers, knocked in 106 runs, and batted .280. The following year, he hit 32 homers, had 116 RBI, and batted .283. The next year, he cut down on his swing somewhat, sacrificing power for average. That season, he hit 19 homers, drove in 100 runs, and finished second to teammate Don Mattingly in the A.L. batting race with a .340 average. He had another outstanding season in 1988, when he hit 25 homers, knocked in 107 runs, and batted .322. While with New York, he had five consecutive seasons in which he drove in at least 100 runs, becoming the first Yankee to do so since Joe DiMaggio.

Winfield was also an exceptional outfielder. The winner of seven Gold Gloves, he possessed one of the strongest throwing arms in the game, often intimidating opposing teams' base runners.

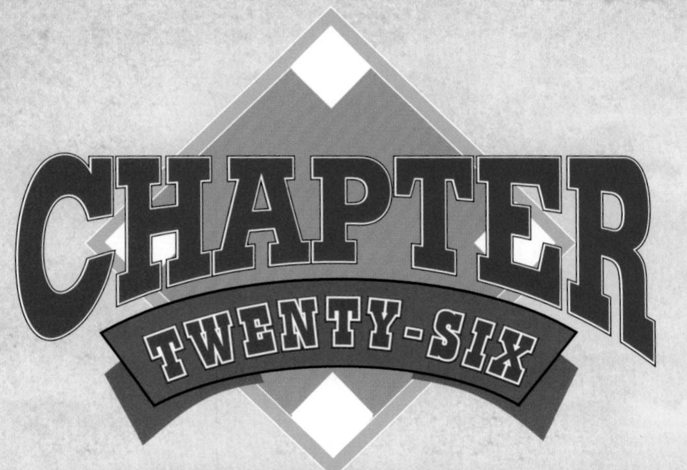

All-Star Utility Man

PLAYER	YEARS	AB	HITS	RUNS	2B	3B	HR	RBI	AVG	SB	OBP	SLG PCT
PETE ROSE	1963–86	14,053	4,256	2,165	746	135	160	1,314	.303	198	.377	.409

PETE ROSE

JUST AS WITH JACKIE ROBINSON IN THE FIRST HALF OF THE CENTURY, PETE ROSE HAS been inserted as a utility player because of his versatility. During his career, he was an All-Star at five different positions: first base, second base, third base, left field, and right field.

Although he is not eligible for the Hall of Fame, Rose's name is all over the record books. He is first all-time in games played, at-bats, and base hits, second in doubles, fifth in runs scored, and sixth in total bases. During his career, he won three batting titles, and led the National League in hits seven times, in runs scored four times, and in doubles five times. He batted over .300 fifteen times, including fourteen out of fifteen seasons from 1965 to 1979, and topped the .330 mark four times. He also had over 200 hits and scored more than 100 runs ten times each, and had more than 40 doubles seven times.

Rose was selected N.L. MVP in 1973, when he helped lead the Cincinnati Reds to the division title by leading the league with a .338 average and 230 hits. However, he had probably his finest season in 1969, when he established career-highs with 16 homers, 82 runs batted in, and a batting average of .348, which led the league. He also had 218 hits and scored 120 runs that season, to finish in the top five in the MVP voting again. Rose would finish in the top five three other times. Rose, who was named "Player of the Decade" of the 1970s by *The Sporting News,* was also an exceptional postseason performer, batting .381 in 118 playoff at-bats.

Unfortunately, Rose's gambling on the sport that made him famous, and his subsequent denial of any accusations of guilt, have made him ineligible for enshrinement at Cooperstown. It's a sad state of affairs, especially when you consider how much his accomplishments on the field of play earned him a place there.

S
SOX
KC

All-Star Designated Hitter

PLAYER	YEARS	AB	HITS	RUNS	2B	3B	HR	RBI	AVG	SB	OBP	SLG PCT
1) EDGAR MARTINEZ*	1987–2003	6,722	2,118	1,173	491	15	297	1,198	.315	48	.423	.525
2) HAROLD BAINES	1980–2001	9,908	2,866	1,299	488	49	384	1,628	.289	34	.356	.465
3) HAL MCRAE	1968–87	7,218	2,091	940	484	66	191	1,097	.290	109	.351	.454

* Indicates player is still active

PRIOR TO NAMING THE SELECTIONS FOR BEST DESIGNATED HITTER, IT SHOULD BE pointed out that the three players mentioned here were the top choices because they had most of their finest seasons serving in that capacity. While all three did play the field at one point during their careers, they are generally thought of more as designated hitters and spent the majority of their time there. Several other players, such as Jim Rice, Jose Canseco, and Paul Molitor DH'd quite a bit during their careers as well. However, they had previously established names for themselves playing positions in the field and assumed this lesser role either because of injuries or because they were nearing the end of their careers.

1 EDGAR MARTINEZ

WHILE HAROLD BAINES HAD MORE CAREER HOME RUNS, RUNS BATTED IN, AND RUNS scored than Edgar Martinez has, Baines also had more than 3,000 more at-bats. Martinez's career batting average is 26 points higher, his on-base percentage is almost 70 points higher, his slugging percentage is 60 points higher, and he has as many doubles. He is clearly the best designated hitter the American League has had since it began using the DH thirty years ago.

Although Edgar Martinez originally came up to the Seattle Mariners as a third baseman and played there regularly for a few seasons, he settled into his role as designated hitter ten years ago and has thrived in that capacity ever since. Martinez has won two batting titles and batted over .300 ten times during his

career. He won his first batting title in 1992, with an average of .343. He also led the league with 46 doubles. Martinez captured his second batting title three years later, when he hit a career-high .356—the highest batting average by a right-handed hitter in the American League since Joe DiMaggio posted a mark of .357 fifty-four years earlier. That season, Martinez also hit 29 home runs, knocked in 113 runs, and led the league with 52 doubles to help the Mariners to the division title. He had his most productive season in the year 2000, however, when he hit 37 homers, knocked in 145 runs, and batted .324. In all, Martinez has hit more than 20 homers eight times, knocked in more than 100 runs six times, scored at least 100 runs five times, and had more than 40 doubles five times. He also has an excellent batting eye, having drawn more than 100 bases on balls four times. As a result, Martinez's career on-base percentage of .423 ranks with the best of the last fifty years.

2 HAROLD BAINES

HAROLD BAINES CAME UP TO THE CHICAGO White Sox as an outfielder in 1980, but began playing primarily as a designated hitter during the 1987 season.

Although he never hit 30 homers in a season, Baines topped the 20 mark eleven times during his career. He also drove in over 100 runs twice and batted over .300 eight times. In 1984, he led the American League with a .541 slugging percentage. The following season, he established a career-high with 113 runs batted in.

❸ HAL MCRAE

HAL MCRAE WAS ONE OF THE CATALYSTS ON THOSE outstanding Kansas City Royals teams of the 1970s and early 1980s. Although he originally came up with the Cincinnati Reds as an outfielder, McRae split his time between the outfield and designated hitter his first few seasons in Kansas City, before becoming a full-time DH. During his career, McRae hit over .300 six times, hit more than 20 homers twice, knocked in more than 100 runs once, and had more than 40 doubles three times. He hit a career-high .332 in 1976, narrowly missing winning the batting title. The following season, McRae led the league with 54 doubles. However, he had probably his finest season in 1982, when he hit 27 homers, knocked in a league-leading 133 runs, batted .308, and again led the league in doubles, with 46.

All-Star Right-Handed Pitcher

PITCHER	YEARS	W	L	PCT	ERA	GS	CG	IP	H	BB	SO
1) ROGER CLEMENS*	1984–2003	310	160	.660	3.19	607	117	4,278	3,677	1,379	4,099
2) BOB GIBSON	1959–75	251	174	.591	2.91	482	255	3,884	3,279	1,336	3,117
3) JUAN MARICHAL	1960–75	243	142	.631	2.89	457	244	3,507	3,153	709	2,303
4) GREG MADDUX*	1986–2003	289	163	.639	2.89	571	103	3,968	3,625	838	2,765
5) TOM SEAVER	1967–86	311	205	.603	2.86	647	231	4,782	3,971	1,390	3,640
HONORABLE MENTION:											
JIM PALMER	1965–67, 1969–84	268	152	.638	2.86	521	211	3,948	3,349	1,311	2,212
ROBIN ROBERTS	1948–66	286	245	.539	3.41	609	305	4,688	4,582	902	2,357
FERGUSON JENKINS	1965–83	284	226	.557	3.34	594	267	4,500	4,142	997	3,192
NOLAN RYAN	1966–93	324	292	.526	3.19	773	222	5,386	3,923	2,795	5,714
PEDRO MARTINEZ*	1992–2003	166	67	.712	2.58	288	41	2,079	1,553	554	2,426

* Indicates player is still active

PITCHING HAS PROBABLY CHANGED MORE THAN ANY OTHER ASPECT OF THE GAME OVER the last fifty years. Throughout the 1950s and 1960s, and even through much of the 1970s, starting pitchers were expected to complete about one-half of their starts and throw somewhere between 220 and 300 innings a season. However, as the role of the bullpen gradually evolved into what it is today, that school of thought changed. Previously, a starting pitcher was thought to have given a quality performance if he made it into the ninth inning without surrendering more than two or three runs. These days, a quality start is thought to be getting past the sixth inning without giving up more than three or four runs.

With this change in the role of the starting pitcher, especially during the last fifteen or twenty years, it is very difficult to compare those from earlier eras to those from more recent times. However, that is what must now be done. Therefore, a brief explanation is in order about how the pitchers from these different eras will be viewed.

As with all other players, they will be judged by the quality of their overall performance within the context of the era in which they played, and by their dominance in that era. However, in those situations where pitchers from different eras appear to be quite comparable, the starter from the earlier period will be given a higher ranking, since more was expected from him.

That being said, let's move on to the selections.

1 ROGER CLEMENS

A LEGITIMATE CASE REALLY COULD BE MADE FOR any of the top five selections here being named best right-handed starter of the last fifty years. Some might even make an argument on Nolan Ryan's behalf. However, he was never seriously considered, for a number of reasons. First, while he could be extremely dominant, Ryan's career was marked by inconsistency. As a result, he has the second lowest winning percentage (.526) of any starting pitcher in the Hall of Fame. While he won 324 games, he also lost 292. In addition, Ryan never won the Cy Young award and never even led his league in wins. Some might say that he had the misfortune of playing on bad teams, but that was not entirely true. While many of his peak seasons were spent with a mediocre California Angels team from 1972 to 1979, the Angels became a contender during the latter portion of his tenure there, following the free agent signings of players such as Bobby Grich, Joe Rudi, and Don Baylor. They were a solid team in 1978, and even won the division in 1979. Ryan's record those two seasons was 10-13 and 16-14. This is just an example of the inconsistency that prevented him from meriting serious consideration for the top spot.

Tom Seaver was a great pitcher who played on some very mediocre teams. However, on the two occasions his team did make it into the postseason, he never truly distinguished himself as a big-game pitcher. In fact, he wasn't even the Mets' best pitcher in either the 1969 or 1973 World Series. In 1969, that honor went to Jerry Koosman, and in 1973, to Jon Matlack. So Seaver was the next to be sent to the showers.

Greg Maddux has been a brilliant pitcher throughout his career and, with four Cy Youngs to his credit, has won the award more often than anyone on this list with the exception of Roger Clemens,

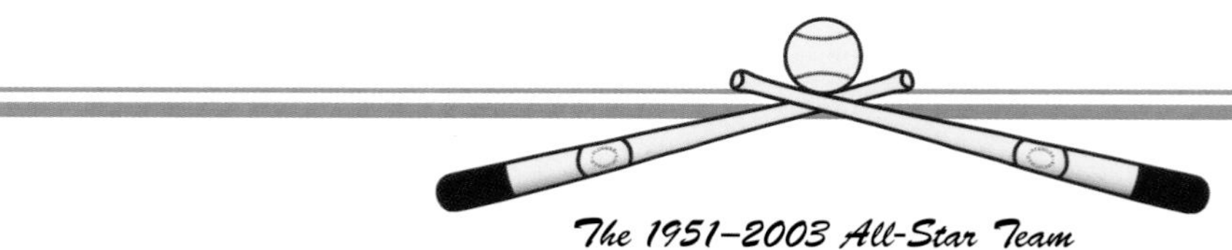

who has six in his trophy case. However, like Seaver, Maddux has faltered somewhat in the postseason, compiling a lifetime record of 11-13 with an ERA of 3.23 in 30 playoff and World Series starts. Meanwhile, Bob Gibson was one of the greatest big-game pitchers in baseball history. In addition, like most modern-day starters, Maddux has been essentially a seven- or eight-inning pitcher throughout his career, having completed as many as 10 games only twice. He has also thrown as many as 250 innings in a season just four times, with his high being 268. In contrast, Gibson completed as many as 20 games seven times during his career, while Juan Marichal topped the 20-mark five times, reaching a high of 30 in 1968. Gibson also threw more than 300 innings twice and surpassed 250 six other times. Marichal topped the 300-mark three times and bettered 250 four other times. With career numbers that were fairly comparable to those of Maddux, the two greats from the 1960s and early 1970s received a higher ranking since more was expected from them when they pitched.

That left Clemens, Gibson, and Marichal. To be honest, selecting Clemens over the other two—and, in particular, over Gibson—was an extremely difficult thing for me to do, for two reasons. For one thing, there was the same durability factor that cropped up with Maddux. Clemens neither completed nearly as many games nor, over the course of any given season, threw as many innings as Gibson or Marichal did. However, he was much more of a workhorse than Maddux was, having completed as many as 18 games in 1987 and reaching double-digits in that department on four other occasions. In addition, he threw more than 250 innings six times in his career, throwing as many as 281 innings one season.

An even bigger obstacle for me in selecting Clemens over Gibson was knowing that, if I had one game I needed to win, Gibson, not Clemens, would be my choice. True, as a member of the Yankees, Clemens has pitched some tremendous games in the postseason. For example, there was the dominating performance against the Mets in the 2000 World Series. There was also the one-hitter he threw against Seattle in the ALCS and the fabulous effort against Curt Schilling and the Arizona Diamondbacks in the 2001 World Series. However, due largely to his volatile and extremely intense disposition, Clemens previously imploded several times in big games. As a result, his lifetime postseason record is a decidedly mediocre 6-6, with a 3.46 ERA and just one complete game in 22 starts. Meanwhile, Gibson seemed to be at his best in pressure situations. For one must-win game, he would be my choice over Clemens.

However, Clemens's career numbers are just too overwhelming to overlook. He had won approximately 60 more games than either Gibson or Marichal did, had a better winning percentage than either pitcher, and also had far more strikeouts. Gibson and Marichal both finished with earned run averages approximately 30 points lower, but they pitched in much less of a hitter's era, and neither ever faced lineups that included a designated hitter. More than anything, though, there is the matter of his six Cy Young awards, which are a testament to his dominance. It is true that both Gibson and Marichal had the handicap of pitching the first half of their careers in a time when only one award was presented to the best pitcher in both leagues combined. It is also true that they had to compete against Sandy Koufax for the award. Nevertheless, Gibson won two Cy Youngs, to Clemens's six, and Marichal failed to win any. Therefore, for his greater level of dominance over a longer period of time, Clemens has to be given the edge.

Further evidence of Clemens's dominance can be seen in the number of times he has led his league in the various pitching categories. He has led American League pitchers in wins four times, ERA six times, complete games three times, strikeouts five times, shutouts six times, and innings pitched twice. The epitome of a power pitcher, Clemens has relied on a high-riding fastball, split-fingered fastball, great slider, and intimidation to take him into third place on the all-time strikeout list. These assets have also helped him to become the only pitcher in major league history to strike out as many as 20 batters in a game on two different occasions. Clemens has been a 20-game winner six times, has finished with an ERA under 3.00 nine times, and under 2.00 four times, and struck out more than 200 batters in a season eleven times.

In addition to being the only pitcher to ever win six Cy Young awards, Clemens is also the only one to win the award with three different teams. He won his first three awards in 1986, 1987, and 1991, as a member of the Boston Red Sox. In 1986, Clemens finished with a record of 24-4, a league-leading 2.48 ERA, and 238 strikeouts, to not only win the Cy Young, but also the A.L. MVP award. The following season, he finished 20-9, with a 2.97 ERA, 256 strikeouts, and a league-leading 18 complete games and 7 shutouts. After winning the award one more time with Boston, Clemens won it twice more as a member of the Toronto Blue Jays. In 1997, he finished 21-7, to lead the league in wins; he also led the league with a 2.05 ERA and 292 strikeouts to win the pitcher's Triple Crown and his fourth Cy Young. He followed that up the next season with another Triple Crown and Cy Young performance, going 20-6 with a 2.65 ERA and 271 strikeouts. Clemens won his sixth Cy Young award as a member of the New York Yankees in 2001 by going 20-3 with a 3.51 ERA and 213 strikeouts.

Almost as impressive as Clemens's six Cy Youngs and one MVP award are his four other top ten finishes in both the Cy Young and MVP voting.

❷ BOB GIBSON

WHENEVER BASEBALL'S GREATEST PITCHERS ARE DISCUSSED, BOB GIBSON'S NAME IS usually mentioned. But for some reason Juan Marichal's name never seems to come up. This is somewhat confusing because, if you look at their numbers, there really was very little that separated the two. In fact, with the exception of strikeouts, Marichal's numbers actually compared quite favorably to Gibson's. Marichal had a higher winning percentage and, in almost the same number of innings, walked slightly more than half the batters that Gibson did. Gibson was a 20-game winner five times, while Marichal topped the 20-mark six times. Gibson finished with an ERA under 3.00 seven times, while Marichal's ERA was under 3.00 nine times. Perhaps what explains the Marichal snub is that Gibson, as was mentioned earlier, established himself as a great big-game pitcher, while Marichal's postseason opportunities were limited to a brief appearance in the 1962 World Series and one start in the 1971 NLCS. Another reason could be that Marichal's reputation was greatly damaged by an incident that occurred in a 1965 game between his San Francisco Giants and the Los Angeles Dodgers. In that contest, the heated rivalry between the two teams turned into an ugly brawl.

At some point during the game, Marichal had hit one of the Dodger batters with a pitch. The next time Marichal came up to hit, Dodger catcher John Roseboro called for Dodger starter Sandy Koufax to retaliate. However, it was not in Koufax's nature to intentionally throw at batters, so he chose not to. Roseboro then took matters into his own hands and, when returning Koufax's pitch to the mound, threw the ball right by Marichal's ear. Marichal responded by hitting Roseboro over the head with his bat, thereby opening up a huge gash on the Dodger catcher's forehead. Needless to say, both benches emptied and a huge brawl ensued. As a result, Marichal's image suffered irreparable damage, to the point that he was not elected to the Hall of Fame until his third year of eligibility.

In any case, Marichal is not usually ranked as high as Gibson in any of the opinion polls. For that reason, Gibson gets the nod as number two right-handed starter.

Bob Gibson's first several big league seasons were not particularly happy ones. He had to struggle with his control those first few seasons, as well as with the racial stereotypes that were prevalent at that time about black pitchers. The view that many unfortunately held was that blacks didn't have the intelligence, or the heart, to become great pitchers. It was probably this attitude that caused Gibson to become the fierce competitor that he was and that gave him the burning desire to prove everyone wrong. Once Johnny Keane took over as Cardinals manager in the early 1960s, however, Gibson was given the vote of confidence he so badly needed, and he began to show what a truly great pitcher he would become.

From 1963 to 1972, Gibson won at least 18 games every season except two, and struck out more than 200 batters each year except one. He won 20 or more games five times and had an ERA under 3.00 seven times. Gibson led the National League in wins, ERA, strikeouts, and complete games once each, and in shutouts four times.

Gibson's finest season came in 1968, when he won both the N.L. MVP and Cy Young awards. That year, his record was 22-9 and he led the league with a 1.12 ERA, 268 strikeouts, and 13 shutouts.

He also threw 28 complete games. His 1.12 ERA was the fourth lowest ever by a starting pitcher, and the lowest ever by any pitcher with more than 300 innings pitched. Gibson had another outstanding season in 1969, when he finished 20-13 with a 2.18 ERA, 269 strikeouts, and a league-leading 28 complete games. The following season, Gibson won his second Cy Young award by compiling a 23-7 record, a 3.12 ERA, and 274 strikeouts.

Gibson is twelfth all-time in strikeouts and shutouts and was the first major leaguer to strike out more than 200 batters in nine seasons. He was also an excellent hitting pitcher, totaling 24 home runs during his career, and an exceptional fielder, having won nine Gold Gloves.

However, it was Gibson's performances in the World Series that truly defined his career. He won two games in the 1964 World Series, and then three more in the 1967 Series. In that '67 Series, he threw three complete games against the Red Sox and only gave up three earned runs. Then, in Game One of the 1968 World Series against the Detroit Tigers, he set a World Series record that still stands: 17 strikeouts. He also won Game Four to set a Series record with seven consecutive victories. Although he lost Game Seven to Mickey Lolich, he finished with a Series record of 7-2, an ERA of 1.89, and eight complete games in nine Series starts to establish himself as one of the greatest big-game pitchers of all time.

❸ JUAN MARICHAL

JUAN MARICHAL WAS A TRULY GREAT pitcher who had a habit of finishing second best. As a result, although he had some truly remarkable seasons, he never won a Cy Young award. Sandy Koufax thwarted him three times in his attempt to come away with the coveted trophy.

In 1963, Marichal finished 25-8 with a 2.41 ERA, 248 strikeouts, and 321 innings pitched, but Koufax won the award. In 1965, Marichal finished 22-13, with a 2.13 ERA, 240 strikeouts, 10 shutouts, 295 innings pitched, and 24 complete games, but Koufax won the award. In 1966, he finished 25-6, with a 2.23

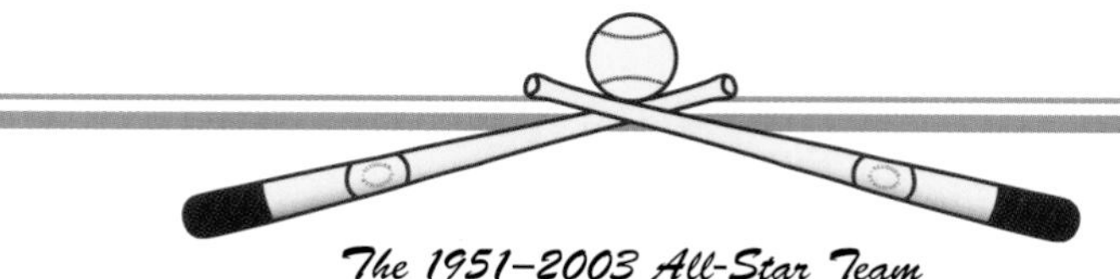

ERA, 222 strikeouts, 307 innings pitched, and 25 complete games, but yes—Koufax, once again, won the award.

But even when it wasn't Koufax, someone *else* always seemed to be standing in Marichal's way. In 1964, he had another fine season, but the award went to the American League's Dean Chance, who finished that season with 20 wins and a 1.65 ERA. Then, in 1968, Marichal led the N.L. with 26 wins and 326 innings pitched, and finished with a 2.43 ERA, 218 strikeouts, and 30 complete games. However, that year, Bob Gibson finished with an ERA of 1.12 and came away with the award. Marichal came close one more time, in 1969, when he won 21 games, and led the league with a 2.10 ERA and eight shutouts. Tom Seaver, however, won 25 games for the Mets that year and walked off with the award.

So Marichal will have to settle for the distinction of having won more games (191) during the 1960s than any other pitcher. He also led the N.L. in wins, complete games, shutouts, and innings pitched twice each, and in ERA once. In all, he was a 20-game winner six times, winning at least 25 games three times, and he finished with an ERA under 3.00 nine times, also bettering the 2.50 mark six times. He may very well be the most underrated and overlooked great pitcher in baseball history.

4 GREG MADDUX

THERE IS VERY LITTLE SEPARATING GREG Maddux and Tom Seaver. Both are—in the case of Seaver, were—great right-handers who had the distinction of being the best pitcher in the National League for much of their careers. While the two had completely different styles on the mound, the results were very similar. Maddux is all finesse, working the corners of the plate to perfection, and relying mostly on his superb control and ball movement. Seaver, while also possessing excellent control, was more of a power pitcher, relying on a great fastball, as well as an excellent change-up.

The two primary factors that earned Maddux fourth place, just ahead of Seaver, were his remarkable control (only 838 walks in just under 4,000 innings pitched) and his outstanding ERA of

2.89. While this is slightly higher than Seaver's 2.86, when one considers that Maddux has accomplished this primarily during a hitter's era, it is truly an outstanding feat.

Greg Maddux is one of only a handful of pitchers to have won as many as four Cy Young awards, and one of just two to have won it four consecutive years (Randy Johnson is the other). He won his first while pitching for the Chicago Cubs in 1992. That season, Maddux finished 20-11 with a 2.18 ERA and 268 innings pitched. He won the award the next three seasons as a member of the Atlanta Braves. In 1993, he finished 20-10 with a 2.36 ERA and 267 innings pitched. In the strike-shortened 1994 season, he was 16-6 with a 1.56 ERA. The following year, he finished 19-2 with a 1.63 ERA.

In all, Maddux has led the National League in wins three times and in ERA five times. He has won 20 games twice and at least 18 games seven other times. He also has finished with an ERA under 3 runs a game nine times, and with one below 2.5 runs a game six times. Evidence of Maddux's remarkable consistency can be found in his sixteen consecutive seasons with at least 15 wins, a streak that was continued in 2003.

5 TOM SEAVER

Tom Seaver just edged out Jim Palmer for the number five spot for a couple of reasons. First, he managed to win 311 games even though he spent most of his career pitching for mediocre teams. In addition, while both pitchers finished with a career ERA of 2.86, Seaver was slightly more dominant, having better strikeout-to-walk and hits-to-innings-pitched ratios.

Known simply as "The Franchise" in his years with the New York Mets, Tom Seaver helped bring respectability and a world championship to a team that previously had never finished out of the second division. In his years with the Mets, Seaver won three Cy Young awards and became the greatest player in that organization's history. He won the award for the first time in 1969, when he finished 25-7 with a 2.21 ERA, 208 strikeouts, and 273 innings pitched, while helping to lead his team to the N.L. pennant and world championship. He finished runner-up that season to Willie McCovey in the N.L. MVP voting.

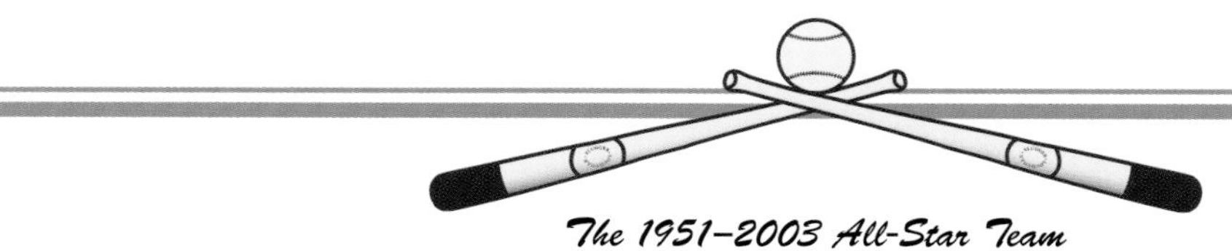

Seaver won the award for the second time in 1973 when he went 19-10 with a league-leading 2.08 ERA and 251 strikeouts, along with 290 innings pitched. He won the award for the last time in 1975, when he finished 22-9 with a 2.38 ERA, a league-leading 243 strikeouts, and 280 innings pitched. Seaver actually had one of his finest seasons in 1971, even though he finished runner-up to Ferguson Jenkins in the Cy Young balloting. That year, Seaver's record was 20-10 and he finished with a league-leading 1.76 ERA and 289 strikeouts. He also finished in the top five in the Cy Young voting two other times.

In all, Seaver led the N.L. in wins and ERA three times each, and in strikeouts five times. He was a 20-game winner five times and finished twelve times with an ERA under 3.00, and five times under 2.50. He also struck out more than 200 batters ten times, including a major league record nine straight seasons from 1968 to 1976.

Honorable mention should be given to Jim Palmer, Robin Roberts, Ferguson Jenkins, Nolan Ryan, and Pedro Martinez:

Jim Palmer was the best pitcher in the American League during the 1970s. Pitching for the Baltimore Orioles, he won at least 20 games eight times, leading the league in wins for three consecutive seasons, beginning in 1975, and winning three Cy Young awards along the way. Palmer won the award for the first time in 1973 when he finished 22-9, led the league with a 2.40 ERA, and had 296 innings pitched. He then won the award in both 1975 and 1976. The first of those seasons, Palmer led the league in wins, as he finished 23-11, and with a 2.09 ERA and 10 shutouts. He had 323 innings pitched and 25 complete games that season. The following year, Palmer once again led the league in wins, as he finished 22-13, with a 2.51 ERA, 23 complete games, and a league-leading 315 innings pitched.

In all, Palmer led the A.L. in ERA twice and in innings pitched four times. He also finished with an ERA under 3.00 nine times, under 2.50 five times, and with more than 300 innings pitched four times.

Robin Roberts was, with the possible exception of Warren Spahn, the most durable pitcher in baseball during the 1950s. Pitching for a Philadelphia Phillies team that was for the most part very mediocre, Roberts led the National League in wins four times, in innings pitched five times, in complete games five times, and in strikeouts twice—all within a five-year stretch beginning in 1951. For the four-year period, from 1952 to 1955, he rivaled Spahn as the game's best pitcher. His numbers for those four seasons:

1952—28 WINS, 7 LOSSES; 2.59 ERA; 330 INNINGS PITCHED; 30 COMPLETE GAMES
1953—23 WINS, 16 LOSSES; 2.75 ERA; 346 INNINGS PITCHED; 33 COMPLETE GAMES
1954—23 WINS, 15 LOSSES; 2.97 ERA; 336 INNINGS PITCHED; 29 COMPLETE GAMES
1955—23 WINS, 14 LOSSES; 3.28 ERA; 305 INNINGS PITCHED; 26 COMPLETE GAMES

In all, Roberts was a 20-game winner six times, finished with an ERA under 3.00 runs a game six times, pitched more than 300 innings six times, and completed more than 20 games eight times.

Although more of a strikeout pitcher, Ferguson Jenkins was a lot like Robin Roberts in that he was extremely durable and pitched mostly for teams that were very mediocre. Having most of his finest seasons while a member of the Chicago Cubs, Jenkins won at least 20 games seven times during his career, including six straight seasons from 1967 to 1972. He led the league in wins twice, in strikeouts once, in innings pitched once, and in complete games four times. Jenkins finished with an ERA under 3.00 four times, which, when one considers that he pitched half his games in Chicago's windy Wrigley Field, was a major accomplishment. He also struck out more than 200 batters six times, had more than 300 innings pitched five times, and had at least 20 complete games eight times.

Jenkins was awarded the National League's Cy Young in 1971, when he finished with a record of 24-13 to lead the league in wins, an ERA of 2.77, 263 strikeouts, and a league-leading 325 innings pitched and 30 complete games. After being traded to the Texas Rangers for Bill Madlock, Jenkins had another outstanding season in 1974. That year, he finished 25-12, with a 2.82 ERA, 328 innings pitched, and 29 complete games, to finish runner-up to Catfish Hunter in the A.L. Cy Young balloting.

Despite bouts with inconsistency that plagued him during his career, Nolan Ryan, at his best, was one of the most dominant pitchers the game has ever seen. His 7 no-hitters and 5,714 career strikeouts, which place him first on the all-time list, are a testament to that. Ryan won 20 games twice, finished with an ERA under 3.00 eight times, under 2.50 twice, struck out over 300 batters six times, and over 200 batters nine other times, and had more than 300 innings pitched twice. He led his league in ERA twice, in shutouts three times, and in strikeouts eleven times.

Ryan had two of his finest seasons for the California Angels in 1973 and 1974. The first of those two seasons, he finished 21-16 with a 2.87 ERA, 383 strikeouts, 326 innings pitched, and 26 complete games. He followed that up the next season by going 22-16 with a 2.89 ERA, 367 strikeouts, 332 innings pitched, and 26 complete games.

He had another outstanding year for the Houston Astros in the strike-shortened 1981 season, when he finished 11-5 with a league-leading 1.69 ERA. Then, pitching for the Texas Rangers in 1989, at the age of forty-two, Ryan finished 16-10 with a 3.20 ERA and a league-leading 301 strikeouts.

From 1997 to 2000, Pedro Martinez put together four of the most dominant seasons of any pitcher since Sandy Koufax was mesmerizing batters during the 1960s. During that period, Martinez won three Cy Young awards and led his league in wins once, in ERA three times, and in strikeouts three times. His numbers over that four-year span:

1997—17 wins, 8 losses; 1.90 ERA; 305 strikeouts
1998—19 wins, 7 losses; 2.89 ERA; 251 strikeouts
1999—23 wins, 4 losses; 2.07 ERA; 313 strikeouts (won pitcher's Triple Crown)
2000—18 wins, 6 losses; 1.74 ERA; 284 strikeouts

If one were to compare Martinez's numbers to the league averages over that period, it might be suggested that those four seasons are among the best by any pitcher in a long, long time.

After suffering through an injury-plagued 2001 season in which he finished 7-3 with a 2.39 ERA, Martinez returned to top form in 2002, compiling a record of 20-4 and an ERA of 2.26 to finish runner-up in the Cy Young voting for the second time in his career. In all, he has won at least 20 games twice, compiled an ERA of less than 3.00 eight times, including the last seven years in succession, and allowed less than 2.50 runs a game in each of the last five seasons. He has led his league in ERA a total of five times.

As was the case in both 2000 and 2001, Martinez experienced occasional tenderness in his pitching arm during the 2003 season that limited his starting assignments and the number of innings he was allowed to work. Yet he still managed to finish with a 14-4 record and a league-leading 2.22 ERA. However, Martinez's durability seems to be somewhat questionable at this point in his career, a fact that may very well prevent him from ever being able to break into the top five.

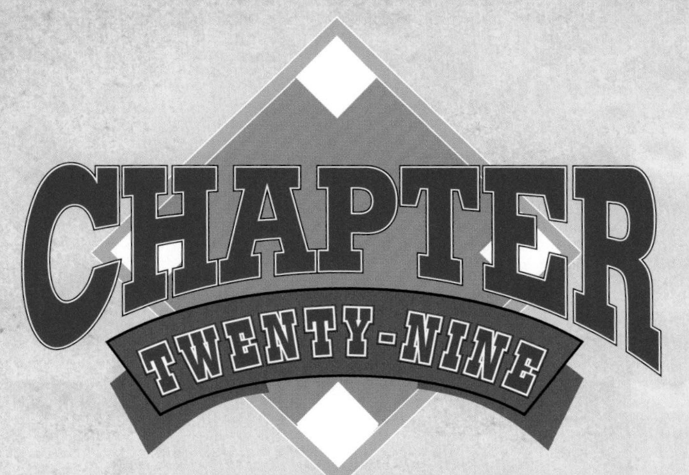

All-Star Left-Handed Pitcher

PITCHER	YEARS	W	L	PCT	ERA	GS	CG	IP	H	BB	SO
1) SANDY KOUFAX	1955–66	165	87	.655	2.76	314	137	2,324	1,754	817	2,396
2) WARREN SPAHN	1946–65	363	245	.597	3.09	665	382	5,243	4,830	1,434	2,583
3) STEVE CARLTON	1965–88	329	244	.574	3.22	709	254	5,217	4,672	1,833	4,136
4) RANDY JOHNSON*	1988–2003	230	114	.669	3.10	444	88	3,122	2,435	1,258	3,871
5) WHITEY FORD	1950, 1953–67	236	106	.690	2.75	438	156	3,170	2,766	1,086	1,956
HONORABLE MENTION:											
TOM GLAVINE*	1987–2003	251	157	.615	3.43	537	52	3,528	3,379	1,206	2,136

* Indicates player is still active

❶ SANDY KOUFAX

ALTHOUGH THE CAREER STATISTICS OF BOTH WARREN SPAHN AND STEVE CARLTON FAR exceed those of Sandy Koufax, the latter is the choice for top left-handed pitcher of the last fifty years. While Spahn and Carlton each had twice as many wins as Koufax, neither had, with the exception of 1972 when Carlton had one of the finest seasons a pitcher has ever had, the kind of dominant seasons that Koufax strung together from 1963 to 1966. He was so great, and stood so far above all others of his time, that he must be given the nod over Spahn and Carlton.

Don Sutton, when discussing Koufax in a television interview, said: "In my thirty-three years around major league baseball, I've seen some remarkable pitchers. Greg Maddux is a remarkable artist. Bob Gibson was a dominator. Tom Seaver was outstanding. Carlton was magnificent. But the man who stands alone as the most dominating pitcher I ever saw, without a doubt, and with no equal, is Sandy Koufax."

High praise from an outstanding pitcher in his own right, but well-deserved. Though Koufax struggled mightily with his control his first six big league seasons, he began putting it all together in

1961. That year, and the next, he developed into an outstanding pitcher, winning 18 games and finishing with a league-leading 269 strikeouts in 1961 and winning 14 games, striking out 216, and leading the league with a 2.54 ERA in 1962, despite missing part of the season due to arm problems. Then in 1963 Koufax became a truly great pitcher, very possibly the greatest the game has ever seen. Over the next four seasons, he would win the Cy Young award three times, even though only one was given out for both leagues combined, and win the pitcher's Triple Crown three times. He would also win the N.L. MVP award once, finish runner-up two other times, lead the league in wins three times, in ERA every year, in strikeouts three times, in innings pitched twice, in shutouts three times, and in complete games twice. In all, Koufax would lead the league in ERA five times, win more than 20 games, finish with an ERA under 2.00, strike out more than 300 batters, pitch more than 300 innings, and complete more than 20 games three times each, and throw 4 no-hitters and 1 perfect game. His win-loss record from 1962 to 1966 was a remarkable 111-34. Let's look at his numbers from 1963 to 1966:

1963—25 WINS, 5 LOSSES; 1.88 ERA; 306 STRIKEOUTS; 311 INNINGS PITCHED; 11 SHUTOUTS; 20 COMPLETE GAMES
1964—19 WINS, 5 LOSSES; 1.74 ERA; 223 STRIKEOUTS; 7 SHUTOUTS
1965—26 WINS, 8 LOSSES; 2.04 ERA; 382 STRIKEOUTS; 335 INNINGS PITCHED; 8 SHUTOUTS; 27 COMPLETE GAMES
1966—27 WINS, 9 LOSSES; 1.73 ERA; 317 STRIKEOUTS; 323 INNINGS PITCHED; 5 SHUTOUTS; 27 COMPLETE GAMES

Unfortunately, during that 1964 season Koufax missed some time due to an arthritic condition he was developing in his arm; the problem would eventually cause him to retire when he was still at the top of his game, at the age of thirty. However, he was so dominant over that four-year period that he not only won three Cy Youngs, but also won the N.L. MVP award in 1963, and finished a close second to Willie Mays in 1965, and to Roberto Clemente in 1966.

Mays once said that Koufax was so difficult to hit that, even though he knew what he was going to throw him on virtually every pitch, "it didn't make any difference. He would still strike me out two or three times every game."

John Roseboro, Koufax's catcher with the Dodgers for most of his career, once told the story of the first time Mickey Mantle faced Koufax, in the 1963 World Series. In the bottom of the second inning of Game One, Koufax started Mantle off with a sharp-breaking curve ball that Mickey could do nothing but look at. The next pitch was a fastball on the outside corner. As Roseboro tells it, Mantle then stepped out of the batter's box, looked at him, and muttered, "How the *bleep* are you supposed to hit stuff like that?" Koufax went on to set a World Series record with 15 strikeouts in that game (a record that would eventually be broken by Bob Gibson), and the Dodgers would go on to sweep the Yankees in four straight games.

Koufax was usually at his best in the World Series. In 1965, after refusing to pitch the first game against the Minnesota Twins because it conflicted with Yom Kippur, the holiest of Jewish holidays, he went on to pitch shutouts in Games Five and Seven, the last being a three-hitter on only two days' rest. In eight World Series games, he had a 0.95 ERA. Perhaps that is why, when asked who he would most like to have pitch for him if he had only one game he had to win, Casey Stengel once said: "I'll take the Jewish kid."

❷ WARREN SPAHN

CHOOSING BETWEEN WARREN SPAHN AND STEVE Carlton was difficult. Although Carlton accumulated many more strikeouts in almost the same number of innings pitched, Spahn won more games, had a higher winning percentage, and finished with a lower earned run average. Carlton won four Cy Young awards to Spahn's one, but that argument loses all credibility when you consider that the award wasn't presented until 1956, halfway into Spahn's career. Had it been presented earlier, there is little doubt that Spahn would have come away with two or three others. Let's look at his numbers in some of those seasons: In 1947, he finished with a record of 21-10 and he led the N.L. with a 2.33 ERA, 289 innings pitched, and 7 shutouts, while throwing 22 complete games. In 1949, Spahn finished 21-14 to lead the league in wins. He also led the league with 302 innings pitched and 25 complete games, and finished with a 3.07 ERA. In 1953, he led the league in both wins and ERA, finishing 23-7, with a 2.10 ERA, 265 innings pitched, and 24 complete games. However, the greatest argument that can be made in Spahn's behalf were his thirteen 20-win seasons, the most by any major league pitcher during the 20th century. That, more than anything else, earned him a spot on the second team, just ahead of Carlton.

Warren Spahn won more games during his career (363) than any other left-handed pitcher in baseball history. He is fifth on the all-time list in wins, sixth in shutouts, and eighth in innings pitched. He led the National League in wins eight times, including five consecutive seasons from 1957 to 1961. He also led the league in ERA three times, in strikeouts, innings pitched, and shutouts four times each, and in complete games nine times, including seven in a row from 1957 to 1963. Spahn finished with an ERA under 3.00 nine times, with more than 300 innings pitched twice, and with at least 20 complete games twelve times. He finished in the top five in the Cy Young voting in five of the first six years it was presented (1956–1961), and won the award himself in 1957. That season, Spahn finished 21-11 with a 2.69 ERA, 271 innings pitched, and 18 complete games to help lead the Milwaukee Braves to the N.L. pennant and world championship. He finished in the top five in the league MVP voting that year, one of four times he'd do so in his career.

Spahn was so durable that, in 1963, at the age of forty-two, he finished with a record of 23-7, an ERA of 2.60, 259 innings pitched, and 22 complete games.

Stan Musial once said of him: "I don't think Spahn will ever get into the Hall of Fame. He'll never stop pitching."

❸ STEVE CARLTON

STEVE CARLTON RECEIVED STIFF COMPETITION from Randy Johnson for a spot on the third team. True, Carlton won almost 100 more games during his career than the still-active Johnson has thus far won. However, Carlton also lost well over 100 more and finished with a much lower winning percentage. Johnson's ERA is also slightly lower and, considering the hitter's era in which he is pitching, that is quite impressive. Johnson has also struck out almost as many batters in far fewer innings. A legitimate case could therefore be made for picking him over Carlton.

However, the latter should be given a certain amount of credit for his greater consistency over a longer period of time. He was an outstanding pitcher for a very long time—most of his career in fact. From the late 1960s to 1982, when Carlton won the last of his four Cy Young awards, he was a superb pitcher. Johnson, on the other hand, struggled with his control early in his career, three times walking well over 100 batters,

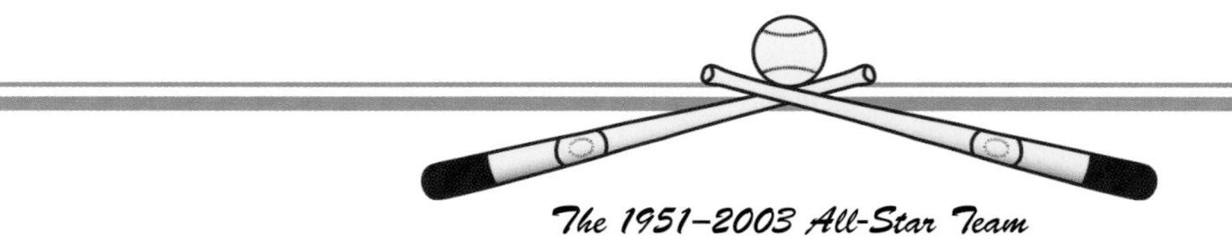

and failed to establish himself as a top starter during his first five seasons. He has, however, been extremely dominant over the last decade, even more dominant than Carlton was in most of his finest seasons.

Neither pitcher truly distinguished himself in the postseason. Carlton's record in the playoffs and World Series was 6-6 with a 3.17 ERA, while Johnson has posted a record of 4-5 and an ERA of 3.09. Johnson has won five Cy Youngs to Carlton's four, but the latter also finished in the top five in the league MVP voting three times, while Johnson has never finished any higher than sixth.

It was a difficult choice and to be honest, it wouldn't take too much to sway me to Johnson's side. But the decision went to Carlton. The determining factors were his sixteen seasons with more than 10 complete games (including 30 one season) and 200 innings pitched, and his twelve seasons with more than 250 innings pitched (including two with more than 300). These are numbers that Johnson cannot even approach. However, it should be added that one or two more outstanding seasons from Johnson would probably be enough to move him into the third slot.

In 1972, Steve Carlton had one of the greatest seasons a pitcher has ever had. Pitching for the last-place Philadelphia Phillies, he won a record 45 percent of his team's 59 wins, en route to winning the first of his four Cy Young awards. Carlton won the pitcher's Triple Crown that season, by finishing 27-10 with a 1.97 ERA and 310 strikeouts. He also led N.L. pitchers with 346 innings pitched and 30 complete games.

However, "Lefty," as Carlton would come to be known, was not a one-season phenomenon. He would win the Cy Young three more times during his career: in 1977, in 1980, and in 1982. In 1977 he led the league with 23 wins against only 10 losses, and finished with a 2.64 ERA, 198 strikeouts, and 283 innings pitched. In 1980 he finished 24-9 to once again lead the league in wins, and compiled a 2.34 ERA, while totaling a league-leading 286 strikeouts and 304 innings pitched. And in 1982 he finished 23-11 with a 3.10 ERA and a league-leading 286 strikeouts, 295 innings pitched, 6 shutouts, and 19 complete games.

In all, Carlton led National League pitchers in wins four times, ERA once, strikeouts five times, innings pitched five times, and complete games three times. He won 20 games six times, and finished with an ERA under 3.00 eight times, over 300 innings pitched twice, and more than 200 strikeouts eight times. He is second on the all-time strikeout list, behind only Nolan Ryan, and ninth in career victories.

4 RANDY JOHNSON

HAVING JUST MISSED OUT ON THE THIRD SPOT, RANDY JOHNSON WAS NOT GOING TO BE denied his spot on the fourth team. While Whitey Ford had a higher winning percentage and a lower earned run average, that was due mostly to the excellent Yankees teams he played on and the ballpark that he pitched half his games in (the "old" Yankee Stadium was a left-handed pitcher's paradise). Ford was not nearly as dominant as Johnson has been over the last ten seasons. Whitey struck out approximately half as many batters in about the same number of innings, won one Cy Young award to Johnson's five, and did not lead his league in the various pitching categories nearly as often as Johnson has.

Randy Johnson, now forty years old, just seems to get better with age. Always known as a hard thrower, he struggled with his control early in his career. However, after gaining a better command of the strike zone several seasons ago, Johnson has become one of the most dominant pitchers the game has seen in a long

time. Currently fourth on the all-time strikeout list, he struck out more than 200 batters in all but one season from 1992 to 2002. He also surpassed the 300-mark in each year from 1998 to 2002. Johnson has led his league in wins, ERA, complete games, and innings pitched four times each, and in strikeouts eight times. He has won more than 20 games three times, and won at least 18 games four other times. He has finished with an ERA under 3.00 six times, under 2.50 five times, and with more than 300 strikeouts six times.

Johnson won the first of his five Cy Youngs pitching for the Seattle Mariners in 1995. That season, he finished 18-2, with a league-leading 2.48 ERA and 294 strikeouts. He won the N.L. Cy Young award four consecutive seasons, beginning in 1999, pitching for the Arizona Diamondbacks. In the first of those years, he finished 17-9 with a 2.48 ERA and a league-leading 364 strikeouts. In 2000, his record was 19-7 with a 2.64 ERA and 347 strikeouts. The following season, he won the pitcher's Triple Crown by compiling a 21-6 record with a 2.49 ERA and 372 strikeouts. Johnson won the Triple Crown a second consecutive time in 2002, finishing the year with a 24-5 record, a 2.32 ERA, and 334 strikeouts. Johnson missed much of the 2003 campaign due to injury and, at age forty, one can only wonder if his best days are behind him. If they aren't, he is within striking distance of Steve Carlton for a spot on the third team.

5 WHITEY FORD

WHITEY FORD AND TOM GLAVINE WERE SIMILAR pitchers in that neither was particularly overpowering, but both had tremendous control of their pitches and a great command of the strike zone. Both also pitched for outstanding teams during their careers, in good pitcher's ballparks.

A look at their career statistics also illustrates how similar the two men were on the mound. Both had extremely high winning percentages and a similar number of innings pitched, bases on balls, and strikeouts. However, Ford had a much lower earned run average and approximately three times as many complete games in fewer starts. Those numbers, plus his reputation as an exceptional big-game pitcher, earned Ford a spot on the fifth team.

Whitey Ford was one of the best big-game pitchers in baseball during the era in which he played. He holds World Series records for most wins (10) and most consecutive scoreless innings pitched (32). He also has the highest career winning percentage of any pitcher since 1900 (.690).

During his career, Ford led the American League in wins three times, and in ERA, innings pitched, and shutouts twice each. He won more than 20 games twice, and had at least 18 wins three other times. He finished with an ERA under 3.00 ten times, and with one under 2.50 five times.

Ford won his only Cy Young award in 1961 when he finished 25-4 to lead the league in wins, and compiled a 3.21 ERA, 209 strikeouts, and a league-leading 283 innings pitched. He also had outstanding seasons in 1955, 1956, 1963, and 1964. Let's look at his numbers from those seasons:

1955—18 WINS, 7 LOSSES; 2.63 ERA; 253 INNINGS PITCHED; 18 COMPLETE GAMES
1956—19 WINS, 6 LOSSES; 2.47 ERA; 18 COMPLETE GAMES
1963—24 WINS, 7 LOSSES; 2.74 ERA; 269 INNINGS PITCHED
1964—17 WINS, 6 LOSSES; 2.13 ERA

Pitching most of his career under manager Casey Stengel, Ford only won 20 games twice because Stengel liked to manipulate the pitching rotation so that he would pitch mostly against the better teams in the league. Otherwise, his statistics might have been even more impressive. When Ralph Houk took over as manager of the Yankees in 1961, he chose to pitch Ford more regularly, on just three days' rest. The change in philosophy became quite apparent in Ford's win totals, as he won more than 20 games in two of the next three seasons. Even so, Ford managed to finish in the top five in the league MVP voting twice during his career.

Honorable mention should be given to Tom Glavine:

Tom Glavine has been one of the best and most consistent pitchers in the National League for more than a decade. While in his days in Atlanta, he frequently pitched in the shadow of his teammate, Greg Maddux, Glavine still managed to win two Cy Young awards. The first came in 1991 when he finished 20-11 to lead the league in wins, and compiled a 2.55 ERA and a league-leading nine complete games. The second came in 1998 when he led the league with 20 wins against only 6 losses, and finished with a 2.47 ERA. In all, Glavine has led the N.L. in wins four times. He has also been a 20-game winner five times and pitched to an ERA under 3.00 six times.

SOX
A's
NY
A's

All-Star Relief Pitcher

PITCHER	YEARS	W	L	PCT	SV	ERA	IP	H	BB	SO
1) DENNIS ECKERSLEY	1975–98	197	171	.535	390	3.50	3,285	3,076	738	2,401
2) ROLLIE FINGERS	1968–85	114	118	.491	341	2.90	1,701	1,474	492	1,299
3) MARIANO RIVERA*	1995–2003	43	29	.597	283	2.49	649	515	177	582
4) BRUCE SUTTER	1976–88	68	71	.489	300	2.83	1,042	879	309	861
5) HOYT WILHELM	1952–72	143	122	.540	227	2.52	2,254	1,757	778	1,610
HONORABLE MENTION:										
RICH GOSSAGE	1972–94	124	107	.537	310	3.01	1,809	1,497	732	1,502
LEE SMITH	1980–97	71	92	.436	478	3.03	1,289	1,133	486	1,251
JEFF REARDON	1979–94	73	77	.487	367	3.16	1,132	1,000	358	877
TREVOR HOFFMAN*	1993–2003	45	44	.506	352	2.78	709	533	217	806

* Indicates player is still active

1 DENNIS ECKERSLEY

IT WASN'T EASY TO DECIDE WHO THE NUMBER ONE RELIEF PITCHER SHOULD BE BETWEEN Rollie Fingers and Dennis Eckersley. Both were the premier closers of their time. Both won a Cy Young and an MVP award. In the end, the thing that tipped the scales in favor of Eckersley is that he was able to accomplish so much in his twelve years as a relief pitcher, after spending the first half of his career as a starter for three different teams.

Dennis Eckersley came up to the Cleveland Indians in 1975 as a starting pitcher. After spending three seasons there, he moved on to Boston where, pitching for the Red Sox in 1978, he had his finest season as a starter. That year, he finished with a 20-8 record, a 2.99 ERA, and 268 innings pitched. From there, Eckersley moved onto the Chicago Cubs, where he remained a starter until 1986.

However, after being acquired by the Oakland Athletics prior to the start of the 1987 season, manager Tony LaRussa elected to convert Eckersley into a relief pitcher, and, as they say, the rest is history. Eckersley would go on to become the best closer in the game, totaling more than 30 saves eight times and more than 40

four times, and leading the A.L. in that department twice. Showing remarkable control, he established a better than three-to-one strikeout-to-walk ratio as a reliever. In his second season as a closer, Eckersley was so effective that he finished runner-up to Minnesota's Frank Viola in the Cy Young balloting. The following year, he finished 4-0 with a 1.56 ERA and 33 saves, and surrendered only 32 hits in 57 innings pitched. In 1990, Eckersely finished 4-2 with 48 saves and an almost unbelievable 0.61 ERA, while giving up only 41 hits in 73 innings of work.

Eckersley had his biggest season in 1992, though, when he won both the A.L. Cy Young and MVP awards. That year, his record was 7-1, he led the league with 51 saves, and he finished with a 1.91 ERA. He also surrendered only 62 hits in 80 innings pitched, and walked only 11 batters while striking out 93. Eckersley was so dominant as a closer that he finished in the top five in the league MVP voting two other times during his career.

❷ ROLLIE FINGERS

ONE OF THE FIRST TRULY GREAT RELIEF PITCHERS, AND only the second to be elected to the Hall of Fame, Rollie Fingers served as closer for three different teams during his career. He first gained recognition when he filled that role on the Oakland

Athletics teams that won three consecutive world championships from 1972 to 1974. From there, he moved on to the San Diego Padres and then to the Milwaukee Brewers. It was with Milwaukee in 1981 that Fingers had his greatest season, winning both the A.L. Cy Young and MVP awards. In that strike-shortened season, Fingers compiled a record of 6-3, a 1.04 ERA, a league-leading 28 saves, giving up only 55 hits in 78 innings pitched and walking only 13 batters, while striking out 61.

In all, Fingers led his league in saves three times and in appearances three times. He had more than 30 saves twice, more than 10 wins four times, and finished with an ERA under 2.00 three times.

3 MARIANO RIVERA

IT WAS CLOSE BETWEEN MARIANO RIVERA AND Bruce Sutter for the number three spot, but Rivera got the nod because of his higher winning percentage, lower earned run average, better than three-to-one strikeout-to-walk ratio, and integral role in one of the greatest postseason runs in baseball history.

Although he has only been in the big leagues for nine seasons, Mariano Rivera has already shown that he deserves to be mentioned with the best closers ever. Originally the Yankees' set-up man for closer John Wetteland, Rivera assumed the closer role himself in 1997. In the seven seasons since, he has had more than 30 saves six times, topping the 40 mark four times and leading the league in that department twice. He also has finished with an ERA under 2.00 four times. His numbers were particularly impressive from 1997 to 2001. They read as follows:

1997—6 WINS AND 4 LOSSES; 43 SAVES; 1.88 ERA; 71 INNINGS PITCHED, 65 HITS
1998—3 WINS AND 0 LOSSES; 36 SAVES; 1.91 ERA; 61 INNINGS PITCHED, 48 HITS
1999—4 WINS AND 3 LOSSES; 45 SAVES; 1.83 ERA; 69 INNINGS PITCHED, 43 HITS
2000—7 WINS AND 4 LOSSES; 36 SAVES; 2.85 ERA; 75 INNINGS PITCHED, 58 HITS
2001—4 WINS AND 6 LOSSES; 50 SAVES; 2.34 ERA; 80 INNINGS PITCHED, 61 HITS

More importantly, in Rivera's first seven full seasons as a member of the New York Yankees, they won five pennants and four World Series. He has been practically unhittable in the postseason, compiling through 2002 a lifetime record of 6-1 with 25 saves and a 0.90 ERA. Perhaps more than any other player, he was responsible for the success the Yankees had in the playoffs and World Series between 1996 and 2000.

4 BRUCE SUTTER

WHEN HE WAS AT THE TOP OF HIS GAME DURING THE late 1970s and early 1980s, Bruce Sutter was one of the most dominant closers the game has seen. Pitching mostly for the Chicago Cubs and St. Louis Cardinals, Sutter led the National League in saves five times, including four times in a row from 1979 to 1982. He compiled more than 30 saves four times and finished with an ERA under 2.00 twice.

Pitching for the Cubs, in 1977, Sutter finished 7-3 with 31 saves, a 1.34 ERA, gave up only 69 hits in 107 innings of work, and walked only 23 batters while striking out 129. He won the N.L. Cy Young award in 1979 when he finished 6-6 with a league-leading 37 saves and an ERA of 2.22. He also surrendered only 67 hits in 101 innings pitched, and walked only 32 batters while striking out 110. In 1984, while pitching for the Cardinals, Sutter led the league with 45 saves, compiled a 1.54 ERA, and walked only 23 batters while striking out 77.

In all, Sutter finished in the top five in the Cy Young balloting four times and finished in the top five in the league MVP voting once.

5 HOYT WILHELM

HOYT WILHELM WAS A BIT OF A PIONEER IN THAT HE became one of the first pitchers to have a lengthy major league career while being used almost exclusively in relief. Although he was employed occasionally as a starter during the first half of his career, Wilhelm gained fame as one of the first relief specialists.

In his first big league season, with the Giants in 1952, Wilhelm, pitching mostly in relief, compiled a record of 15-3 with a league-leading 2.43 ERA and 11 saves in 71 appearances. After being used as a starter by the Baltimore Orioles in 1959, winning 15 games and leading the league with a 2.19 ERA, Wilhelm eventually wound up with the Chicago White Sox, where he became a full-time reliever. He had more than 20 saves three years in a row, from 1963 to 1965, and finished with an ERA under 2.00 seven times, including five straight seasons, from 1964 to 1968. Using a knuckleball that put less stress on his pitching arm, Wilhelm was able to stay in the majors until he was forty-nine, become the all-time leader in appearances (1,070), and become the first relief pitcher to be elected to the Hall of Fame.

Honorable mention should be given to Rich Gossage, Lee Smith, Jeff Reardon and Trevor Hoffman:

Rich "Goose" Gossage, with his scowl and blazing fastball, was the most intimidating relief pitcher of his time. He led the American League in saves three times, compiling more than 30 in a season twice and more than 20 eight other times. He also finished with an ERA under 2.00 four times.

Pitching for the Pirates in 1977, he finished 11-9 with 26 saves and a 1.62 ERA. That season, he gave up only 78 hits in 133 innings of work and walked only 49 batters, while striking out 151. The following season, with the Yankees, he led the A.L. with 27 saves, finished with a 2.01 ERA, surrendered only 87 hits in 134 innings, and walked 59 while striking out 122. In 1980, he finished 6-2 with a league-leading 33 saves and an ERA of 2.27. Gossage was practically unhittable during the strike-shortened 1981 season. That year, he finished 3-2 with 20 saves, a 0.77 ERA, gave up 22 hits in 46 innings, and walked 14 while striking out 48.

Lee Smith is the all-time leader in saves with 478. During his career, he led his league in saves four times, finishing with more than 30 nine times and more than 40 three times. He also finished with an ERA under 2.00 twice.

Smith had his finest seasons pitching for the Cubs and Cardinals. In 1983, with the Cubs, he compiled a 1.65 ERA, led the N.L. with 29 saves, and gave up only 70 hits in 103 innings pitched. With the Cardinals in 1991, Smith finished 6-3 with a 2.34 ERA, a league-leading 47 saves, and walked only 13 batters while striking out 67. He finished each of the next two seasons with 43 saves.

Jeff Reardon had at least 20 saves eleven years in a row from 1982 to 1992. Pitching mostly with the Expos and Twins, he had more than 30 saves seven times, more than 40 three times, and led the league in that department once.

Trevor Hoffman has been the closer for the San Diego Padres since 1994. He's arguably been the best relief pitcher in the National League since 1996. In the seven seasons from 1996 to 2002, he surpassed 40 saves five times, compiling a career-high and league-leading 53 in 1998. In that 1998 season, he finished with a brilliant 1.48 earned run average, surrendered only 41 hits in 73 innings of work, and struck out 86 batters while walking only 21. Two seasons later, he walked only 11 batters in 72 innings of work while striking out 85. After another outstanding season in 2002, in which he saved 38 games in 41 save opportunities, Hoffman missed virtually all of the 2003 campaign due to injury. He will need to return to top form in 2004 and put together two or three more solid years if he is going to have any chance of breaking into the top five.

NOW THAT THE SELECTIONS HAVE BEEN MADE FOR THE SECOND HALF OF THE CENTURY, it is time to make out the lineups.

FIRST TEAM:		SECOND TEAM:	
1.	Willie Mays *CF*	1.	Roberto Alomar *2B*
2.	Joe Morgan *2B*	2.	George Brett *3B*
3.	Stan Musial *1B*	3.	Roberto Clemente *RF*
4.	Hank Aaron *LF*	4.	Mickey Mantle *CF*
5.	Frank Robinson *RF*	5.	Barry Bonds *LF*
6.	Edgar Martinez *DH*	6.	Eddie Murray *1B*
7.	Mike Schmidt *3B*	7.	Yogi Berra *C*
8.	Ernie Banks *SS*	8.	Cal Ripken, Jr. *SS*
9.	Johnny Bench *C*	9.	Harold Baines *DH*
RHP	Roger Clemens	*RHP*	Bob Gibson
LHP	Sandy Koufax	*LHP*	Warren Spahn
R	Dennis Eckersley	*R*	Rollie Fingers

The first-team lineup is a little right-handed heavy, with Morgan and Musial providing the only left-handed bats. But it offers good speed, with Mays, Morgan, Aaron, and Robinson, and excellent power throughout. Mays batting leadoff might seem a bit strange, but the N.L. used to put him there occasionally in the All-Star game, and he always seemed to thrive in that role.

The second-team lineup offers a great deal of versatility, as it features three switch-hitters in Alomar, Mantle, and Murray. It also has good speed and excellent base-running skills from Alomar, Brett, Clemente, Mantle, and Bonds, and good power, especially from the middle of the order in Mantle, Bonds, and Murray.

SEVEN PASS. TOURING CARS
FIVE PASS. TOURING CARS
ALSO BY WEEK OR MONTH

PART FIVE

Baseball's All-Time All-Star Team

Selecting the Best of the Best

WE HAVE ALREADY DISCUSSED MANY OF THE CHANGES THAT HAVE TAKEN PLACE IN THE game over the past hundred or so years. In particular, we looked at the way the game evolved during each half of the past century, and noted how difficult it is to compare players from different eras, within each fifty-year period. Now, the time has come to take things one step further and select the greatest players from both periods, combined. This is an even more difficult task, for a number of reasons.

First, there are the many phases the game went through during the twentieth century, causing it to eventually evolve into the game we know today. Night ball has become far more prevalent, there is a much greater reliance on relief pitching, and, more recently, there has been an increase in offensive productivity.

However, another huge obstacle to selecting an all-time team involves the breaking of the color barrier. Some might ask how the players from an era in which the game was segregated could be compared to those who played after the color line was broken. If the great black and Hispanic players of the day were not permitted to compete against the white major leaguers, are not the achievements of players such as Babe Ruth, Honus Wagner, Rogers Hornsby, and Lefty Grove diminished somewhat? It is certainly true that the general public was deprived of the opportunity to witness the excellence of players such as Josh Gibson, Satchel Paige, and Oscar Charleston. It is also true that the level of competition in the major leagues had to suffer, somewhat, as a result. However, one other important factor must be considered.

For the entire first half of the twentieth century, there were only sixteen major league teams. In fact, it wasn't until 1962 that the majors expanded to twenty franchises, and it took another seven years to increase the number to twenty-four. Of course, six more teams have since then been added. So while it is true that, prior to the integration of the game in 1947, the overall talent pool of players who were eligible to compete in the major leagues was not what it would eventually become, there were also far fewer teams. It therefore follows that there was less dilution of the talent that was available. As a result, while some of the greatest players in the game were not playing in the major leagues, the number of stars, and players of lesser ability as well, who were on the rosters of each club was essentially the same. The level of competition was therefore most likely comparable to what it would have been otherwise.

Others might point out that great hitters such as Lou Gehrig, Jimmie Foxx, and Ty Cobb played before pitches such as the split-fingered fastball and slider came into use, and that they didn't have to hit

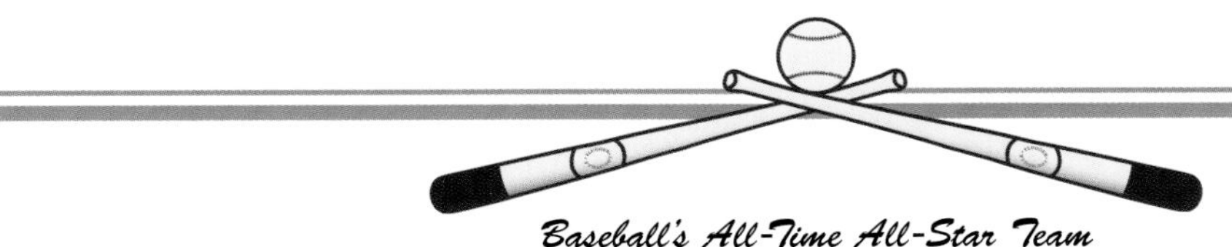

against a fresh relief pitcher in the latter stages of most games. While this is true, it is also true that they didn't have many of the advantages that modern hitters have. They played in an era when the ball was not as lively as it would later become. They never had an opportunity to view themselves on film to look for flaws in their hitting mechanics. They played before weight training became the norm. Steroids were the stuff of science fiction. And pitchers were far less tentative about pitching inside to hitters, and even knocking them down. So how can the advantages and disadvantages that the players from different periods had be weighed against each other, and how much of an effect did they have on their overall performance? There really is no definitive answer, since no one will ever know for sure. However, the attitude I've adopted is that a great player from one era would be a great player in any era, and he should be judged within the context of the era in which he played.

Finally, the task of making this last set of selections is made even more difficult by the fact that it involves picking the greatest players of *all time*—the best of the best. The top players of each period have already been named, and now they must be whittled down to an even more select group. In some cases, the choices will not be too difficult. However, in others, a great deal of contemplation and deliberation will be required.

As was done in the previous rankings, the top five players at each position will be listed, in order, and an explanation will be given as to why each player was selected. However, many of the players' career highlights, and their statistics, will not be repeated here since they were touched on in the previous sections.

It is now time to move on to the final selections.

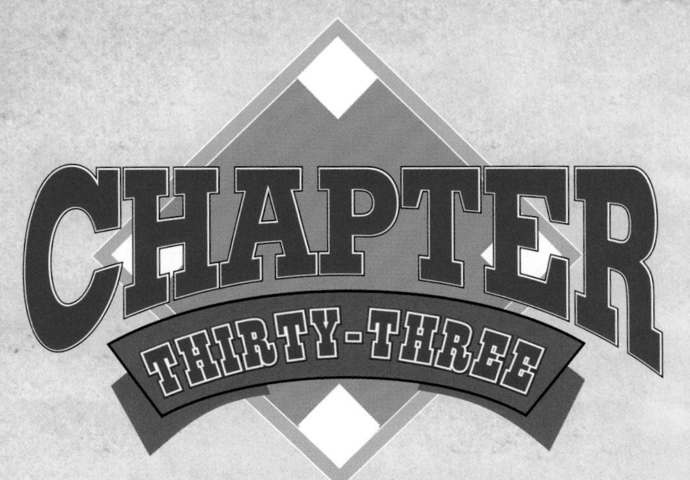

All-Time All-Star First Baseman

LOU GEHRIG

JIMMIE FOXX

STAN MUSIAL

GEORGE SISLER

HANK GREENBERG

1 LOU GEHRIG

AS WAS MENTIONED EARLIER, LOU GEHRIG IS GENERALLY CONSIDERED TO BE THE greatest first baseman in baseball history. You'll find no disagreement with that opinion here. Gehrig was the greatest run producer, the most consistent, and the most durable. Having survived the challenge of Jimmie Foxx earlier, there was no one else who was going to dethrone him.

While Stan Musial was a great player, Gehrig was far more productive and had much more power. In almost 3,000 fewer career at-bats, Gehrig had more home runs, more runs batted in, a higher batting average, a higher on-base percentage, a much higher slugging percentage, only 60 fewer runs scored, and almost as many triples. While Musial won seven batting titles to Gehrig's one, he never led the league in home runs—something Gehrig did three times—and he only led the league in RBI twice—something Gehrig did five times. Also, while Musial never hit 40 homers in a season, Gehrig did so five times. He also had a Triple Crown to his credit and still holds the American League RBI record with 184 in 1931. So Lou Gehrig remains the greatest first baseman of all time.

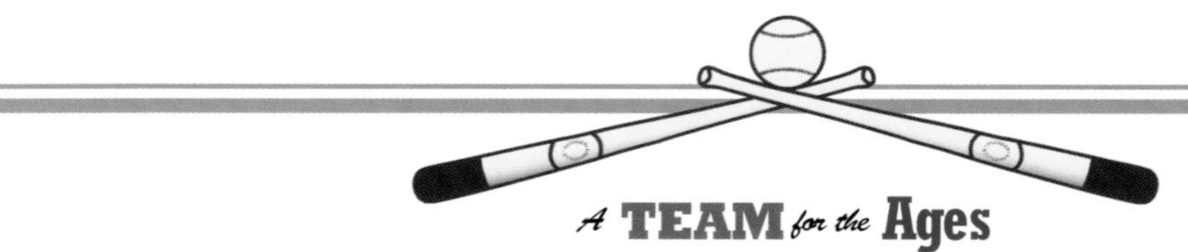

❷ JIMMIE FOXX

THIS WAS A CLOSER MATCH-UP. WHILE POPULAR OPINION MIGHT SUGGEST THAT STAN Musial was a slightly better player, the numbers do not bear that out. Like Gehrig, Jimmie Foxx was a far more productive and powerful hitter than Musial. In almost 3,000 fewer at-bats, Foxx hit more home runs, knocked in only 30 fewer runs, and had a slightly higher on-base percentage and a much higher slugging percentage. Musial had a slightly higher batting average for his career and had the edge in doubles and triples. But the quality that is most essential in a first baseman is productivity, and Foxx clearly had the edge there.

Each player won three MVP awards, but Foxx also won a Triple Crown, led the league in home runs four times, and hit more than 50 homers twice. Musial's seven batting titles outnumbered Foxx's two, but the latter led the league in runs batted in three times to Musial's two. Also, Musial's peak seasons were during the 1940s and early 1950s, before the National League became the more dominant of the two leagues with the arrival of many young stars such as Willie Mays, Hank Aaron, Eddie Mathews, Ernie Banks, and Frank Robinson. When he was in his prime, the N.L. was still considered to be the weaker of the two leagues. Meanwhile, Foxx had his greatest seasons during the 1930s, when the American League was stronger. He had to compete every year for league batting honors with players such as Lou Gehrig, Hank Greenberg, and, later, Joe DiMaggio. The fact that he was considered to be probably the top slugger in the game at that time says quite a bit for him. In addition, for what it's worth, when Ted Williams selected his 20 greatest hitters of all-time, Foxx was number three on his list, while Musial finished seventh. So even though Musial might have the better-known name, Foxx was the more dominant player and deserves a spot on the second team.

❸ STAN MUSIAL

WHILE HE WAS DENIED A SPOT ON THE FIRST TWO TEAMS BECAUSE OF THE GREAT slugging and productivity of Gehrig and Foxx, Stan Musial clearly is deserving of a spot on the third team. One of the greatest hitters the game has ever seen, Musial finished well ahead of George Sisler in almost every offensive category. He had far more home runs, runs batted in, runs scored, and doubles, and finished with a much higher on-base percentage and slugging percentage. Due to his superior ability as a base runner, Sisler had a big edge in stolen bases. He was also a far better defensive first baseman. While Sisler did have two incredible offensive seasons in which he led the league in batting by topping the .400 mark, Musial's seven batting championships more than compensate for that. In addition, his greater power and run production make up for any advantages that Sisler may have had as a base runner and fielder. Therefore, Musial is the clear-cut choice for the third team.

❹ GEORGE SISLER

EARLIER WE SAW THAT EVEN THOUGH HANK GREENBERG WAS A MORE DEVASTATING hitter and run producer than George Sisler, the latter excelled at more aspects of the game and was more of a complete player. That is what earned Sisler a higher spot in the rankings for the first half of the century in what was actually one of the most difficult choices of the entire selection process.

Having survived the challenge from Greenberg, Sisler was not about to be thwarted by Frank Thomas, Mark McGwire, or Jeff Bagwell. While it is true that both Thomas and McGwire, like Greenberg, were far superior to Sisler as home run hitters, and were greater run producers as well, they were also far more one-dimensional.

In about three-quarters the number of at-bats, McGwire hit almost six times as many home runs as Sisler, while Thomas has hit more than four times as many. Both men also knocked in approximately 200 more runs, compiled slugging percentages 100 or more points higher, and, in spite of the fact that Sisler finished with a much higher batting average, compiled higher on-base percentages. In fact, Thomas's career on-base percentage is some 50 points higher. Both players also scored runs at a faster pace. Sisler did, however, out-hit Thomas by 30 points and McGwire by almost 80. He stole more than eight times as many bases and compiled almost ten times as many triples as the two players combined. It would seem, though, that the statistical edge would have to be given to both Thomas and McGwire for their greater slugging and run production.

However, other things need to be considered. For one thing, the numbers of both Thomas and McGwire are inflated somewhat by the era in which they played. While there is little doubt that both men were superior to Sisler as sluggers and run-producers, the discrepancy would not be as great as it appears to be if all three played during the same era. Sisler's 164 career triples indicate that he did indeed have good power, since that was generally the benchmark that was used for sluggers when he played. He also managed to both knock in and score more than 100 runs four times despite the fact that he played on relatively weak teams that did not score a lot of runs. So in truth, Sisler was quite proficient as a run producer.

More important, though, is the fact that Sisler was a far more complete player than either McGwire or Thomas. While the latter, in spite of his lack of running speed and base running ability, is probably a superior overall offensive player to Sisler, he has always been a total liability in the field. As a result, Thomas has spent the better portion of the last several seasons in the role of designated hitter. Meanwhile, Sisler was not only an excellent base runner, but he was the finest defensive first baseman of his time.

McGwire was not quite the defensive liability that Thomas is, but he was hardly nimble around the bag, and he was far more one-dimensional as a hitter. Although a great home run hitter, he batted only .263 for his career, managing to raise his average several points during the late 1990s when numbers throughout baseball as a whole were skyrocketing. In essence, for the better part of his career, McGwire offered three options at the plate: a home run, a walk, or a strikeout. He finished with only 6 triples and 252 doubles in almost 6,200 at-bats, with almost 40 percent of his hits being home runs.

So, all things considered, George Sisler, with his superior defense, excellent base running, and greater versatility on offense, was a better and more complete player than either Frank Thomas or Mark McGwire.

However, both Jeff Bagwell and Eddie Murray were far less one-dimensional than either McGwire or Thomas. Bagwell is a good base runner and a solid fielder at first. We also saw earlier that, while perhaps just a notch below Thomas, he is actually quite comparable to him as a hitter and run producer. Bagwell would, therefore, probably have to be considered to be at least the equal of Sisler as an offensive player. However, while Bagwell is both a *good* base runner and fielder, Sisler was an *excellent* one. As noted earlier, he was considered to be the finest defensive first baseman of his time, and one of the best of the first half of the last century. He was also considered to be one of the finest all around players of that period. So it would seem that Bagwell falls just a bit short of Sisler.

Eddie Murray also had several outstanding qualities. He was a Gold Glove first baseman who was one of the most complete and dangerous hitters of his era. In addition, his numbers compare quite favorably to those of Sisler.

In roughly 3,000 more at-bats, Murray hit almost five times as many home runs, drove in almost 750 more runs, scored almost 350 more, and finished with 135 more doubles and a slightly higher slugging percentage. However, Sisler out-hit Murray by more than 50 points, stole more than three times as many bases, finished with almost five times as many triples, and compiled an on-base percentage that was 20 points higher. In addition, considering that he finished with only about 75 percent as many at-bats as Murray, Sisler was actually quite comparable as a run-producer. Although he knocked in only about 61 percent as many runs, Sisler scored almost 80 percent as many times.

So while each player had an edge in certain offensive categories, it would seem that, for the most part, their respective advantages cancel each other out—with the exception, of course, of Murray's huge statistical edge in home runs. Yet when one considers that Sisler's first few seasons were spent hitting in the dead ball era, and that his best years came before home run totals started to grow, even that discrepancy loses some of its significance. It should additionally be noted that while Murray hit almost five times as many home runs, his slugging percentage was only 8 points higher than Sisler's.

In the end, this decision came down to which player was more dominant during the time in which he played. Murray was an outstanding player for many years and one of the most consistent performers of his era, but he was generally not considered to be a truly dominant player. He led his league in a major offensive category only twice and was never named league MVP. Sisler, however, was a league leader no fewer than six times and won the American League's MVP award in 1922. Accordingly, for his slightly greater level of dominance, the man considered to be one of the very finest players of the first quarter of the last century gets the nod for fourth-team honors.

5 HANK GREENBERG

SORRY, FANS OF MARK MCGWIRE, BUT BIG MAC DOESN'T MAKE IT INTO THE TOP FIVE. As an all-around hitter, Hank Greenberg was by far McGwire's superior. His career batting average was 50 points higher than McGwire's, his on-base percentage was 18 points higher, and his slugging percentage was 17 points higher. He had far more doubles and triples, and he knocked in runs and scored them at a faster pace. In approximately 1,000 fewer career at-bats (roughly the equivalent of two full seasons), Greenberg had only about 140 fewer runs batted in, and scored only about 120 fewer runs. The only real edge that McGwire had was in his home run total, where he outnumbered Greenberg by 262. However, that discrepancy loses some of its significance when one considers several factors. First, there is the greater number of at-bats that McGwire accumulated during his career. Then there is the fact that Greenberg was in the service for almost five full years when he was at his athletic peak. Finally, it must be remembered that McGwire hit many of those home runs during the last seven or eight years of his career, when home run totals throughout the game of baseball, as a whole, were reaching astronomical proportions. In the end, it becomes quite clear that Greenberg deserves a higher ranking than McGwire.

The men who actually mounted a more serious challenge to Greenberg for the number five spot were Eddie Murray, Frank Thomas, and Jeff Bagwell. Due to the fact that he had more than twice the number of career at-bats as Greenberg, Murray's totals far surpass those of the Tiger slugger. He had 173 more homers,

600-plus more runs batted in, almost 500 more runs scored, and twice as many hits. But Greenberg hit home runs, drove in runs, and scored them at a faster pace, had a career batting average that was 26 points higher, an on-base percentage that was 53 points higher, and a slugging percentage that was 131 points higher. He also won two MVP awards, something Murray never did, and led the league in home runs and runs batted in four times each, to Murray's once. Greenberg hit 58 home runs one year and more than 40 three other times, while Murray never hit more than 33 homers in any season. He also knocked in 183 runs in another season, and more than 150 two other times—numbers Murray never approached during his career. As consistent and as outstanding a player as Murray was, he has to be rated just behind the more dominant Greenberg.

The career statistics of Frank Thomas are actually fairly similar to those of Greenberg. In approximately 1,200 more at-bats, he has hit almost 100 more home runs, driven in just over 100 more runs, scored about 200 more runs, and compiled an almost identical batting average. His on-base percentage is almost 20 points higher, but his slugging percentage is 40 points lower. Greenberg had far more triples, but Thomas has slightly more doubles. Both players won two MVP awards and were (or are, in Thomas's case) among the most feared hitters of their time.

Greenberg had three distinct advantages, though. First, while Thomas has won a batting title—something Greenberg never did—he has never led the league in either home runs or runs batted in, two important categories for a first baseman. Greenberg led the league in both departments four times. Secondly, while Greenberg was hardly known for his defense, he was adequate as a first baseman and played all his games in the field, something Thomas has not done for a good portion of his career. Finally, Greenberg lost almost five full seasons in the prime of his career to military service. Had that not been the case, his numbers would have been far more impressive than those of Thomas. All things considered, Greenberg was the better all-around player and is deserving of a higher ranking.

The career numbers of Jeff Bagwell are also quite comparable to those of Greenberg. In almost 2,000 more at-bats, Bagwell has hit almost 90 more home runs, driven in almost 150 more runs, and compiled an almost identical on-base percentage. He has, however, scored 350 more runs and stolen more than three times as many bases. Greenberg, though, finished with a batting average that was 13 points higher and a slugging percentage that was more than 50 points higher. He also collected more than twice as many triples. Once again taking into consideration that Greenberg missed almost five full seasons at the peak of his career, it becomes apparent that he was the superior offensive player. Had he not missed that time, he would have hit more home runs than Bagwell, driven in far more runs, and scored more runs. Further evidence of his superiority can be found in the greater number of times he led his league in a major offensive category. In addition to leading the American League in home runs and runs batted in four times each, he also led in doubles twice and in both runs scored and slugging percentage once. Meanwhile, Bagwell has led his league in runs scored three times, and in slugging percentage and doubles one time each, but has never led in home runs, and has topped the league in runs batted in just once.

In addition, while Bagwell has been named league MVP once and has finished in the top ten in the voting five other times in his thirteen full seasons, Greenberg won two MVP awards and made it into the top ten four other times in just nine full big league seasons. In fact, he finished lower than third in the voting just once in his five full seasons between 1935 and 1940 (he missed most of the 1936 campaign with an injury). So Hank Greenberg was clearly the more dominant player of the two. He is therefore most deserving of a spot on the fifth team.

All-Time All-Star Second Baseman

ROGERS HORNSBY
CHARLIE GEHRINGER
JOE MORGAN
ROBERTO ALOMAR
NAPOLEON LAJOIE/
EDDIE COLLINS

1 ROGERS HORNSBY

ROGERS HORNSBY WAS WITHOUT QUESTION THE GREATEST OFFENSIVE SECOND BASEMAN in the history of baseball. His .358 career batting average is the second highest in the history of the game, his 301 home runs are the most by any second baseman, and his .577 slugging percentage is not even approached by anyone else who played the position. His three .400-plus seasons and .400 average over a five-year period are a testament to his greatness as a hitter.

Hornsby dominated his league for the better part of a decade—something no other second baseman has ever done—and was by far the greatest run-producing second baseman in the history of the game. While Joe Morgan, Paul Molitor, and Eddie Collins each scored more runs, they also had many more career at-bats, and none of them approached Hornsby's RBI total. Charlie Gehringer was the next greatest run producer at the position, but his batting average was 38 points lower, his slugging percentage was almost 100 points lower, and he had more than 100 fewer home runs. Eddie Collins and Roberto Alomar were outstanding hitters, better base runners than Hornsby, and far better defensively. But their power numbers and run production don't compare to Hornsby's. Joe Morgan was also better defensively, was a better base runner, and had a comparable number of home runs. But his batting average was almost 100 points lower, his slugging percentage was 150 points lower, and in approximately 1,000 more career at-bats, he had 450 fewer runs batted in. A case could be made for Napoleon Lajoie, who, while playing in the dead ball era, compiled a career batting average only 20 points less than Hornsby's and knocked in 15 more runs. But Lajoie had more than 1,400 more at-bats, and finished with an on-base percentage that was 54 points lower and a slugging percentage that was 110 points lower.

So in spite of the fact that he was just an average fielder, Rogers Hornsby is the only possible choice for first-team second baseman. Indeed, Joe Morgan himself, when analyzing *The Sporting News'* selections of the top 100 players from the 20th century, said that if he were choosing his top five players of all-time Rogers Hornsby would be one of them.

❷ CHARLIE GEHRINGER

IT WAS REALLY A DIFFICULT CHOICE BETWEEN CHARLIE GEHRINGER AND JOE MORGAN for second-team second baseman. Both were the catalysts on world championship teams: Gehringer's Tigers won one World Series, while Morgan's Reds won two. Gehringer was voted MVP in his league once, while Morgan won the award twice in his. Gehringer had a much higher career batting average (.320 to .271), but Morgan walked a lot, so his on-base percentage was only 9 points lower. Gehringer had a much higher slugging percentage, but some of that could be attributed to the higher offensive numbers that were prevalent throughout baseball as a whole during much of his career. Gehringer was the greater run producer of the two, but Morgan, with 689 career stolen bases, was the far better base runner. So even though Gehringer was the better hitter, it was really very close, offensively. There was also very little to choose between the two defensively. Both were extremely steady, consistent and smooth, and were considered to be among the best fielding second basemen of their time.

What finally tipped the scales in Gehringer's favor was the fact that he was a great player for a longer period of time. While Morgan was a very good player throughout much of his career, he didn't become a great one until he came to the Cincinnati Reds in 1972. For the next six seasons, he was probably the best all-around player in the game, and certainly the equal of Gehringer in his prime. Morgan hit more than 20 homers four times during that stretch, had his only 100-RBI season, batted no lower than .288 (surpassing the .300 mark twice), stole more than 50 bases five times, and scored well over 100 runs, while drawing well over 100 walks each year. However, those six seasons represented the peak of his career, and were the only ones in which he was truly a great player. He never hit more than 16 homers, knocked in more than 75 runs, hit any higher than .289, or stole more than 49 bases in any other season. On the other hand, Gehringer was a great player for twice as long. From 1927 to 1938, he hit below .300 only once (.298 in 1932), batted over .320 eight times, knocked in over 100 runs seven times, scored more than 100 runs eleven times, and had more than 200 hits seven times. Over that twelve-year period, Gehringer was not only considered to be the finest second baseman in the game (with the exception of the first few seasons, when Rogers Hornsby was still at the top of his game), but one of the best all-around players in both major leagues. For this longer period of excellence, Charlie Gehringer gets the nod over Morgan for second-team honors.

❸ JOE MORGAN

ANOTHER CLOSE CALL, THIS TIME THE CHOICE WAS BETWEEN JOE MORGAN, ROBERTO Alomar, Napoleon Lajoie, and Eddie Collins. During the selections for the last half of the century, I compared Morgan and Alomar, and the former came out just ahead. Therefore, there's no need to review that match-up again. I'll instead focus on Morgan, Lajoie, and Collins.

Some might ask how someone with a .271 career batting average could be rated ahead of either a player with a .338 average or another with a mark of .333. While it is true that Nap Lajoie's career average of .338 was 67 points higher than Morgan's, he didn't walk nearly as often and therefore his on-base percentage of .380 was actually lower than Morgan's .395. Lajoie's slugging percentage of .467 was 40 points higher than Morgan's, and he also had far more doubles and triples. However, in approximately 300 fewer at-bats, Morgan hit more than three times as many home runs and scored about 150 more runs. Lajoie did knock in almost 500 more runs, but much of that could be explained by the fact that Morgan batted either first or second in the lineup for much of his career. He only batted in the third spot in the order, which is far more conducive to driving in runs, during three or four of his best seasons in Cincinnati. However, even if the concession is made that Lajoie was a better and more productive hitter, the fact remains that Morgan, with his 689 stolen bases to Lajoie's 380, was a far better base runner and more of an offensive catalyst. He was the driving force behind the Big Red Machine's two world championships, and for that reason gets the nod over Lajoie.

Eddie Collins, on the other hand, was very similar to Morgan in many ways. He walked a lot and therefore had a very high career on-base percentage (.424). His slugging percentage was almost identical to Morgan's, and he actually stole 55 more bases. He had almost the same number of doubles, but had almost twice as many triples and scored runs at a slightly faster pace. Also, like Morgan, he was a catalyst for his teams, helping to lead the Philadelphia A's and, later, the Chicago White Sox to championships. However, Morgan had a huge edge in power. His 268 home runs were almost six times as many as Collins hit during his career. For that reason, Morgan must be ranked above Collins and slotted into the number three spot.

❹ ROBERTO ALOMAR

THERE IS VERY LITTLE SEPARATING ROBERTO ALOMAR FROM NAP LAJOIE AND EDDIE Collins. Lajoie's on-base percentage was 8 points higher than Alomar's, and his slugging percentage was 23 points higher. In almost 700 more at-bats, Lajoie finished with approximately twice as many triples and with almost 160 more doubles. His batting average was 37 points higher than Alomar's, and he drove in runs at a considerably faster pace. However, Alomar scores runs at a slightly faster pace, has hit more than twice as many home runs, and has stolen almost 100 more bases. Of course, much of the home run discrepancy could be attributed to the fact that Lajoie played during the dead ball era.

It would seem that Lajoie was a slightly better offensive player. However, as solid and steady as Nap was defensively, Alomar was the better fielder. He is an artist in the field, possessing great hands and agility and possibly the most range of any man who has ever played the position. For that reason, he just barely edges out Lajoie.

Collins was also very close to Alomar. His slugging percentage was somewhat lower, but his on-base percentage was almost 50 points higher. The two players drove in runs at a very similar rate. Collins stole more bases, hit for a higher average, had more than twice as many triples, and scored runs at a faster pace. However, Alomar, in slightly more than 1,000 fewer at-bats, has more doubles and has hit four times as many home runs. He, like Collins, is an offensive catalyst and has played for two world championship teams in Toronto. It's a close call, but Alomar is the choice based on his offensive versatility. Collins was more of a leadoff or number two-type hitter, even though he frequently batted third because of the style of play employed during the dead ball era. He never knocked in 100 runs in a season. Meanwhile, though not considered a slugger, Alomar has hit over 20 homers three times and driven in over 100 runs twice during his career. He is equally comfortable batting first, second, or third in the lineup. So, we'll find a spot for him on the fourth team.

5 NAPOLEON LAJOIE EDDIE COLLINS

AS WAS MENTIONED DURING THE RANKINGS FOR THE FIRST HALF OF THE CENTURY, there is very little separating Napoleon Lajoie and Eddie Collins. It would therefore be unfair to include one in the top five without including the other. They were clearly the top two second basemen of the dead ball era. Lajoie was the slightly better hitter of the two, had more power, and was the greater run producer. However, Collins, with his propensity for drawing bases on balls, had a higher on-base percentage, scored more runs, stole more bases, and was a better base runner. They were both exceptional fielders, with Lajoie being extremely steady, but Collins having greater quickness and more range. So both deserve recognition here as being among the top second basemen of all-time.

Rod Carew, it should be mentioned, provided the greatest amount of competition to the two for the final spot. With his seven batting titles, Carew was actually just as good a scientific hitter as either Lajoie or Collins. However, in approximately the same number of at-bats, Carew hit only 9 more home runs than Lajoie, and finished far behind him in doubles, triples, and runs batted in. Considering that Carew played with a livelier ball, this is an indication of Lajoie's superior power. In fewer career at-bats, Carew did hit almost twice as many homers as Collins, but the latter negated that by knocking in more runs.

What really kept Carew from breaking into the top five was his defense. As was mentioned earlier, one of the reasons he was shifted to first base midway through his career was because of his inconsistent play at second. Both Lajoie and Collins were far superior as fielders and therefore deserve a higher ranking.

All-Time All-Star Third Baseman

MIKE SCHMIDT

GEORGE BRETT

EDDIE MATHEWS

BROOKS ROBINSON

PIE TRAYNOR

1 MIKE SCHMIDT

MIKE SCHMIDT IS CONSIDERED BY MOST PEOPLE TO BE THE FINEST ALL-AROUND THIRD baseman in baseball history, and with good reason. His 548 career home runs place him in the top ten all-time, his eight home run titles are a National League record, and his .527 career slugging percentage is a record for third basemen. Schmidt is also the only third baseman to lead his league in runs batted in as many as four times, in slugging percentage as many as five times, to hit more than 30 homers thirteen times, and to win as many as three MVP awards.

George Brett is once again Schmidt's closest competition. As powerful and as productive a hitter as Schmidt was, Brett may very well have been the superior batsman. His .305 average was almost 40 points higher than Schmidt's, and while his 317 homers do not approach Schmidt's total, he had more than twice as many triples (137 to 59), and more than 50 percent more doubles (665 to 408). However, in 2,000 fewer at-bats, Schmidt knocked in the same number of runs. In addition, with his ten Gold Gloves, he was a much better defensive player than Brett. In fact, with the exception of Brooks Robinson, he was the best defensive third baseman of all the finalists. Therefore, Mike Schmidt is the clear-cut choice for first-team honors at third base.

② GEORGE BRETT

GEORGE BRETT MAY VERY WELL HAVE BEEN THE GREATEST HITTING THIRD BASEMAN IN baseball history. In comparing him to his nearest competition for a spot on the second team, it could be argued that Eddie Mathews, with 512, hit many more home runs and, with only 142 fewer runs batted in and 74 fewer runs scored in almost 2,000 fewer at-bats, drove in runs and scored them at a faster pace. However, Brett's .305 batting average was 34 points higher than Mathews's .271, he had almost twice as many doubles and triples, he was a tremendous clutch hitter, and he didn't have the advantage that Mathews had in having Hank Aaron batting behind him throughout much of his career. Brett was also the superior base runner, having stolen 201 bases to Mathews's 68. Mathews was a bit more consistent in the field, and had the edge defensively. Overall, though, Brett was the more complete player and deserves recognition as the second greatest third baseman of all time.

③ EDDIE MATHEWS

AS HE DID IN THE RANKINGS FOR THE SECOND HALF OF THE CENTURY, EDDIE MATHEWS once again edges out Brooks Robinson. While the latter was clearly the better fielder, there really is no comparison on offense. Mathews had much more power and was a far greater run producer. In more than 2,000 fewer at-bats, he hit almost twice as many home runs, had almost 100 more runs batted in, scored almost 300 more runs, and finished with an on-base percentage that was more than 50 points higher and a slugging percentage that was more than 100 points higher. In spite of Robinson's reputation and popularity, Mathews was clearly the better player.

In 1969, when the Baseball Writers Association of America voted Pie Traynor the greatest third baseman of the first 100 years, they were obviously basing their selection more on reputation and sentiment than on numbers. Perhaps Mathews's then recent retirement swayed them, or perhaps it was because he had been overshadowed by teammate Hank Aaron throughout much of his career. Still, when you look at the numbers, it becomes obvious that Mathews should have been ranked higher than Traynor. In approximately 1,000 more career at-bats, he hit almost *nine times* as many homers (512 to 58), knocked in almost 200 more runs, scored more than 300 more runs, and finished with a slugging percentage that was almost 75 points higher. While it is true that Traynor's .320 batting average was almost 50 points higher than Mathews's .271, he didn't walk nearly as often. As a result, his .362 on-base percentage is actually lower than Mathews's .378. Clearly, Eddie Mathews is deserving of a spot on the third team.

④ BROOKS ROBINSON

PIE TRAYNOR WAS CLEARLY A BETTER HITTER THAN BROOKS ROBINSON. TRAYNOR'S career batting average was more than 50 points higher, his on-base percentage was almost 40 points higher, and his slugging percentage was almost 35 points higher. In approximately 3,000 fewer career at-bats, he had more than twice as many triples and scored only about 50 fewer runs. He also drove in runs at a slightly faster pace. However, it must be remembered that Traynor had his best seasons during the 1920s, when offensive numbers, as a whole, were higher than the norm. Robinson's best years were during the pitching-dominated 1960s. Thus, when you factor in the respective eras in which they played, the discrepancy between their numbers doesn't loom quite as large. Also, Robinson's 268 career homers far exceed Traynor's 58, Robinson won an MVP award—something Traynor never did—and, while Traynor never led his league in any major offensive category, Robinson led the A.L. in RBI in his MVP season of 1964.

However, even conceding Traynor's superiority as a hitter, there are obviously other desirable attributes in a third baseman. One of these is power and run production. Robinson clearly had more power, was relatively close in run production, and, as can be evidenced by his performances in postseason and All-Star play, was a solid clutch hitter. The other quality that is most important in a third baseman is that he be a good fielder. Here, Robinson had no equal. Although Traynor is still considered to have been a good fielder, his reputation as a glove man has suffered through the years. In no way was he anywhere near the fielder that Robinson was. While Traynor led N.L third basemen in putouts seven times, in chances five times, and in double plays four times, Robinson led A.L. third basemen in fielding eleven times, and in putouts and assists eight times each. He also holds major league records for third basemen with highest fielding percentage (.971), most putouts (2,697), most assists (6,205), and most double plays (618). Therefore, the edge that Robinson had over Traynor in the field was more conclusive than Traynor's edge over Robinson at the plate and earns Brooks Robinson a spot on the fourth team.

5 PIE TRAYNOR

IT WAS STATED EARLIER THAT IF PIE TRAYNOR WERE TO BE COMPARED TO THE TOP THIRD basemen in the major leagues over the last fifty years he might not make it into the top five. Well, he just does make it in, at number five, edging out Wade Boggs.

Traynor and Boggs were similar in that they didn't hit many home runs, but hit for a high average. Boggs actually hit twice as many homers as Traynor, had a slightly higher average (.328 to .320), had a much higher on-base percentage (.415 to .362), and had far more doubles. On the other hand, Traynor had almost three times as many triples and stole many more bases (158 to 24). Boggs scored 330 more runs, but also had approximately 1,600 more at-bats (roughly three full seasons). So, essentially, they scored runs at the same rate. However, Traynor was the far more productive hitter of the two, knocking in about 260 more runs.

In addition, Boggs was no more than adequate as a fielder, while, as noted, Traynor was solid with the glove. For his greater run production and superior ability as a fielder, Traynor beats out Boggs for the fifth spot.

All-Time All-Star Shortstop

HONUS WAGNER

ERNIE BANKS

CAL RIPKEN, JR.

JOHN HENRY LLOYD

ALEX RODRIGUEZ

1 HONUS WAGNER

AFTER ALL THESE YEARS, HONUS WAGNER IS STILL THOUGHT TO HAVE BEEN, BY A fairly wide margin, the greatest shortstop the game has ever seen. He was the best player in the National League for almost fifteen years, the most dominant player in the league throughout the first decade of the 20th century, and one of the finest all-around players in baseball history.

Wagner's .327 career batting, his 1,732 runs batted in, 1,736 runs scored, 252 triples, 640 doubles, 722 stolen bases, and 3,415 hits are all records for major league shortstops. Some of those numbers even place him in the top ten all-time. He was also a marvelous fielder who could play almost any position on the diamond.

Wagner's closest competition here was Ernie Banks, who in approximately 1,000 fewer at-bats, hit more than five times as many homers, knocked in runs at a slightly faster pace, and finished with a higher slugging percentage. However, Wagner was well ahead in every other offensive category. He out-hit Banks by 53 points, scored more than 400 more runs, had almost three times as many triples, had more than 50 percent more doubles, stole almost fifteen times as many bases, collected more than 800 more hits, and finished with an on-base percentage that was almost 60 points higher. In addition, while Banks won two MVP awards and led his league twice in both home runs and runs batted in, Wagner won eight batting titles, led his league in runs batted in and stolen bases five times each, slugging percentage six times, and doubles seven times. Had the MVP award been presented in the National League while Wagner was playing, he undoubtedly would have won at least two or three.

So until Alex Rodriguez shows that he can do for another seven or eight seasons what he has done over his first eight full seasons, Honus Wagner will remain the greatest shortstop in baseball history.

2 ERNIE BANKS

BECAUSE OF HIS GREATER POWER AND RUN PRODUCTION, ERNIE BANKS ONCE AGAIN finishes ahead of Cal Ripken, Jr. in the shortstop rankings. In more than 2,000 fewer career at-bats, Banks hit 81 more homers and knocked in only 59 fewer runs. In most other offensive categories, the players were relatively close. Banks had the edge in slugging percentage, triples, and stolen bases, while Ripken had more doubles and a slightly higher on-base percentage. The two had an almost identical batting average and scored runs at a similar rate. Both players won two MVP awards, but Banks led his league in both home runs and runs batted in twice, while Ripken was never able to lead his league in either. Also, Banks hit more than 40 homers five times, something Ripken was unable to do even once.

John Henry Lloyd also merited consideration here, but since he was never allowed to play in the majors it would be very difficult to slot him ahead of a player with Banks's credentials. Therefore, Ernie Banks is the choice for the second-team shortstop.

3 CAL RIPKEN, JR.

JOE CRONIN WAS SIMILAR TO CAL RIPKEN, JR. IN THAT HE HAD EXCELLENT POWER FOR a shortstop. Cronin, in fact, may have been the slightly better hitter of the two. In approximately two-thirds the number of at-bats, Cronin knocked in only about 270 fewer runs, scored about three-quarter the number of runs, compiled almost three times as many triples, had only about 90 fewer doubles, out-hit Ripken by 25 points, and finished with an on-base percentage that was 50 points higher and a slugging percentage that was 21 points higher. However, Ripken hit well over twice as many homers and was far more durable. Playing almost the same number of seasons as Ripken, Cronin appeared in far fewer games, and as a result had far fewer plate appearances. In addition, he was considered to be no better than average defensively, while Ripken was an outstanding shortstop.

Once again, John Henry Lloyd merited serious consideration. However, other than a few very sketchy statistics and the raves of those who were fortunate enough to have seen him play, too little is known about him to place him ahead of someone with Ripken's qualifications. Therefore, with his two MVP awards, twelve seasons of more than 20 homers, four 100-RBI campaigns, and five .300 seasons, Cal Ripken, Jr. settles into his spot on the third team.

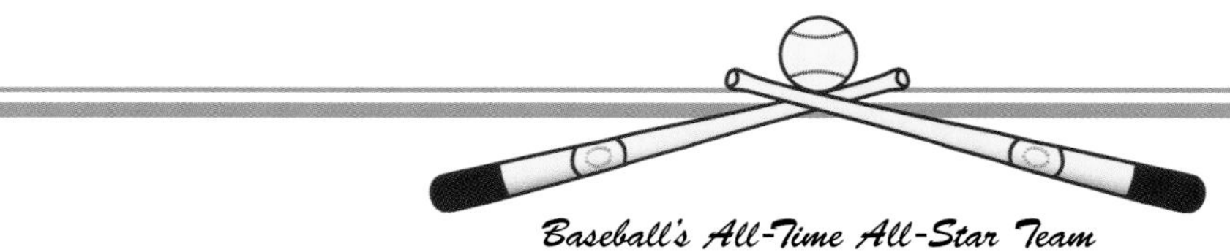

❹ JOHN HENRY "POP" LLOYD

THERE IS NO ONE ELSE TO STAND IN THE WAY OF JOHN HENRY LLOYD AND HIS SELECTION to the fourth team. Joe Cronin had good offensive numbers but was neither the fielder nor the complete player that Lloyd was. After all, we are talking about someone who was likened to Honus Wagner in his abilities, and whom Wagner himself said he felt honored to be compared to.

As good as Lloyd may have been in the field, chances are he was not as good as Ozzie Smith. However, Smith had to work hard to turn himself into a slightly above average offensive player and was clearly never the hitter Lloyd was.

Alex Rodriguez is quite possibly a better hitter and all-around player than Lloyd was, but even that's debatable. It bears mentioning that Lloyd once appeared in a series of exhibition games in Cuba against Ty Cobb's Tigers when the Detroit great was at the height of his career. Lloyd outplayed Cobb, out-hitting him .500 to .369, playing brilliantly in the field and on the basepaths and embarrassing Cobb to the point that Cobb vowed never to play against blacks again. In addition, Babe Ruth once called Lloyd the greatest baseball player he had ever seen. So while little is available about him in the way of statistics, John Henry Lloyd was clearly a great player. Before Alex Rodriguez can be rated above such a superb player he must continue to perform at the same level for a few more seasons. Therefore, Lloyd claims a spot on the fourth team.

❺ ALEX RODRIGUEZ

OZZIE SMITH WAS A BRILLIANT DEFENSIVE PLAYER, BUT WE SAW EARLIER THAT HIS offensive skills did not approach those of Alex Rodriguez. Joe Cronin was a fine hitter and was considered to be quite possibly the finest all-around shortstop of his day. However, he was neither the offensive player nor the fielder that Rodriguez is. In approximately two-thirds the number of at-bats, the latter has already hit twice as many home runs, stolen twice as many bases, and scored only about 200 fewer runs. The two are very close in batting average and on-base percentage, but Rodriguez's slugging percentage is more than 100 points higher and he drives in runs at a much faster pace.

While it is true that Rodriguez has always played in excellent hitters' parks in Seattle and Texas, the right-handed swinging Cronin had many of his finest seasons playing in Boston's Fenway Park, an excellent park for righties. Also, just as Rodriguez has spent his entire career playing in a hitter's era, most of Cronin's peak years came during the 1930s, another excellent era for hitters. In addition, Cronin was considered to be an average defensive player, while Rodriguez is one of the best fielding shortstops of his time. So, the comparison here really is not even a close one. The bigger questions are how high on this list Rodriguez will eventually be able to climb, and whether or not he will, in time, be able to unseat Honus Wagner as the greatest shortstop in baseball history.

Only time will tell.

G

All-Time All-Star Catcher

JOSH GIBSON
JOHNNY BENCH
YOGI BERRA
BILL DICKEY
MICKEY COCHRANE

1 JOSH GIBSON

THE SELECTION OF JOSH GIBSON OVER JOHNNY BENCH AS FIRST-TEAM CATCHER WILL undoubtedly draw much criticism because of the lack of reliable statistical data to support it. However, the bottom line is this: Johnny Bench was the greatest catcher ever to play in the major leagues, but Josh Gibson was the greatest catcher in baseball history.

When analyzing Bench's career, it becomes apparent that while he was an outstanding player for several seasons, he was truly a dominant one for only five. In addition, it becomes even more obvious that during the second half of his career, he got by more on reputation than anything else.

Let's take a closer look.

After winning the N.L. Rookie of the Year award in 1968, Bench had an outstanding season in 1969 to begin to establish himself as a true star. In winning his first MVP award the following year, Bench had his first dominant season, hitting 45 homers, knocking in 148 runs, and batting .293. After an off year in 1971 (one in which he drove in only 61 runs and batted just .238), Bench rebounded in 1972 by hitting 40 homers and knocking in 125 runs to win his second MVP award. He had a good year in 1973, then two more outstanding ones in 1974 and 1975, and one more in 1977. However, during this

period, he began suffering some fairly serious injuries that had a major impact on his performance. As a result, after 1977, he would never again hit more than 24 homers or knock in more than 80 runs in any season. Although he was awarded the Gold Glove every year and was elected to the starting All-Star team, he was no longer the best catcher in the league, having been surpassed by both Ted Simmons and Gary Carter. So in actuality Bench had five outstanding seasons and two very good ones. The rest of his career was built largely on his reputation.

Meanwhile, Josh Gibson was not only considered to be the greatest *catcher* in the Negro Leagues, but many thought him to be its greatest *player*. Rivaled only by Oscar Charleston in his early years, Gibson was the Negro Leagues' most dominant player for well over a decade.

While not the handler of pitchers or overall defensive player that Bench was, Gibson was a fine catcher with an outstanding throwing arm. As a hitter, though, he had few if any equals, and was plainly Bench's superior. Although the unreliability of stat-keeping in the Negro Leagues is well-documented, Gibson is on record as having batted at least .354 during his career, with as few as 800 or as many as 962 home runs. His single-season highs have been listed as .517 and 84 homers. As was mentioned earlier, in 16 exhibition games against major league pitching, he hit .424 with 5 home runs.

So while Bench was a terrific player and a great receiver, he was not the dominant player that Gibson was. Consider the words of Hall of Famer Monte Irvin, who played against Gibson in the Negro Leagues and later played with Willie Mays on the New York Giants: "I played with Willie Mays and against Hank Aaron. They were tremendous players, but they were no Josh Gibson. You saw him hit, and you took your hat off."

As good as Bench was, not too many people would compare him favorably to Willie Mays and Hank Aaron. Therefore, Josh Gibson is the choice for first-team catcher.

2 JOHNNY BENCH

WE SAW EARLIER HOW JOHNNY BENCH, IN HIS PRIME, WAS A MORE DOMINANT PLAYER than Yogi Berra. While Berra's offensive numbers rival those of Bench, he was able to go through his career essentially injury-free, thereby allowing him to compile excellent career numbers while experiencing more good seasons. However, Bench's peak years were better than Berra's. While Berra never led his league in either home runs or runs batted in, Bench led the N.L. in homers twice and in runs batted in three times. Also, while Berra reached the 30-homer mark twice and knocked in more than 100 runs five times, Bench hit 40 or more homers twice and drove in over 100 runs six times. However, Bench's greatest advantage was in his defense, where he had no peer.

Perhaps closest to Bench, defensively, was Berra's tutor, Bill Dickey. He was a magnificent catcher, called a great game, did a marvelous job of handling a pitching staff, and had many of the intangibles that you look for in a catcher. Bench probably had a slight edge because of his quickness behind the plate and his cannon for an arm, but the difference was not that great. Offensively, Bench also had the edge. While the two players were relatively close in most hitting categories, Dickey, at .313, had a much higher career batting average than Bench, at .267. However, Bench, in about 1,250 more at-bats, hit 389 homers to

Dickey's 202. Also, like Berra, Dickey never led the league in any major hitting category. In addition, while a solid hitter throughout his career, Dickey only had four seasons, 1936–1939, where he was an extremely productive one, hitting more than 20 homers and knocking in over 100 runs. Meanwhile, Bench, in addition to those two 40-homer seasons, had nine others with more than 20 homers, and also knocked in more than 100 runs six times.

So, even though the gap between Bench, Berra, and Dickey might not be quite as large as public perception would seem to indicate, Bench must be given the nod over both former Yankees catchers for a spot on the second team.

❸ YOGI BERRA

WHILE YOGI BERRA IS GENERALLY CONSIDERED TO BE, WITH THE EXCEPTION OF JOHNNY Bench, the greatest catcher in major league history, many people seem to forget how good his predecessor with the New York Yankees, Bill Dickey, was. Dickey's .313 career batting average is the third highest of any catcher with more than 5,000 at-bats, and is 28 points higher than Berra's .285. He hit more than 20 homers, knocked in over 100 runs, and batted over .300 in four consecutive seasons. He was also a superb receiver, considered to be the finest defensive catcher of his time, an excellent handler of pitchers, and a team leader. That is what made this selection so difficult.

A look at their offensive numbers reveals that there was very little separating Bill Dickey and Yogi Berra. They were almost identical in slugging percentage, stolen bases, and doubles. As was mentioned earlier, Dickey hit for a higher average and also had more triples and a higher on-base percentage, but Berra hit 358 homers to Dickey's 202. Even though Berra had more runs batted in and runs scored, when you factor in his 1,255 more career at-bats, you realize that the two players produced runs at, basically, the same rate.

It was a difficult choice to make, but Berra gets the nod over Dickey for three reasons. First, in spite of the fact that Dickey set a major league record by catching more than 100 games for thirteen consecutive seasons, Berra was the more durable of the two. In those thirteen seasons, Dickey caught as many as 130 games only five times, and 140 only once. Meanwhile, Berra caught at least 130 games for seven consecutive seasons, from 1950 to 1956. He also caught at least 140 games five times during his career.

Second, while Dickey was an excellent hitter, Berra was the more dangerous of the two. While Dickey had those four seasons with more than 20 homers and 100 RBI, he only had as many as 15 homers and 90 RBI one other time. Berra, on the other hand, had eleven seasons with more than 20 homers, including two with 30, knocked in over 100 runs five times, and had another four seasons with at least 90 runs batted in.

Finally, Berra had three MVP awards, fourteen pennants, and ten world championships to his credit. He also finished in the top five in the MVP voting four other times. While Dickey's nine pennants and eight world championships were also quite impressive, he was never elected MVP, and only finished in the top five once. It could be argued that Dickey was often overlooked in the MVP balloting because he was overshadowed by teammates such as Lou Gehrig and Joe DiMaggio. Meanwhile, Berra's MVP seasons came right at the end of DiMaggio's career and at the beginning of Mickey Mantle's, before the latter had firmly established himself as the team's best player. Nevertheless, the fact remains that Berra won the award three times and was recognized as the most important player on some of those great Yankees teams. Yogi Berra therefore just edges out Bill Dickey for a spot on the third team.

4 BILL DICKEY

WHILE MICKEY COCHRANE, ROY CAMPANELLA, AND MIKE PIAZZA ALL MERITED consideration for this spot as well, Bill Dickey is clearly deserving of a spot on the fourth team. Earlier, it was discussed how his defensive skills and ability to handle a pitching staff earned him a higher ranking than his contemporary, Mickey Cochrane. The same can be said with regard to current-day slugger Mike Piazza. While Piazza is a tremendous hitter, he is not nearly the defensive player or team leader that Dickey was. Roy Campanella, on the other hand, approached Dickey in both categories. However, when you look at Campanella's numbers, they fall far short of Dickey's except in home runs and slugging percentage. True, Campanella had approximately two-thirds the number of at-bats, but his batting average was 37 points lower, his on-base percentage was 20 points lower, he had half as many doubles, and he only had one-fourth as many triples. Also, Dickey drove in runs and scored them at a comparable rate. It is true that Dickey's finest seasons came during the 1930s, a notoriously good era for hitters. However, Campanella's best years were during the 1950s, another pretty good decade for hitters. When you also factor into the equation the fact that Campanella played his home games in tiny Ebbets Field, a great ballpark for hitters, there is really no legitimate argument for ranking him ahead of Dickey.

5 MICKEY COCHRANE

THIS WAS ANOTHER DIFFICULT CHOICE BECAUSE A CASE COULD BE MADE FOR COCHRANE, Campanella, or Piazza. In approximately the same number of at-bats, Piazza has three times as many homers as Cochrane, almost 300 more runs batted in, virtually the same batting average, and a slugging percentage that is almost 100 points higher. However, Cochrane's on-base percentage was some 30 points higher, he stole almost four times as many bases, he had ten times as many triples, he had far more doubles, and he scored about 150 more runs. So even though Piazza has far more power and is more dangerous a hitter than Cochrane ever was, Cochrane was more versatile and, overall, was not that far behind as an offensive player.

Defensively, it has already been noted that Piazza, though an adequate handler of pitchers and a decent signal-caller, has a difficult time throwing runners out on the bases. Cochrane was no more than adequate behind the plate either, but he moved around a little better and was known for being a team leader. Therefore, he has to be given the edge there.

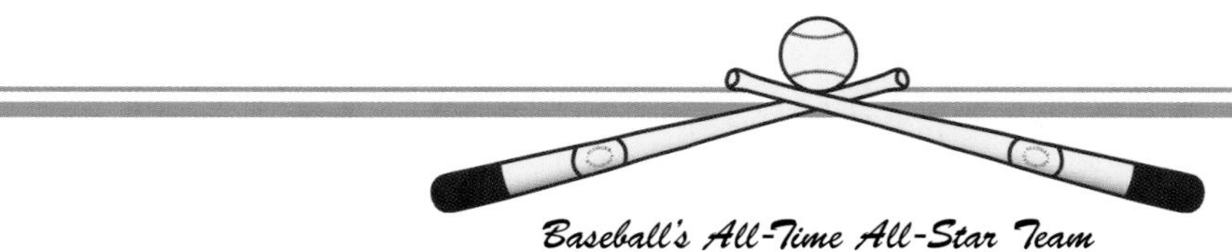

Where Cochrane had the biggest advantage, though, was in his two MVP awards. Piazza has yet to win one, and when one reflects on some of the great players who were in the American League during Cochrane's time, it was quite an achievement for him to have won the award twice.

Roy Campanella, however, won *three* MVP awards. In addition, in about 80 percent the number of at-bats, he hit twice as many homers as Cochrane, knocked in 24 more runs, and finished with a slugging percentage that was 22 points higher. On the other hand, Cochrane out-hit Campanella by 44 points, had an on-base percentage that was 57 points higher, scored far more runs, and had far more doubles, triples, and stolen bases. In addition, while Campanella did put up some outstanding numbers in his three MVP seasons of 1951, 1953, and 1955, hitting more than 30 homers, driving in over 100 runs, and batting over .300 each year, his career was marked by inconsistency. Mixed in with those three very productive seasons were three years in which he hit 22, 19, and 20 homers, and two in which he drove in 51 and 73 runs, while batting only .207 and .219. Therefore, for his greater consistency, Mickey Cochrane edges out Campanella for the final spot.

Braves

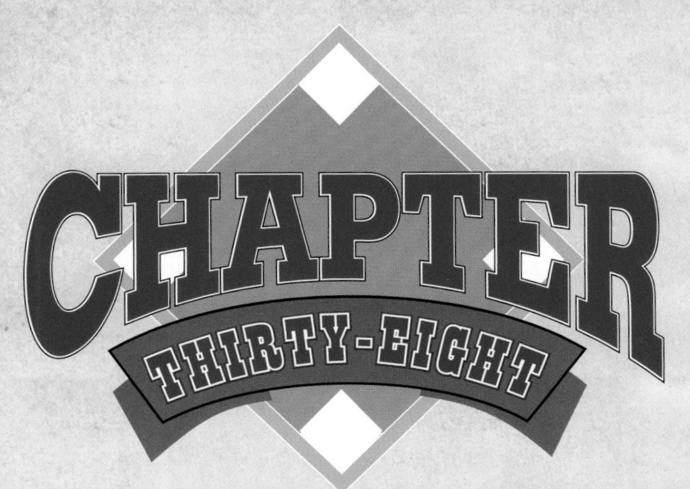

All-Time All-Star Left Fielder

HANK AARON

TY COBB

BARRY BONDS

RICKEY HENDERSON

AL SIMMONS

1 HANK AARON

LEFT FIELD PRESENTS A TRULY UNIQUE SITUATION IN THAT THE TOP FIVE PLAYERS chosen represent, at least to some degree, each decade of the 20th century. Ty Cobb's career spanned portions of the first three decades; Al Simmons played from the 1920s into the early part of the 1940s; Hank Aaron came up in the mid-1950s and played until 1976; and both Rickey Henderson and Barry Bonds have endured from the 1980s into the 21st century. As a result, this position presents perhaps the greatest challenge in terms of player evaluation and comparison. With the exception of Bonds and Henderson, each player competed in an era in which the style of play differed drastically. For Cobb, the game was a low-scoring chess match, featuring slap-hitting, speed, and base-running. For Simmons, the game was played at a slower pace, with runs not being so scarce, and with power taking precedence over speed. In Aaron's time, things were a bit more balanced, with the sport having both its share of sluggers and speed merchants. For most of Henderson's and part of Bonds's careers, the game was played in a similar fashion to the way it was played during Aaron's time. However, they both have been part of the

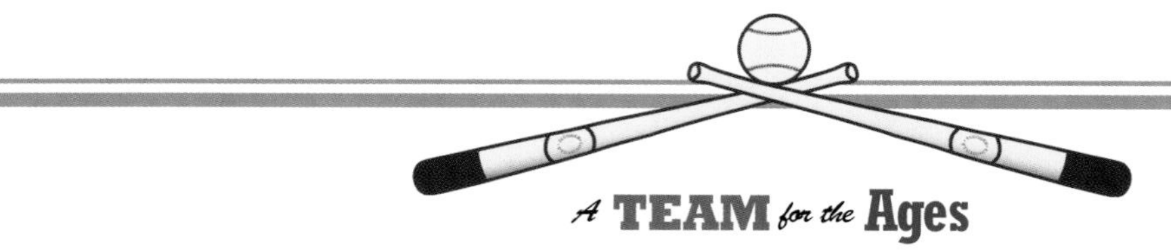

offensive explosion that began in the early part of the 1990s. So ranking these players is truly no easy task, and probably the greatest challenge is picking the number one man: Ty Cobb or Hank Aaron?

With the exception of Babe Ruth, Ty Cobb dominated his era the way no other player ever has. We saw earlier that he led his league in batting ten times over a thirteen-year period, hit over .300 every season from 1906 to 1928, batted over .350 sixteen times in his career, surpassing the .400 mark three times, and finished with the highest lifetime batting average of any player who ever lived. He also led the league in stolen bases six times, runs batted in four times, triples four times, doubles three times, hits eight times, runs scored five times, on-base percentage six times, and slugging percentage eight times, won a Triple Crown, and won an MVP award. He did all this in a flamboyant manner, drawing attention to himself by fighting with opposing players, teammates and fans alike. While widely regarded as the game's greatest player, due to his competitive and combative nature he also became its most hated.

Hank Aaron, on the other hand, had a completely different disposition and style of play. Mild-mannered and low-key, he remained relatively inconspicuous throughout most of his years in Milwaukee and, later, Atlanta. He wasn't as flashy or as exciting to watch as Willie Mays. Mickey Mantle hit longer home runs and was better known to the general public because he played in New York and appeared in the World Series almost every year. But when all was said and done, Hank Aaron was very possibly the finest player of his generation, and one of the very greatest of all time.

Aaron didn't dominate the game in the obvious way that Ruth or Cobb did. He never hit 50 home runs, drove in 150 runs, batted .370, or stole 75 bases. Rather, he dominated the game in a more subtle manner, putting up superb numbers year after year until, by the time his career was over, people came to realize what a great player he really was. Aaron finished first all-time in home runs, runs batted in, and total bases, third in runs scored and base hits, and ninth in doubles. He led the National League in home runs, runs batted in, doubles, and slugging percentage four times each, in runs scored three times, and in both batting average and base hits twice. He hit over 40 homers eight times, and hit more than 20 a record 20 consecutive seasons. He also drove in more than 100 runs eleven times, batted over .300 fourteen times, had 200 hits three times, scored more than 100 runs fifteen times, and won an MVP award.

In looking at Aaron's numbers versus Cobb's, the latter, in 900 fewer career at-bats, finished well ahead in doubles, triples, hits, stolen bases, on-base percentage, and batting average (.367 to .305). He also finished with 72 more runs scored. Aaron, on the other hand, had 755 home runs to Cobb's 117, had a slugging percentage that was 43 points higher, and finished with 360 more runs batted in. Overall, the statistical edge would seem to go to Cobb. However, the advantage is not a very big one. In addition, the level of his dominance was really not much greater than that of Aaron when you consider their numbers within the context of the eras in which they played. Let's take a closer look.

One could say that when Ty Cobb played a dominant season was considered to be one in which a player batted over .350, stole 50 bases, knocked in 100 runs, and scored 100 runs. Using those criteria, Cobb had ten such seasons. In a couple of those years, he may have fallen a little short in one or two of the categories, but his numbers were good enough in the others to compensate for that and still have the years categorized as dominant.

In Aaron's time, with more of an emphasis being placed on power and run production, it could be said that a dominant season was one in which a player hit around 40 homers, batted around .320, knocked in approximately 120 runs, and scored about 120 others. Using those as benchmarks, Aaron had six such seasons. So even though he had fewer than Cobb, and even though he never set any single-season records, Aaron was an extremely dominant player.

In addition, there is no aspect of the game in which Aaron did not excel. Aside from being a great hitter, he had outstanding speed, was an excellent base runner, had a strong and accurate throwing arm, and was an outstanding outfielder. Cobb, on the other hand, was considered to be only a slightly above average outfielder.

Finally, there is the issue of continuity. Aaron was a true team player, blended in well with the rest of the team, and was very popular. Cobb, meanwhile, was a distraction and a divisive force. He not only fought with his opponents, but with his own teammates as well.

All things considered, Henry Aaron is a better choice to play left field on the first team.

❷ TY COBB

A STRONG CASE COULD BE MADE FOR PUTTING EITHER TY COBB OR BARRY BONDS ON the second team. Each was the greatest player of his era. Each had a presence that made him the central figure in any game he appeared in. Even statistically, an argument could be made on either's behalf.

Cobb drove in almost 200 more runs and scored approximately 300 more as well. However, he also had almost 3,000 more at-bats. It would thus seem that Bonds was the greater run-producer of the two. But it must also be remembered that Cobb played during the dead ball era when runs were much more difficult to come by. All things considered, the two were probably fairly close as run-producers. Regardless of the eras in which they played, though, Bonds had a clear advantage in power, as can be evidenced by his greater home run total and higher slugging percentage. He has hit almost six times as many homers as Cobb did, and his slugging percentage is 90 points higher.

However, those are the only statistical advantages that Bonds holds over Cobb. The two men have identical on-base percentages, and Cobb stole almost 400 more bases, collected four times as many triples, and finished with almost 200 more doubles. So neither player has a clear-cut advantage based strictly on career statistics.

Cobb does, however, have an edge over Bonds in other areas. For one thing, he was a league-leader in the various offensive categories far more often than Bonds has been. During his career, Cobb led his league in a major offensive category a total of *fifty-five* times. Bonds has led his league a total of seventeen times. At the time of his retirement, Cobb held almost every major career and single-season batting and base running record.

In addition, Cobb dominated the game for more than a decade. While he received stiff competition from other outstanding players such as Tris Speaker, "Shoeless" Joe Jackson, Eddie Collins, and even the great Walter Johnson, Cobb was generally considered to be *the* dominant player in the game for a period of almost fifteen years. On the other hand, while Bonds has been the finest all-around player of his generation, he has really been regarded as baseball's most dominant player in only a few seasons. He has clearly been the most dominant player in the game since 2001. He was also the greatest player in the game in his third MVP season of 1993. However, even after he had already established himself as a star with the Pittsburgh Pirates in the early 1990s, he was not generally thought of as being baseball's most dominant player. For several seasons he was usually rated behind Ken Griffey, Jr., and, in other years, he has taken a back seat to Alex Rodriguez. Thanks to his dominance over a longer period of time, Ty Cobb therefore gets the nod over Bonds for second-team honors.

3 BARRY BONDS

WE SAW EARLIER THAT BARRY BONDS IS MORE OF A COMPLETE PLAYER THAN RICKEY Henderson, and therefore deserves to be ranked ahead of him. The same thing can be said when comparing him to Al Simmons. While Simmons was a tremendous hitter, he didn't have either the fielding or base running ability that Bonds had in his youth.

If you look at Bonds and Simmons, strictly as hitters, the discrepancy is not as great as most might think. In almost the same number of at-bats, Simmons had almost 100 more runs batted in, out-hit Bonds by almost 40 points, and had twice as many triples. Bonds, on the other hand, has more than twice as many homers, has scored more than 400 more runs, and has an on-base percentage that is more than 50 points higher and a slugging percentage that is 67 points higher. Overall, Bonds would have to be given the edge as a hitter. He has an even greater edge, though, as a base-stealer, having stolen more than five times as many bases. In addition, while Simmons was a good outfielder, Bonds was a Gold Glove caliber one, with eight to his credit. Bonds, in short, is clearly the better all-around player and is well deserving of a spot on the third team.

4 RICKEY HENDERSON

THIS SELECTION WAS NOT AN EASY ONE BECAUSE AL SIMMONS HIT FOR A MUCH HIGHER average, had more power, and was a far more dangerous hitter than Rickey Henderson. In approximately 2,000 fewer at-bats, Simmons hit 10 more homers, knocked in more than 700 more runs, out-hit Henderson by 55 points, compiled more than twice as many triples, collected almost 30 more doubles, and had a slugging percentage that was 116 points higher. However, Henderson walked much more and therefore possesses an on-base percentage that is some 20 points higher than Simmons's. Henderson has also scored almost 800 more runs and has stolen more than 1,300 more bases. Henderson's advantage in runs scored negates Simmons's edge in runs batted in. However, when you consider that the latter had 2,000 fewer at-bats, it becomes apparent that he was actually the greater run producer of the two. But it should also be noted that Henderson has been a leadoff hitter throughout his career and, as such, has had fewer opportunities to drive in runs. Overall, then, Simmons's edge as a run producer is minimal.

What finally earned Henderson a higher ranking was the realization that, with him, statistics do not tell the whole story because he always made the other players around him better, and because he had the ability to take over a game with his legs. Henderson had a way of disrupting the other team's defense and upsetting their pitcher to the point of distraction. Opposing fielders became tense, and opposing pitchers frequently gave the hitters batting behind Henderson better pitches to hit. In addition, by drawing a walk, stealing second and third base, and then scoring on a sacrifice fly or an infield out, he could manufacture a run all by himself. As the greatest leadoff hitter the game has ever seen, Henderson is the all-time leader in stolen bases, runs scored, and walks. Having fulfilled this role better than any other man ever has, he has to be given the nod, just slightly, over the better hitter, Al Simmons.

5 AL SIMMONS

JOE MEDWICK AND CARL YASTRZEMSKI WERE ALSO CONSIDERED FOR THIS SPOT, BUT Simmons was clearly better than both. Playing in the same era as Medwick, Simmons finished well ahead of him in every offensive category, except for doubles, and was the more feared hitter of the two.

Carl Yastrzemski might have been a slightly better outfielder than Simmons, and he had two or three truly exceptional seasons that could be put up against some of Simmons's best. But he was only a great player for those few seasons; the rest of his career he was merely a very good one. Simmons, on the other hand, had those eleven consecutive seasons, twelve in all, in which he drove in more than 100 runs and batted over .300. Six of those years could be classified as dominant ones, with him batting over .350 six times and knocking in more than 120 runs five times. In more than 3,000 fewer at-bats, Simmons knocked in only 17 fewer runs, scored only 300 fewer, had more than twice as many triples, and finished with a batting average that was 49 points higher and a slugging percentage that was 73 points higher. Yastrzemski did hit 145 more homers, but much of that could be attributed to his greater number of plate appearances. So due to his better overall numbers and greater number of dominant seasons, Al Simmons deserves to be ranked higher than Yastrzemski.

All-Time All-Star Center Fielder

WILLIE MAYS

JOE DIMAGGIO

MICKEY MANTLE

TRIS SPEAKER

OSCAR CHARLESTON

1 WILLIE MAYS

FOR THE FIRST SEVEN YEARS OF HIS CAREER, FROM 1936 TO 1942, JOE DIMAGGIO MAY have been not only the finest center fielder in baseball history, but perhaps the greatest all-around player the game has ever seen. In five of those seasons, he hit at least 30 homers, once hitting as many as 46. In each of those seasons, he knocked in well over 100 runs, six times driving in at least 125, and once knocking in as many as 167. He also batted well over .300 in each of those years, topping .350 three times, and hitting as high as .381 one year. In addition, he was a superb outfielder, possessing a very strong throwing arm, and an excellent base runner.

However, after spending three years in the military, DiMaggio's last six seasons, 1946–1951, were not nearly as productive. Although still an excellent player, he would only hit as many as 30 homers and knock in more than 100 runs two more times. He did still bat over .300 four more times, and even had one more great season left in him, when, in 1948, he hit 39 homers, knocked in 155 runs, and batted .320. But he clearly was not the same player he was prior to World War II.

Willie Mays, on the other hand, was a great player from the time he completed his stint in the military in 1954, until he finally started to slow down following the 1966 season. He therefore had thirteen outstanding seasons to DiMaggio's eight. In addition, while DiMaggio played only thirteen seasons, Mays's career spanned twenty-two years. As a result, he was able to accumulate numbers that make DiMaggio's pale by comparison. DiMaggio did finish with a higher career average (.325 to .302), and with slightly higher on-base and slugging percentages. Also, if you were to project his numbers over the same number of at-bats that Mays had, he would finish ahead of Willie in every offensive category, except home runs and stolen bases. But superiority is not achieved by number projections. It is achieved by performance and long-term excellence. In that regard, Willie Mays was clearly the superior player.

Mays hit 300 more home runs during his career, knocked in 366 more runs, scored 672 more runs, had 134 more doubles, and stole 300 more bases. In addition, he was a great outfielder, considered by many to be even better than DiMaggio himself. Just listen to what Joe Gordon, DiMaggio's teammate for several seasons, said when asked to compare DiMaggio and Mays, as reported by Charles Einstein in *The Fireside Book of Baseball*: "You are not going to like this, but the greatest player I ever saw is Willie Mays."

❷ JOE DIMAGGIO

MICKEY MANTLE WAS THE ONLY PLAYER WHO POSED A SERIOUS THREAT TO JOE DiMaggio's spot on the second team. We saw earlier that Tris Speaker did not offer the power or run production that DiMaggio did, and we also noted that it would be difficult to rank Oscar Charleston above a player as great as DiMaggio, due to the lack of statistics from Charleston's career. Ken Griffey, Jr. has approximately the same number of career at-bats as DiMaggio, but is well behind in every offensive category, except home runs and stolen bases.

So it came down to the two greatest Yankees center fielders ever. Mantle, like DiMaggio, would have been able to put up far better numbers had he not been affected by external factors. There were the debilitating injuries that hampered him throughout much of his career, and, of course, Mantle himself was partly to blame for not taking care of himself the way he should have. Nevertheless, the two men must be judged by what they *were* able to accomplish during their careers, not by what *might have been*.

In those terms, Joe DiMaggio has to be rated just a little higher than Mickey. In approximately 1,300 fewer at-bats, he knocked in 28 more runs, batted .325 to Mantle's .298, had almost twice as many triples, had 45 more doubles, and finished with a slugging percentage that was 22 points higher. Mantle did hit 175 more homers, though, scored almost 300 more runs, stole five times as many bases, and finished with a higher on-base percentage (.423 to .398). Offensively, it's close—but because he was the better RBI man, the edge has to go to DiMaggio.

Defensively, though, DiMaggio had a more decided advantage. While Mantle, in his youth, was the faster of the two, he didn't have DiMaggio's instincts. Mantle was fast enough to occasionally outrun the ball, but he didn't get the same jump on a ball that DiMaggio got, nor did he have the knack that DiMaggio had of always being in the right place at the right time.

❸ MICKEY MANTLE

TRIS SPEAKER'S DEFENSIVE SKILLS, SUPERIOR BATTING AVERAGE, AND ABILITY TO AMASS large numbers of extra-base hits made this relatively close, but in the end, Mickey Mantle's power and greater run-production won out. Speaker did hit .345 to Mantle's .298, had three times as many triples and more than twice as many doubles, and stole almost three times as many bases. However, Mantle, in approximately 2,000 fewer at-bats, hit almost five times as many homers, knocked in only 20 fewer runs, and scored only 205 fewer runs. He also finished with a slugging percentage that was 57 points higher and, because of his ability to draw bases on balls, negated Speaker's batting average advantage by finishing with an on-base percentage that was only 5 points lower.

So the center field spot on the third-team belongs to the greatest switch-hitter in baseball history, and the man who may have been blessed with the greatest natural ability of any player who ever lived. Many baseball historians feel that Mickey Mantle had the greatest combination of speed and power the game has ever seen, and that he had the potential to be the greatest player ever.

As it turned out, he was still an exceptional player who accomplished a great deal during his career. There were his 536 home runs, which place him high on the all-time list, his four home run titles, his two 50-homer seasons, his Triple Crown season of 1956, and his three MVP awards. In addition, he was an almost mythic figure, and a hero to millions.

4 TRIS SPEAKER

IT WAS MENTIONED EARLIER THAT IT WOULD BE DIFFICULT TO RANK OSCAR Charleston above an all-time great such as Tris Speaker. Therefore, the only other man who presented a challenge to Speaker for a spot on the fourth team was Ken Griffey, Jr. However, Griffey has yet to accomplish enough in his career to be rated above a player with Speaker's credentials. While Griffey has hit four times as many home runs and has a slugging percentage that is 62 points higher than Speaker's, the latter is well ahead in every other offensive category. His .345 batting average is some 50 points higher than Griffey's, he knocked in almost 150 more runs, scored almost 600 more runs, had more than six times as many triples, more than twice as many doubles, almost 1,500 more hits, and finished with an on-base percentage that was almost 50 points higher. In addition, as good a fielder as Griffey is, Speaker's reputation as the greatest defensive center fielder of the first half of the 20th century is well-documented.

So the man who ranks among the top ten all-time in batting average, doubles, triples, runs scored, base hits, and total bases takes his spot on the fourth team.

5 OSCAR CHARLESTON

KEN GRIFFEY, JR. FANS MAY NOT LIKE THIS, BUT IN SPITE OF THE GREAT NUMBERS HE put up in his first several seasons prior to being slowed by injuries over the last few years, Junior has not yet done enough to be considered one of the all-time greats. In fact, since his trade to the Cincinnati Reds, his performance has fallen off dramatically. While it is true that injuries are the primary reason for his decrease in productivity, there is also the factor that he is no longer swinging for the shallow fences of Seattle's Kingdome. Until Griffey shows he can remain healthy for an extended period of time and add considerably to the resume he has created for himself thus far, it really would be a bit premature to group him with the greatest players ever.

It should be remembered that Charleston, along with Josh Gibson and Satchel Paige, was considered to be among the greatest of all Negro League players. In addition, Buck O'Neill, who played against Charleston in the Negro Leagues, called him the greatest player he ever saw, including Willie Mays.

NY

All-Time All-Star Right Fielder

BABE RUTH

FRANK ROBINSON

ROBERTO CLEMENTE

"SHOELESS" JOE JACKSON

SAMMY SOSA

1 BABE RUTH

FRANK ROBINSON WAS A TREMENDOUS PLAYER WHO IS NEVER GIVEN THE CREDIT HE deserves as one of the very best players of all time. However, he was not the greatest player who ever lived. That distinction belongs to Babe Ruth.

Babe Ruth's name is synonymous with the game of baseball—and well it should be. He brought the game out of the dark ages, creating an excitement that had never existed before. He almost single-handedly saved the sport following the "Black Sox" scandal of 1919. He set records that stood for thirty or forty years, others that stood longer, and still others that may never be broken.

Ruth set single-season records for home runs, walks, and slugging percentage, and career records for home runs and walks, all of which were eventually broken. However, his single-season records for runs scored (177) and total bases (457), and his career record for highest slugging percentage (.690), still stand, and probably always will. He led his league a record twelve times in both home runs and slugging percentage, six times in runs batted in, once in batting average, eight times in runs scored, eleven times in walks, and ten times in on-base percentage. He hit more than 50 homers in a season four times and more than 40 seven other times. He also knocked in more than 100 runs thirteen times, including five seasons with more than 150. He was more than just a slugger, though, batting over .370 six times during his career.

Thus, Ruth was not only the most charismatic player in the history of the game, but the most dominant for the time in which he played. In short, no matter how many of his records are broken, there can never be another Babe Ruth.

2 FRANK ROBINSON

FRANK ROBINSON WAS CLEARLY THE SECOND GREATEST RIGHT FIELDER IN THE HISTORY of the game. Harry Heilmann, Joe Jackson, Paul Waner, Roberto Clemente, and Tony Gwynn were all great hitters, but none of them came close to Robinson as run-producers. Sammy Sosa does come close, but as we saw earlier, he is not the player Robinson was.

Mel Ott was one player whose numbers were on a par with Robinson's. In fact, in 550 fewer at-bats, Ott knocked in 48 more runs and scored 30 more. He also finished with a slightly higher batting average and on-base percentage. On the other hand, Robinson finished slightly ahead in doubles and slugging percentage, well ahead in stolen bases, and with 586 home runs to Ott's 511.

Statistically, it's very close. However, as noted earlier, Ott had the huge advantage of playing his home games in the Polo Grounds, with its right field wall a mere 258 feet from home plate. As was also noted earlier, only 187 of Ott's 511 home runs were hit on the road. Therefore, his home run and RBI totals were greatly inflated. In addition, he played mostly during the 1920s and 1930s, in an era in which offensive statistics were generally much higher than they were when Robinson played. When those two factors are taken into consideration, it becomes apparent that Ott was not the player that Robinson was.

Which leaves us with Frank Robinson, the most underrated of all the great superstars to ever play the game. He settles into the number two slot, with his 586 career home runs, two MVP awards, one Triple Crown, and five pennants and two world championships to his credit.

3 ROBERTO CLEMENTE

WE SAW EARLIER THAT ROBERTO CLEMENTE'S SUPERIOR POWER AND RUN-PRODUCTION, as well as his unparalleled defensive skills, earned him a higher ranking than Tony Gwynn. We also saw that he was a more complete player than Sammy Sosa. However, Mel Ott, Paul Waner, Harry Heilmann, and "Shoeless" Joe raised different issues.

A comparison of Clemente's statistics to those of Ott would seem to indicate that the latter was the superior player. After all, in almost exactly the same number of at-bats, he finished ahead of

Clemente in every offensive category, except batting average, base hits, and triples. He hit more than twice as many home runs, drove in 555 more runs, scored more than 440 more, had more doubles, compiled an on-base percentage that was some 50 points higher and a slugging percentage that was some 60 points higher, and even stole 6 more bases. Clemente did out-hit Ott by 13 points, collected more than 100 more hits, and totaled more than twice as many triples, but overall, Ott's numbers far exceed his.

However, as was noted before, Ott's statistics were greatly inflated by both the ballpark and the era in which he played. Had he not played half his games in the Polo Grounds, Ott would not have hit nearly as many home runs as he did. And had Clemente not spent the majority of his career playing in Forbes Field, he would have hit many more than the 240 home runs he managed to hit. So the power differential was not nearly what it seemed to be. The disparity in run-production would have been greatly reduced as well had the two men played in different ballparks. The numbers would have been impacted even further had Clemente and Ott played in the same era. Playing under the same conditions, Ott would probably still have hit several more home runs, driven in and scored slightly more runs, and compiled a higher on-base and slugging percentage. However, one has to think that playing in Ott's time would have added at least another 10 or 15 points to Clemente's already impressive .317 career batting average and greatly increased his RBI and runs scored totals. Thus it would seem that even though both men had their areas of superiority, overall they were fairly equal as offensive players.

Defensively, while Ott was considered to be a good outfielder, he certainly was not in the same class with Clemente. The latter also held an edge in the league MVP voting. Ott finished in the top five three times during his career, and made it into the top ten another three times. However, he never finished any higher than third, and he could do no better than sixth in any season that his Giants won the National League pennant. When the Giants won the pennant in 1933, Ott received no support in the voting whatsoever, failing to receive even a single point. When New York repeated as pennant-winners in 1936 and 1937, Ott finished sixth and seventh in the voting, respectively. However, in both years, he finished well behind teammate Carl Hubbell in the balloting, and in 1937 he received less support than another teammate, Dick Bartell. In essence, Ott was generally not considered to be even the most valuable player on his own team.

The same could not be said about Clemente, who for much of his career was the heart and soul of his Pirates teams. In addition to his MVP season of 1966, Clemente finished in the top five of the voting three other times. He also made it into the top ten four other times. It would seem, therefore, that he was consistently held in somewhat higher esteem by the voters than Ott ever was. In addition, the National League was generally considered to be the weaker of the two leagues when Ott played. However, throughout virtually all of Clemente's career, it was thought to be superior to the American League. Therefore, Clemente fared better in the voting even though he was playing in a league that was somewhat more competitive than the one in which Ott played. All things considered, Clemente was the better player of the two and deserves a higher ranking.

A look at the career numbers of Paul Waner versus those of Clemente indicates that the two players were quite evenly matched. Each won four batting titles and an MVP award. In virtually the same number of at-bats, they finished with practically the same number of runs batted in, stolen bases, and triples, and with almost exactly the same slugging percentage. Waner hit for a higher average, had more doubles, scored more runs, and had a higher on-base percentage. Clemente, however, hit more than twice as many home runs. The slight edge that Waner would seem to have based on statistics disappears, though, when one considers that, like Ott, he played during an era in which offensive numbers tended to be higher than in most other periods. In addition, even though Clemente did not attempt to steal many bases during his career, he was much faster than Waner, and a far better base runner. For that reason, and also for his greater ability as an outfielder, Clemente deserves to be ranked higher than Waner.

Harry Heilmann was another great hitter who won four batting titles. However, unlike Waner, his power was more comparable to Clemente's, and he was actually a slightly better run-producer. Just looking at the numbers, one would tend to give the advantage to Heilmann. But when you consider that he, too, played mostly in the 1920s, his numbers tend to take on less significance. In addition, he was considered to be a mediocre outfielder, not even close to Clemente in ability. Once again, Clemente must be given the nod.

In the case of "Shoeless" Joe Jackson, other factors come into play, the most important of which is that he played just ten full seasons in the major leagues. As a result, he had little more than half the number of at-bats that Clemente had. If you project his numbers over the same number of at-bats, he would have finished well ahead of Clemente in every offensive category, except home runs. As it is, he finished with more triples and stolen bases, a much higher batting average, and much higher on-base and slugging percentages. However, had he not been banned from baseball because of his involvement in the 1919 "Black Sox" scandal, Jackson's skills inevitably would have begun to erode as he got older. He certainly would not have finished his career with a .356 batting average. Most likely his on-base and slugging percentages would have dropped somewhat as well, although there is little doubt he still would have finished with better numbers than Clemente in all three categories.

All things considered, it would seem that Jackson was the slightly better offensive player of the two. However, Clemente was a great player for a longer period of time. That should count for something. In addition, it is extremely difficult to project exactly what Jackson's numbers would have looked like had he played another six or seven years. He probably would have out-hit Clemente by 25 or 30 points and finished with a comparable number of runs batted in and runs scored. But Clemente's numbers are part of history, not merely projections. Rather than speculating about what might have been, I'll take the numbers that are on the board and, for the third team, go with the man who was arguably the greatest defensive right fielder in the history of the game: Roberto Clemente.

4 "SHOELESS" JOE JACKSON

THE THREE PLAYERS WHO RECEIVED THE GREATEST AMOUNT OF CONSIDERATION FOR the number four spot were Joe Jackson, Sammy Sosa, and Tony Gwynn.

When comparing Jackson to Gwynn, the determining factor was Jackson's greater power and run-production. That might seem strange when a look at their career statistics reveals that, even though he had slightly less than twice the number of at-bats, Gwynn actually out-homered Jackson by a better than two-to-one ratio, and both knocked in and scored significantly more runs. However, as was mentioned earlier, the number of home runs a player hit was not the measure of his power when Jackson played, but rather the number of triples he had. In little more than half the number of at-bats, Jackson had twice as many triples as Gwynn. He also had about 70 percent the number of runs batted in and almost two-thirds the number of runs scored. When it is considered that runs were much harder to come by when Jackson played, he really was far superior to Gwynn as a run producer. In addition, his on-base percentage was 35 points higher and his slugging percentage was 58 points higher.

Both players were fine outfielders, excellent base runners, and great hitters. But Jackson was considered to be one of the top sluggers of his day, something Gwynn never was. Therefore he deserves a higher ranking.

However, comparing Jackson to Sammy Sosa is another matter since Sosa is one of the top sluggers and run producers of his time. In fact, one might wonder how one player whose power numbers so far exceed those of another could receive a lower ranking than the other player. Sosa has *ten* times as many home runs as Jackson and drives in runs at a faster pace. In roughly two-thirds the number of at-bats that Sosa has accumulated thus far, Jackson knocked in only 54 percent as many runs (785 to 1,450). Sosa's slugging percentage is also 30 points higher, and he has scored about 450 more runs. However, Jackson actually scored runs at a similar rate and compares quite favorably to Sosa in every other offensive category. His batting average and on-base percentage were each approximately 75 points higher than Sosa's, he collected four times as many triples, and he finished with almost as many doubles and stolen bases, in far fewer at-bats. Jackson was also a better outfielder and base runner than Sosa is.

While it is clear that Sosa has more power than Jackson did, it is somewhat debatable how much of an edge he has over him as a run producer. It was noted earlier that Jackson scored runs at a comparable rate to Sosa, and when one considers that he played during the dead ball era when runs were often at a premium, the fact that Jackson drove in runs at a somewhat slower rate loses some of its significance. In 1920, Jackson's final season in the majors, with a livelier ball being used, he knocked in a career-high 121 runs. Had he played in a different era, it is quite possible that Jackson would have been able to post RBI totals similar to those of Sosa. In addition, Jackson was banned from the game when he was only thirty-one years old, with several of his finest seasons still presumably ahead of him. Coming off his most productive season in the big leagues, and with the dead ball era having come to a close, it is highly likely that Jackson still had another three or four 100-plus RBI seasons left in him.

So even though the intent throughout these rankings has been to stay away from making projections, it seems that as an overall hitter, outfielder, and base runner, Joe Jackson was a more complete player than Sammy Sosa. Therefore, the man proclaimed by both Babe Ruth and Ty Cobb to be the greatest hitter either one of them ever saw claims his spot on the fourth team.

❺ SAMMY SOSA

JUST AS HE DID EARLIER WITH TONY GWYNN, SAMMY SOSA NOW RECEIVES A HIGHER ranking than Paul Waner because of his greater power and run production. True, Waner's batting average and on-base percentage were both more than 50 points higher than Sosa's, and he finished with more than four times as many triples and almost twice as many doubles. However, Sosa, in roughly three-quarters the number of at-bats, has hit almost five times as many home runs, driven in almost 150 more runs, stolen twice as many bases, and compiled a slugging percentage that is some 70 points higher. He has also scored runs at a slightly faster pace. Because of his greater productivity, Sosa gets the nod over Waner.

Harry Heilmann, on the other hand, was quite comparable to Sosa as a run producer. In only about 200 more at-bats, he knocked in almost 100 more runs, while scoring about 25 less. He also compiled a batting average and on-base percentage that was some 60 points higher, collected more than three times as many triples, and also amassed more than 200 more doubles. However, Sosa has hit three times as many home runs, stolen twice as many bases, and compiled a slugging percentage that is 26 points higher. Nevertheless, it would seem that Heilmann was the more complete hitter of the two.

As outfielders, both could be described as adequate. However, in his youth, Sosa was the better base runner. Both men spent most of their careers hitting in excellent parks for hitters. Heilmann played most of his home games in Tiger Stadium, while Sosa has been in Wrigley Field for the past twelve seasons.

Heilmann did have one advantage over Sosa. In his years in Detroit, Heilmann usually had other excellent hitters surrounding him in the Tiger lineup. In the late teens through the mid-1920s, he had Ty Cobb and Bobby Veach, another excellent-hitting outfielder, playing alongside him. Later, it was Charlie Gehringer and Hall of Fame outfielder Heinie Manush. So Heilmann always had players who could get on base coming up in front of him, and hitters quite capable of driving him in coming up after him. Sosa has not had that luxury. For the better part of his career, he has had very little protection in the Cubs' lineup, and he has been the only real threat in their batting order. Mark Grace was a fine player, but he was not the kind of hitter who instilled fear in pitchers, or who drove in a lot of runs. With a better supporting cast, Heilmann's opportunities to either drive in or score runs were far more frequent. As a result, one would have to conclude that Sosa was actually the better run-producer of the two. For that reason, he deserves a higher ranking than Heilmann.

Mel Ott's numbers compare even more favorably to those of Sosa. Although he hit 30 fewer home runs in almost 2,000 more at-bats, Ott finished well ahead of Sosa in runs batted in, runs scored, on-base percentage, triples, and doubles. Sosa, though, has stolen more than twice as many bases and compiled a slugging percentage that is almost 15 points higher. Also, factoring in Ott's 2,000 additional at-bats, the two players actually scored and drove in runs at a very similar pace. However, Ott drew far more bases on balls and, as a result, his on-base percentage, which is 65 points higher than Sosa's, is difficult to ignore. Overall, the numbers seem to favor Ott.

However, once again, the diminutive Giant slugger's place in the rankings is hurt by the ballpark he played in. Since the Polo Grounds greatly inflated his home run and RBI totals, the inevitable conclusion is that Sosa is the greater slugger and run producer of the two. He therefore finishes just ahead of Ott and claims the fifth spot.

Chapter Forty-One: All-Time All-Star Utility Man

PETE ROSE

JACKIE ROBINSON

❶ PETE ROSE

JACKIE ROBINSON WAS A SUPERB NATURAL ATHLETE WHO EXCELLED IN FOUR SPORTS—baseball, football, basketball, and track and field—while attending UCLA. His great athletic ability enabled him to also excel at four different positions during his major league career with the Brooklyn Dodgers. Robinson, at different times, performed admirably at first base, second base, third base, and left field. He was also an outstanding hitter, with good power, and was the finest base-runner of his day.

Pete Rose, on the other hand, did not possess great athletic ability. He wasn't particularly big, didn't run particularly fast, and didn't have a very strong throwing arm. But, as former teammate Joe Morgan once said: "He always ran as fast as he could and threw the ball as hard as he could." Because of his hustle and determination, Rose was able to turn himself into one of the best players of his era, becoming an All-Star at five different positions: first base, second base, third base, left field, and right field.

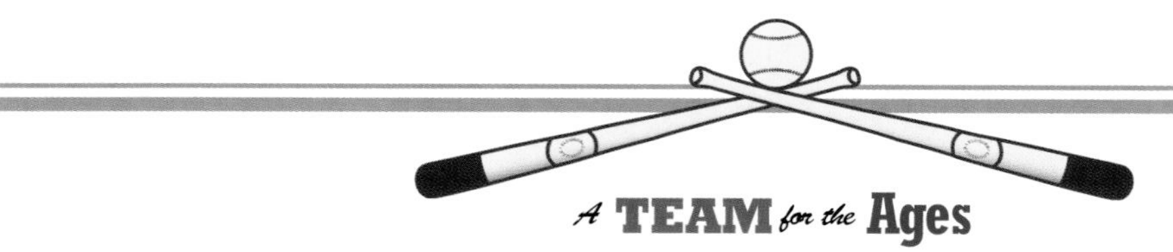

It really is unfair to compare Robinson's statistics to those of Rose because the former only played ten years in the majors, as opposed to the latter's twenty-four, and only had slightly more than one-third the number of plate appearance. Due to time spent in the military and, of course, the unwritten laws of the day prohibiting blacks from playing in the major leagues, Robinson's career was short and we probably never even got to see much of his best. However, one of the two men must now be chosen, and the main criterion for making that selection has to be their numbers.

Predictably, the only categories that Robinson finished ahead in are those that are not tied to longevity. He finished with a higher batting average (.311 to .303), a higher on-base percentage (.410 to .377), and a higher slugging percentage (.474 to .409). If his other numbers were projected over the same number of at-bats that Rose had, Robinson would have finished well ahead in virtually every other offensive category as well, except for doubles and triples. However, even though Rose had less hitting power and running speed than Robinson, because of his longevity he had more home runs (160 to 137), almost twice as many runs batted in (1,314 to 734), more than twice as many runs scored (2,165 to 947), and almost three times as many hits (4,256 to 1,518), doubles (746 to 273), and triples (135 to 54). He even finished with one more stolen base. So even though Robinson had more talent, and may have been a slightly better player during the time he did spend in the majors, it would be difficult to justify selecting him over Rose for the first-team. Therefore, that honor goes to Pete Rose.

In addition to being the all-time leader in base hits, an All-Star at five different positions, a three-time batting champion, an MVP winner, and the man named "Player of the Decade" of the 1970s by *The Sporting News,* Pete Rose was a winner. During his career, he helped lead two different teams—the Cincinnati Reds and Philadelphia Phillies—to six division titles, five pennants, and three world championships. While some may oppose his induction into the Hall of Fame from a moral perspective, there is little doubt that his performance on the field earned him a place in Cooperstown.

2 JACKIE ROBINSON

WE HAVE ALREADY DISCUSSED JACKIE ROBINSON'S CAREER, HIS ABILITY AS BOTH AN athlete and a baseball player, and some of the difficulties he encountered during his major league career. The only thing left to say is that it is sad that he had to go through what he did, and that we didn't get to see more of him. It is also unfortunate that he never had the opportunity to just go out and play the game, relax, and enjoy it the way other players could. Perhaps the greatest tragedy, though, is that this courageous man was taken from us at such an early age.

All-Time All-Star Designated Hitter

TED WILLIAMS

EDGAR MARTINEZ

1 TED WILLIAMS

When completing the lineup for the first half of the century, Ted Williams was inserted as the designated hitter, even though that role was not created until well after he retired. He, therefore, is also being treated as a DH in this section—and with good reason.

If the role of designated hitter were created for one particular man, it would seem that Ted Williams would be that man. He was obsessed with hitting, to the point that he alienated many of the hometown Boston fans by practicing his swing in between pitches when he was in the outfield. Williams took his hitting so seriously that he admitted to keeping a careful watch on any player who happened to be hitting as well as him at any particular time. Joe DiMaggio's younger brother, Dominick, was an outstanding center fielder who played alongside Williams in the Boston outfield for many years. Dominick once said that, in 1941 during Joe's 56-game hitting streak, he would usually find out if his brother had been able to extend the streak directly from Williams. He said that the two players would be in the outfield when Williams, who obviously had been scoreboard watching, would call out to him, "Dommie,

Dommie, Joe got his hit." Any man so obsessed with not only his own hitting, but the hitting of others, would clearly have thrived in the role of designated hitter.

Thought of by many as having been the greatest hitter who ever lived, Ted Williams has the distinction of being the only one of the truly great hitters whose career spanned parts of four decades. He first came up to Boston in 1939, when the game was still played almost exclusively during the day, and when it was still segregated. By the time his final season of 1960 arrived, night ball had become more the norm, the game had been integrated, and relief pitching was starting to become an integral part of the game. Through it all, Williams remained baseball's greatest hitter. He is one of only two players (Rogers Hornsby being the other) to have won as many as two Triple Crowns, he is the last player to have hit .400, he has the highest career on-base percentage in baseball history, and he is second only to Babe Ruth in career slugging percentage. More than just a great slugger, Williams won seven batting championships, hitting .388 in 1957 at the age of thirty-eight. When it was suggested to him that hitting .388 at that age might have been a greater accomplishment than batting .406 in 1941, he rejected the notion. Williams, the perfectionist, responded that he didn't pull the ball as much, or hit it as consistently hard, in 1957 as he had sixteen years earlier.

A man who turned hitting into such a science would clearly have made the greatest designated hitter in history.

❷ EDGAR MARTINEZ

THE FINEST DESIGNATED HITTER THE AMERICAN LEAGUE HAS SEEN IN THE ALMOST thirty years since the role was created, Edgar Martinez finishes second only to the great Ted Williams. We saw earlier that he has not only been the best DH, but one of the best hitters in the game over the past dozen or so seasons. He has won two batting titles, batted over .300 ten times, surpassing the .340 mark twice, hit more than 20 homers eight times, knocked in more than 100 runs six times, and has one of the highest career batting averages (.315) and on-base percentages (.423) of the past fifty years.

All-Time All-Star Right-Handed Pitcher

WALTER JOHNSON
CHRISTY MATHEWSON
GROVER CLEVELAND ALEXANDER
SATCHEL PAIGE
ROGER CLEMENS

1 WALTER JOHNSON

THE FACT THAT THE FIRST THREE SELECTIONS FOR GREATEST RIGHT-HANDED PITCHER all come from the pitching-dominated dead ball era may seem somewhat unjust. However, Walter Johnson, Christy Mathewson, and Grover Cleveland Alexander were not only the finest pitchers of that era, but they were the most dominant right-handers in the history of the game. In fact, they were so dominant that they were not only considered to be the greatest *pitchers* of the dead ball era, but along with Ty Cobb, Honus Wagner, and Tris Speaker, the game's greatest *players*.

While Bob Gibson, Juan Marichal, Bob Feller, Roger Clemens, and Greg Maddux were all great pitchers who had some truly dominant seasons, they, for the most part, did not dominate their league the way Johnson, Mathewson, and Alexander did. These three were not only considered to be the best players on their own teams, but arguably the best and most valuable players in their leagues. Had Gibson, Marichal, and the others pitched during this era, it is possible they would have been just as dominant. But when they pitched a pitcher was not generally looked upon as being the most important player on his team, and if he was his team's ace, he wasn't expected to start as many as one-third of his team's games or throw as many innings as the earlier iron men did.

By way of comparison, consider that during his career Bob Gibson threw as many as 20 complete games seven times, and Juan Marichal completed at least 20 games five times. These days, those numbers seem extremely impressive, and were even in their own time. However, both Christy Mathewson and Grover Cleveland Alexander completed as many as *30* games on six separate occasions. Gibson threw at least 300 innings twice and topped the 250 mark six other times. Marichal topped 300 on three occasions and reached 250 four other times. Mathewson threw at least 300 innings *eleven* times, topping 350 on three occasions, including a high of 390 one season. Alexander threw at least 300 innings seven times and reached the 350 mark six of those times, peaking at 387 one season.

As you can see, when Johnson, Mathewson, and Alexander pitched, the game was played differently than it would be in future generations. As a result, these three became a more integral part of their teams' success and were given the opportunity to become more dominant forces. Therefore, they must be given the highest ranking.

When *The Sporting News* selected its one hundred greatest players of the twentieth century, there were five pitchers among the top twenty, and Johnson, Mathewson, and Alexander were three of them (Cy Young and Satchel Paige were the others). Walter Johnson was the first of these, and earlier we saw why. In spite of the fact that the team he pitched for, the Washington Senators, was a second-division team for much of his career, Johnson still managed to win 416 games (a 20th-century record) and finish with a .599 winning percentage. His 2.16 ERA is among the lowest ever and, pitching in an era when hitters didn't strike out nearly as often as they would in later years, he accumulated over 3,500 strikeouts during his career. (As a basis for comparison, Cy Young, in over 1,400 more innings, struck out 700 fewer batters.) In addition, Johnson holds the major league record for lifetime shutouts with 110, won more than 30 games twice, more than 20 games ten other times, and finished with an ERA under two runs a game ten times. He also led the American League in wins six times, in ERA five times, and in strikeouts a remarkable twelve times. Lastly, Johnson won the pitcher's Triple Crown three times and is one of only three pitchers to win as many as two league MVP awards.

❷ CHRISTY MATHEWSON

JUST A FEW NOTCHES BEHIND WALTER JOHNSON IN *THE SPORTING NEWS* POLL WAS Christy Mathewson, the man generally considered to be the greatest right-handed pitcher in National League history. Although almost as great as Johnson, Mathewson was a completely different type of pitcher, relying more on razor-sharp control and his favorite pitch, known as the "fadeaway," than on a blazing fastball to dominate opposing hitters. And dominate he did, winning 373 games during an illustrious career that included twelve seasons of more than 20 wins, four seasons with more than 30 wins, and five seasons with an ERA under 2.00. He also finished with one of the lowest ERAs in baseball history (2.13), one of the highest winning percentages (.665), and a remarkable strikeout-to-walk ratio of better than three-to-one. Mathewson also won two pitcher's Triple Crowns.

❸ GROVER CLEVELAND ALEXANDER

ON THE SAME LEVEL AS MATHEWSON WAS A MAN WHO FINISHED ONLY SLIGHTLY BEHIND him in most pitching categories: Grover Cleveland Alexander. Alexander finished his career with exactly

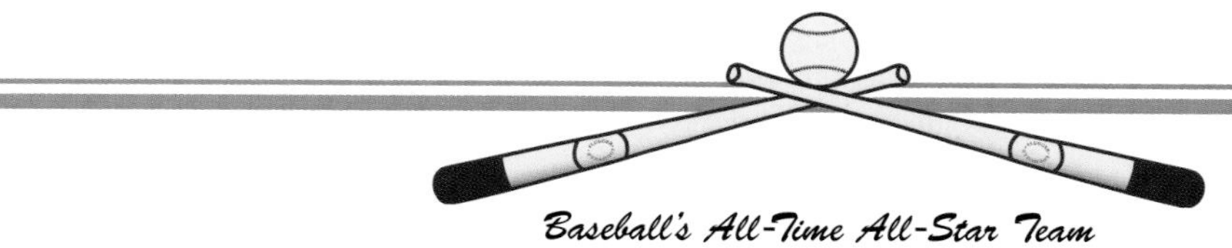

the same number of wins, a slightly lower winning percentage, and a slightly higher earned run average. However, during his peak seasons of 1915–1917, he was as dominant as any pitcher who ever lived. As was mentioned earlier, he won the pitcher's Triple Crown in each of those seasons, winning at least 30 games and finishing with an ERA under two runs a game each time. His combined win-loss record for those three seasons was an astounding 94-35. In all, he won more than 20 games nine times during his career, leading the N.L. in wins five times, ERA four times, strikeouts six times, and shutouts seven times. He is second to only Walter Johnson in career shutouts, with 90, and he holds the National League record for lifetime complete games, with 437.

4 SATCHEL PAIGE

SATCHEL PAIGE MAY VERY WELL HAVE BEEN AS GOOD AS JOHNSON, MATHEWSON, OR Alexander, but since the statistics are not readily available to prove it he must be slotted just behind them. He was unquestionably the greatest pitcher in Negro League history, dominating the circuit for twenty years. Paige was also recognized by *The Sporting News* as one of the twenty greatest players of all-time. He is therefore clearly deserving of the number four spot, just ahead of the likes of Roger Clemens, Bob Gibson, Juan Marichal, and Bob Feller.

Although his opportunities to compete against major leaguers were limited, Paige always made the most of them. On barnstorming tours, he regularly out-dueled the best pitchers the majors had to offer—pitchers such as Bob Feller and Dizzy Dean—and dazzled hitters with his wide assortment of pitches, thrown from many different angles. Joe DiMaggio once said that Paige "was the best I ever faced," and Buck O'Neill, who saw him play in the Negro Leagues, said: "Satch was awesome. He could throw his fastball one hundred miles an hour."

5 ROGER CLEMENS

IT WAS DIFFICULT TO EXCLUDE BOB GIBSON AND JUAN MARICHAL FROM THE TOP FIVE since they were the two finest pitchers I saw in my youth (I didn't get to see much of Sandy Koufax). However, as was mentioned earlier, the career statistics of Roger Clemens are just too overwhelming to ignore, and his unprecedented six Cy Young awards are further evidence of his greater level of dominance over a longer period of time.

Bob Feller was quite possibly just as dominant as Clemens and was perhaps his equal as a power pitcher. However, due to his time away from the game during World War II, Feller finished with 44 fewer wins than Clemens had. Although both pitchers finished with similar hits-to-innings-pitched ratios, Clemens walked far fewer men in more innings of work, accumulated approximately 1,500 more strikeouts, finished with a higher winning percentage, and, pitching against lineups that always included a designated hitter, ended his career with a lower earned run average. Once again, the numbers are in Clemens's favor, and he must be slotted just ahead of Feller.

B

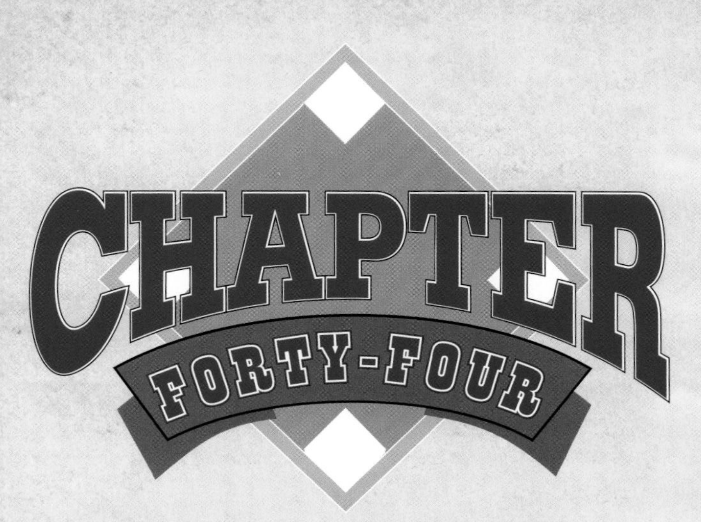

All-Time All-Star Left-Handed Pitcher

LEFTY GROVE
SANDY KOUFAX
WARREN SPAHN
STEVE CARLTON
RANDY JOHNSON

1 LEFTY GROVE

IT WAS STATED EARLIER THAT IN SITUATIONS WHERE ONE PLAYER HAD BETTER CAREER statistics than another due to excellence over a longer period of time, the second player would only be rated above him if, at his peak, his performance far exceeded that of the other player. That is what enabled Sandy Koufax to finish ahead of both Warren Spahn and Steve Carlton in the rankings for the second half of the century. As we saw, while both Spahn and Carlton were superb pitchers who had very long and distinguished careers, Koufax, in his prime, was far more dominant. The same cannot be said, though, when comparing Koufax to Lefty Grove.

Sandy Koufax, from 1963 to 1966, was probably the greatest pitcher who ever lived. Over those four seasons, he won three Cy Young awards, three pitcher's Triple Crowns, led the league in wins three times, in ERA four times, in strikeouts three times, in innings pitched twice, in shutouts three times, and in complete games twice. He also won one MVP award and finished runner-up two other times. His win-loss record during those four years was a phenomenal 97-27. He was also outstanding in 1961 and 1962. So, in all, Koufax was a great pitcher for four years, and an outstanding one for six.

Lefty Grove at his best, however, was not very far behind Koufax. He won at least 20 games seven seasons in a row from 1927 to 1933. He led the league in ERA a record nine times, including four seasons in a row from 1929 to 1932, led the league in wins four times, in winning percentage five times, and in strikeouts seven consecutive seasons. Like Koufax, he won one MVP award, and he also won two pitcher's Triple Crowns. In addition, he strung together six seasons that were comparable to the four greatest seasons Koufax had. From 1928 to 1933, Grove's win-loss record was an amazing 152-41. Although, during those six seasons, his ERA was never less than 2.00 (as Koufax's was three times during his streak), it was far below the league average, and taken within the context of his era, was comparable to the ones that Koufax posted. In essence, it could be said that while Koufax was a great pitcher for four seasons and an excellent one for another two, Grove was a great one for six and an excellent one for another five or six. While Koufax may have had the edge when he was at his best, Grove was close enough to deserve a higher ranking based on his excellence over a longer period of time. Therefore, Lefty Grove is the choice as the greatest left-handed pitcher ever.

2 SANDY KOUFAX

WHILE SANDY KOUFAX DID NOT HAVE ENOUGH GREAT SEASONS TO OVERTAKE LEFTY Grove for the top spot, his short-term brilliance was enough to surpass any other left-handed pitcher. He was so great that when players from his era discuss him more than thirty years later, they still talk about him with reverence. He was without question the greatest pitcher of the last half of the twentieth century. The only unfortunate thing is that we were cheated out of seeing more of him because of the arthritic condition he developed in his pitching arm. But, as he once said: "I had a choice—continue pitching, or risk becoming a cripple later in life, and I was not about to become a cripple."

3 WARREN SPAHN

JUST AS WARREN SPAHN'S THIRTEEN 20-WIN SEASONS ENABLED HIM TO EDGE OUT Steve Carlton in the rankings for the second half of the century, they now allow him to finish ahead of Carl Hubbell as well. Hubbell was, at his peak, perhaps slightly more dominant, having won two MVP awards and more than 20 games for five consecutive seasons. In fact, from 1933 to 1937, his record was 115-50, he led the N.L. in wins and ERA three times each, and he was rivaled by only Dizzy Dean as the league's best pitcher. However, after 1937 Hubbell never won more than 13 games in a season. Prior to 1933, he had been a very solid pitcher for five seasons, winning as many as 18 games twice, but he didn't become a great one until he perfected his screwball that year. Even after Hubbell hit his stride, however, the level of his performance did not exceed that of Spahn by enough to overtake him in the rankings. Therefore, the man with more wins than any other left-hander in the history of the game settles into the third slot.

Not only did Warren Spahn have more 20-win seasons than any other pitcher in the twentieth century, but he finished fifth on the all-time list in wins, sixth in shutouts, and eighth in innings pitched. He led the league in wins eight times, finished with an ERA under 3.00 nine times, finished in the top five in the Cy Young voting in five of the first six years it was presented, and won the award once himself. He also finished in the top five in the league MVP voting four times. Accordingly, the man who Stan Musial once said "will never stop pitching" clearly deserves to be included with the all-time greats.

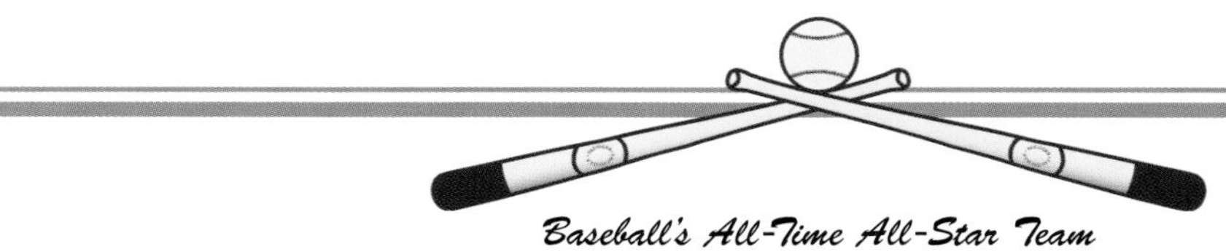

4 STEVE CARLTON

IT WAS EXTREMELY CLOSE FOR THE FOURTH SPOT BETWEEN STEVE CARLTON, RANDY Johnson and Carl Hubbell. I discussed earlier why Carlton was rated just ahead of Johnson. He now edges out Hubbell for two reasons. First, he was outstanding for a longer period of time. As was just mentioned, Hubbell had five outstanding seasons and two other very good ones. Carlton, on the other hand, won more than 20 games six times during his career and had five other very strong seasons. In four of those, he won at least 16 games. The other was the strike-shortened 1981 season. That year, Carlton finished 13-4 with a 2.42 ERA.

Secondly, Carlton was a bit more dominant, being much more of a strikeout pitcher. While Hubbell struck out just over four batters every nine innings, Carlton fanned just over seven. "Lefty" therefore gets the nod at number four.

In addition to his four Cy Young awards, Steve Carlton finished in the top five in the league MVP voting three times. He also is second on the all-time strikeout list to Nolan Ryan.

5 RANDY JOHNSON

IT WAS DIFFICULT TO CHOOSE BETWEEN CARL HUBBELL AND RANDY JOHNSON FOR A spot on the fifth team since, at their peaks, both were such dominant pitchers. In approximately the same number of starts, Hubbell completed three times as many games and threw about 500 more innings than Johnson has in his career so far. Hubbell also won almost 25 more games, but that is countered by Johnson's higher winning percentage. In fewer innings pitched, Johnson has also walked approximately 500 more batters, but his strikeout-to-walk ratio of better than three-to-one is much better than Hubbell's ratio of slightly better than two-to-one.

Hubbell's two MVP awards are certainly a point in his favor, but Johnson's five Cy Youngs, including four in a row from 1999 to 2002, are equally impressive. Another argument that could be made on Hubbell's behalf is that, pitching mostly in the 1930s, when hitting statistics were generally higher than normal, he finished his career with an outstanding 2.98 earned run average. As a basis for comparison, Lefty Gomez, considered to be the top left-hander in the A. L. for much of that period, finished his career with a mark of 3.34. So Hubbell's 2.98 ERA, a dozen percentage points lower than Johnson's career mark, was truly an outstanding achievement. However, Johnson has also spent his entire career pitching in a hitter's era, and it could be argued that his mark of 3.10 is actually just as impressive as Hubbell's.

What finally swung the pendulum in Johnson's favor, though, were two things. First, there is his mound presence, the feeling of intimidation he instills in hitters, and his greater ability to dominate a game. The second factor is the greatness he has shown over a longer period. While Hubbell dominated the N. L. for a period of five years, Johnson was a dominant pitcher from 1993 to 2002, with the exception of the 1996 campaign, most of which he missed due to injury. Particularly impressive were his six consecutive seasons, from 1997 to 2002, with at least 17 wins (including three 20-victory seasons), five seasons during that span with more than 300 strikeouts, and four seasons with an ERA of less than 2.50. For this level of dominance, Johnson barely edges out Hubbell for a spot on the fifth team.

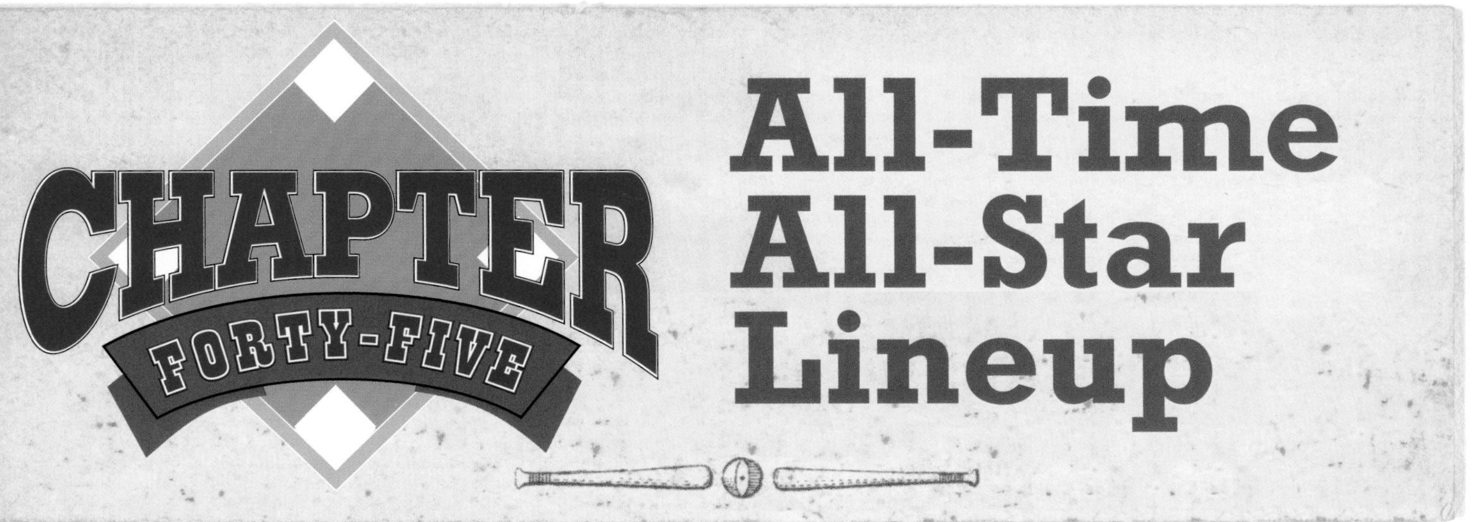

All-Time All-Star Lineup

Now it's time to make out the All-Time All-Star lineup. For the second team, let's insert Stan Musial as the designated hitter: with all due respect to Mickey Mantle, Barry Bonds, and Roberto Clemente, Musial was the best all-around hitter of all the players who made it onto the third-team, and was also better than Edgar Martinez, who, otherwise, would have been the second-team DH. Also, since the only relief pitchers named were for the last half of the century, they automatically became part of the all-time team. Here goes:

	FIRST TEAM:		SECOND TEAM:
1.	Willie Mays *CF*	1.	Ty Cobb *LF*
2.	Honus Wagner *SS*	2.	Charlie Gehringer *2B*
3.	Babe Ruth *RF*	3.	Stan Musial *DH*
4.	Lou Gehrig *1B*	4.	Jimmie Foxx *1B*
5.	Rogers Hornsby *2B*	5.	Joe DiMaggio *CF*
6.	Ted Williams *DH*	6.	Frank Robinson *RF*
7.	Hank Aaron *LF*	7.	George Brett *3B*
8.	Josh Gibson *C*	8.	Ernie Banks *SS*
9.	Mike Schmidt *3B*	9.	Johnny Bench *C*
RHP	Walter Johnson	*RHP*	Christy Mathewson
LHP	Lefty Grove	*LHP*	Sandy Koufax
R	Dennis Eckersley	*R*	Rollie Fingers
U	Pete Rose	*U*	Jackie Robinson

The first-team lineup has six right-handed bats to only three left-handed, but is power-laden, featuring three of the top four all-time home run hitters (Aaron, Ruth, and Mays), and with every player, except for Wagner, having been a multiple home run champion. It also offers good speed, with Mays and Wagner at the top of the order, and with Aaron further down. Also, with fireballers Johnson and Grove on the mound, there figures to be a lot of smoke in our fantasy ballpark.

The second-team lineup is a little more balanced, with five right-handed hitters and four lefties. It offers a little less speed, with Cobb being the only real stolen base threat. However, Gehringer, DiMaggio, Robinson, and Brett all could run and were excellent base runners. The order also presents a good deal of power, with Foxx, Robinson, Musial, DiMaggio, Banks, and Bench leading the way. And with Koufax and Mathewson pitching, the opposition doesn't figure to score too many runs.

Chicago— Pittsburgh

PART SIX

Summary

Baseball's All-Time All-Star Team: A Synopsis

THE SELECTIONS HAVE BEEN MADE AND THE LINEUPS HAVE BEEN COMPLETED. AN evaluation of the players selected reveals some interesting things.

During the selection process for the first half of the century, twenty-one players were chosen to be on either the first or second team. Of those twenty-one, eight played primarily during the dead ball era, ten played mostly during the period of 1920–1939, and three (Joe DiMaggio, Ted Williams, Jackie Robinson) competed mostly during the 1940s. Considering that the last period was a shorter one, made even shorter by the enlistment of many of the nation's greatest players into the military, each period was very well represented.

For the second half of the century, twenty-five players were selected. Of those twenty-five, eleven played primarily during the period from 1951 to 1975, eleven played mostly during the last twenty-five years, and three (Joe Morgan, Johnny Bench, Pete Rose) had careers that overlapped.

The list of players chosen for the first and second all-time teams includes twenty-six names. Of those twenty-six, four were from the dead ball era, ten played mostly from 1920 to 1950, five played during the third-quarter of the century, five were from the last twenty-five years, and two had careers that overlapped from the third-quarter into the fourth.

If nothing else, these observations would seem to suggest that each period in baseball history has had its share of great players, and that the players from one era were not necessarily better than those from any other.

In addition, a look at the players chosen for the first and second teams for each half of the century reveals the following:

For the first half of the century, thirteen were American Leaguers, six were National Leaguers, and two were Negro Leaguers. For the second half of the century, eleven were American Leaguers, thirteen were National Leaguers, and one (Frank Robinson) split time between the two leagues. This would tend to support the theory that the American League was clearly the stronger of the two leagues for much of

the first half of the century, but that the National League became more dominant during the second half because of its greater willingness to sign top black and Hispanic talent.

Two additional points should be made. First, while many great ballplayers have been mentioned, there were many other outstanding ones who haven't been. Many of the players who were not mentioned are in the Hall of Fame. Everyone has his own personal favorites and, needless to say, not all of them have been mentioned. However, an effort was made to name all those players who were truly great and who, therefore, would have been on most people's lists.

Second, the selections made in this book, though *fact-based*, are *opinions*. Especially when evaluating players from different generations, there is no sure way of knowing who was better. For the record, my opinions—as I hope you've seen throughout—were based on a combination of statistical data, the interpretation of that data, the personal viewpoints of people involved in the game, and first-hand knowledge.

GLOSSARY

Abbreviations and Statistical Terms

AB. At-bats. The number of times a player comes to the plate to try to get on base. It does not include those times when a walk was issued, the player hit a sacrifice fly to score a runner, or the player advanced a base runner via a sacrifice bunt.

AVG. Batting average. The number of hits divided by the number of at-bats.

BB. Bases on balls, which are better known as walks. A free trip to first base as a penalty to the pitcher when he fails to get the ball over the plate four times during an at-bat.

CG. Complete games pitched.

ERA. Earned run average. The number of earned runs a pitcher gives up, per nine innings. This does not include runs that scored as a result of errors made in the field and is calculated by dividing the number of runs given up, by the number of innings pitched, and multiplying the result by nine.

GS. Games started by a pitcher.

H. Base hits surrendered by a pitcher to the opposing team's batters.

HITS. Base hits. Awarded when a runner safely reaches at least first base upon a batted ball, if no error is recorded.

HR. Home runs. Fair ball hit over the fence, or one hit to a spot that allows the batter to circle the bases before the ball is returned to home plate.

IP. Innings pitched.

L. Losses.

OBP. On-base percentage. Hits plus walks plus hit-by-pitches, divided by plate appearance.

PCT. Winning percentage. A pitcher's number of wins divided by his number of total decisions (i.e. wins plus losses).

RBI. Runs batted in. Awarded to the batter when a runner scores upon a safely batted ball, a sacrifice or a walk.

RUNS. Runs scored by a player.

SB. Stolen bases.

SLG PCT. Slugging percentage. The number of total bases earned by all singles, doubles, triples and home runs, divided by the total number of at-bats.

SO. Strikeouts.

SV. Saves. A save is recorded by a relief pitcher when he enters the game with the opposing team having the tying run either on base, at home plate, or in the on-deck circle.

3B. Three-base hits. Triples.

2B. Two-base hits. Doubles.

W. Wins.

BIBLIOGRAPHY

Books:

DeMarco, Tony, et al., *The Sporting News Selects 50 Greatest Sluggers. The Sporting News,* a division of Times Mirror Magazines, Inc., St. Louis, MO, 2000.

Dewey, Donald, and Acocella, Nicholas, *The Biographical History of Baseball.* Carroll & Graf, Inc., New York, NY, 1995.

Ford, Whitey, with Phil Pepe, *Few And Chosen.* Triumph Books, Chicago, IL, 2001.

Honig, Donald, *Baseball When the Grass Was Real.* Coward, McCann and Geoghegan, Inc., New York, NY, 1975.

Honig, Donald, *The New York Yankees* (Revised Edition). Crown, Inc., New York, NY, 1987.

Langford, Walter M., *Legends of Baseball.* Diamond Communications, Inc., IN, 1987.

McCarthy, John P., *Baseball's All-Time Dream Team.* Betterway Books, Cincinnati, OH, 1994.

Millikin, Mark R., *Jimmie Foxx, The Pride of Sudlersville.* The Scarecrow Press, Inc., Lanham, MD, & London, 1998.

Nemec, David, et al., *Players of Cooperstown—Baseball's Hall of Fame.* Publications International, Ltd., Lincolnwood, IL, 1994.

Okrent, Daniel, and Lewine, Harris, eds., with David Nemec, *The Ultimate Baseball Book.* Houghton Mifflin Co. / A Hiltown Book, Boston, MA, 1988.

Ritter, Lawrence, *The Glory of Their Times.* Random House, New York, NY, 1985.

Shalin, Mike, and Neil Shalin, *Out by a Step: The 100 Best Players Not in the Baseball Hall of Fame.* Diamond Communications, Inc., IN, 2002.

Thorn, John, and Palmer, Pete, eds., with Michael Gershman, *Total Baseball.* HarperCollins Pub. Inc., New York, NY, 1993.

Williams, Ted, with Jim Prime, *Ted Williams' Hit List.* Masters Press, Indianapolis, IN, 1996.

Videos:

The 500 Home Run Club. Cabin Fever Entertainment, Inc., 1988.

The Life And Times Of Hank Greenberg. The Ciesla Foundation, 1999.

New York Yankees: The Movie. Magic Video Publishing Company, 1987.

The Sporting News' 100 Greatest Baseball Players. National Broadcasting Co., 1999.

Sports Century—Carl Yastrzemski. ESPN, 2000.

Sports Century: Fifty Greatest Athletes—Sandy Koufax. ESPN, 1999.

Sports Century—Frank Robinson. ESPN, 2000.

Sports Century—Stan Musial. ESPN, 2000.

Ted Williams' 20 Greatest Hitters. Across the Street Productions, 1995.

Internet Websites:

The Ballplayers, online at BaseballLibrary.com (http://www.baseballlibrary.com/baseballlibrary/ballplayers).

Historical Stats, online at MLB.com (http://www.mlb.com/stats_historical/individual_stats_player).

Negro Leagues Profiles, online at MLB.com (http://www.mlb.com/history/negro_leagues_profile).

The Players, online at Baseball-Almanac.com (http://www.baseball-almanac.com/players).

The Players, online at Baseballink.com (http://www.baseballink.com/baseballink/players).

The Players, online at Baseball-Reference.com (http://www.baseball-reference.com/players).

INDEX